Starting an
Import/Export Business

The *Entrepreneur Magazine* Small Business Series

ENTREPRENEUR MAGAZINE

Starting an
Import/Export Business

John Wiley & Sons, Inc.

New York • Chichester • Brisbane • Toronto • Singapore

This text is printed on acid-free paper.

Copyright © 1995 by Entrepreneur Media, Inc.
Published by John Wiley & Sons, Inc.

Library of Congress Cataloging-in-Publication Data:

Entrepreneur magazine : starting an import/export business.
        p.   cm. — (The Entrepreneur magazine small business series)
    Includes index.
    ISBN 0-471-11058-2 (cloth : alk. paper). — ISBN 0-471-11059-0
(pbk. : alk. paper)
    1. Trading companies—Management.   2. New business enterprises.
I. Entrepreneur (Santa Monica, Calif.)   II. Series.
HF1416.E577   1995
    658.8'48—dc20   95-16999

Printed in the United States of America

10   9   8   7   6   5   4   3   2   1

ACKNOWLEDGMENTS

ENTREPRENEUR MAGAZINE GROUP

Editor	Charles Fuller
Assistant Editor	Ken Ohlson
Copy Editors	David Pomije
	Heather Page
	Imran Husain
Contributing Editors	Maura Hudson Pomije
	Anne Gene Callot
	Lauren Fischbein
	Meredith Kaplan
Editorial Assistants	Glen Webber
	Lynn Norquist

We would like to thank Richard A. Powell for his participation in the production of this manuscript.

CONTENTS

INTRODUCTION

Thousands of manufacturers throughout the United States and Canada produce products for domestic sales, never considering how they can profit from sales to other countries. Many other manufacturers around the world need help to reach the extensive U.S. market.

That's where import/export services come in. They can help producers find and reach valuable markets and write profitable contracts with businesses throughout the world. Yet an import/export service requires few assets; an understanding of world markets and regulations, a telephone, a fax machine, a prospect file, and lots of rewarding hard work.

Starting an Import/Export Business includes both the guidelines and the resources for success as an import/export agent. Topics include understanding the world market and how it interacts; recent trade agreements and how they impact businesses worldwide; how to plan and start a successful import/export service; and everything you need to know about managing time and money to build a successful business. You'll learn how successful import/export agents effectively market their services and apply advanced techniques to separate themselves from their competitors.

Starting an Import/Export Business covers not only how to plan and start a successful import/export agency, but also how to manage it on a day-to-day basis. Valuable forms, regulations, and worksheets are exhibited, and a comprehensive glossary of international business and trade terms is positioned for easy reference. In addition, the book offers numerous verified contacts, in the United States and around the world, that can help you quickly learn and apply your knowledge of international trade.

Starting an Import/Export Business is not a get-rich-quick scheme. It is a work-smart guide written by *Entrepreneur* magazine, revised and updated by two knowledgeable writers on small business opportunities and import/export. Dan Ramsey is the author of more than a dozen books on business topics. He is also president of a business consulting service that helps small businesses grow. John Song is the co-owner of Western Enterprise Company, an import/export business located in Signal Hill, California. He is a former contributing editor to *Frisko* magazine.

1

UNDERSTANDING THE WORLD MARKET

Perhaps the only constant in the world today is change. New boundaries—political, economic, technological—are crossed, redrawn, and crossed again seemingly every day. The end of the Cold War and the emergence of free market ideas around the world has created an unprecedented opportunity for those interested in entering the import/export business. Market opportunities not only exist in those countries and industries already developed by free market economies, but perhaps are even greater in countries that are just beginning to explore and establish free markets.

Opportunities abound. The "Seven Tigers" and other nations of the Asian Pacific Rim are booming, with China representing the single largest market opportunity in the world. South of our border, Mexico has emerged as one of the largest U.S. trading partners, and the passage of the North American Free Trade Agreement (NAFTA) offers a historic opportunity to create a single unified market from Hudson Bay to the Guatemalan border. Europe is emerging powerfully from a crippling continentwide recession that undercut growth through the early 1990s. Throughout the African continent, nations are slowly beginning to follow the success of South Africa in using economic opportunity to facilitate political and social change.

3

For the beginning import/export entrepreneur, the entire world is a potential market. Whether you're interested in importing products from foreign countries or exporting American products to small and large markets worldwide, this is where you—the start-up entrepreneur—can make an impact.

Import/export is big business. In 1994, the United States imported about $670 *billion* in goods and services and exported approximately $520 billion in goods to the world, according to the U.S. Department of Commerce. Figure 1–1 compares America's 1993 imports with its exports, and Figure 1–2 tracks the growth of American exports from 1991–1994. With world population growing 70% faster than that of the United States, the future of the import/export business is strong.

About 85% of the exports from the United States are produced by approximately 250 large manufacturing companies. This leaves the majority of manufacturers, mostly small and midsize companies, with few foreign sales. This is where the greatest opportunities for import/export entrepreneurs lie.

Figure 1–1   Import/Export Comparison for the United States

Exports	**Billions of Dollars**
Agricultural Merchandise	$41.80
Machinery	136.40
Transport Equipment	36.60
Commodity Groups	250.00
Total	**$464.80**
Imports	
Petroleum	$49.70
Machinery	168.70
Transport Equipment	83.30
Commodity Groups	278.60
Total	**$580.50**
Trade Balance	**$-115.70**

Source: U.S. Bureau of the Census, *Highlights of U.S. Export and Import Trade; U.S. Merchandise Trade: Export, General Imports, and Imports for Consumption,* 1993 data.

Figure 1–2 Growth of U.S. Exports

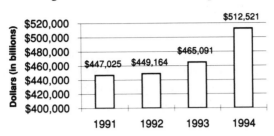

Source: U.S. Department of Commerce.

Some moderate-size companies do not export because:

- They fear the complexities of international trade.
- They are unaware of the potential of foreign markets.
- They believe, "We're doing just fine selling at home."

Many companies do not realize that if they are selling well at home, they may be able to sell just as well, or even better, in a foreign market. With a favorable exchange rate, profits can actually be much higher in some foreign markets than at home.

Importing, too, holds great potential for the right products. Americans love exotic goods, and in many countries products can be manufactured much more inexpensively than in the United States. In some cases—high-fashion clothing from Paris, expensive Russian caviar—there is a market for products that actually cost more than their local equivalent because the foreign products are seen as having higher quality. Sometimes this perception is true, but the demand is frequently just a function of status.

The most important responsibility of an import/export entrepreneur is finding out what U.S. products people in other countries want, and what foreign products are in great demand within the United States. Once these customer preferences are discovered, an import/export business can be rewarding work.

THE WORLD OF TRADE

International trade is the exchange of goods and services among countries. Countries typically export goods and services that they can produce inexpensively, and import goods and services that are produced more efficiently elsewhere.

What makes a product less expensive to produce in one country than in another?

1. Resources—natural resources such as minerals, and human resources such as low-cost labor or highly skilled workers.
2. Technology—the knowledge and tools to process raw materials into finished products.

An oil refinery is an application of technology; so is a fabric loom. A country with extensive oil resources and a refinery will export oil, but may need to import clothing.

There is a third factor in world trade: government. A national government may choose to reserve natural resources by limiting exports of specific products, or may attempt to protect the country's economy by limiting the import of products made by lower-paid workers in other countries. A government can control imports by banning them or, more effectively, by adding a tax—called a tariff—on specific products.

An import/export business matches buyers and sellers of products in different countries. An import/export entrepreneur conducts this business in various ways:

- Acting as an intermediary,
- Buying a product from a manufacturer and selling it to retailers or wholesalers in another country,
- Creating a network of retail distribution agents selling on commission,
- Hiring a separate company to find sales and customer demand.

Some import/export entrepreneurs work as consultants for other countries that want to export their products but do not have the necessary know-how.

UNDERSTANDING IMPORT TRADE

As an importer, you will be bringing goods into the United States. You may, for example, want to import Guatemalan leather goods. You may be able to find a Guatemalan leather goods exporter without traveling, or you may have to go to Guatemala and comparatively evaluate manufacturers. In both instances, you tell the Guatemalan manufacturer that you are interested in importing its goods and ask for a price list and samples to be sent or to take back to the United States. As a sales agent in the United States, you take the samples around to wholesalers or retailers and book their orders. Once you have sales or orders, you buy the goods from the manufacturer and have them shipped directly to the buyer, who then pays you for them.

In both the import and export scenarios, you are the intermediary; you pull all of the strings that bring buyers and sellers together. The actual process by which you put a deal together can vary. For instance, if you work on a commission basis, you do not actually have to put up money in either case.

The most important factor for you is to *make sales*. You can have the best possible plan on paper, with every detail in place, but if you cannot make a sale, or if you do not have a foreign distributor who can, your plan is useless. For this reason, a big part of the job of an importer/exporter is determining what goods and services a country's populace really desires and is willing to buy. An import/export agent is a salesperson.

At first, foreign trade may sound complicated, with such components as financing, customs, trade barriers and tariffs, currency fluctuations, exclusive/nonexclusive distribution rights, and packing/shipping. In reality, these components are not difficult, and it is by understanding them that the import/export businessperson makes a living. This book will explain all of these areas, take the mystery out of the foreign trade game, and help you to set up and manage your import/export business.

UNDERSTANDING EXPORT TRADE

Why would U.S. companies want to export? The reason is simple: profit. The total international market is four times larger than the U.S. market. In addition, growth rates for some products and services in overseas countries far exceed domestic growth.

Let's consider that you want to start exporting Southwestern dresses from Arizona to France. You have seen these particular dresses in local stores and you think they would sell well abroad. You contact the sales manager at the dress manufacturer and indicate that you want to export the product. The first reaction may be skepticism—foreign markets may be something the manufacturer has not thought of before. You calm the fears expressed by explaining that you will buy the dresses at their factory price and take care of the rest yourself. All you need is a price list and some samples, plus information on what quantities you can order and how long it will take to fill any orders you bring in.

After the manufacturer agrees in principle to work with you, the next step is to determine how to generate sales in France, and how much the price of the product should be to cover expenses (including shipping costs, taxes, and tariffs) and still provide an acceptable profit. Unless you have enough staff to develop your own foreign distribution system, you will have to find a foreign partner to distribute the product in France—ideally, a sales representative who already has contacts in the French clothing industry. After discussing a working arrangement, you send the representative some product samples, a price list, and any other literature that may be important to the overseas end of the business.

If the dresses are a hit and your agent is able to generate substantial sales, he or she will send the orders back to you along with a letter of credit from the buyers. The letter of credit releases payment for the order(s) through a local bank as soon as the goods are shipped. With the orders and letter of credit in hand, you buy the dresses and have a shipping company pick them up directly from the factory. Then you take the shipping documents and the letter of credit to the local bank that has arranged to pay you upon presentation of the documents. The last step is to send your foreign agent the agreed-on commission. In a deal such as this, your risk is very low because you will not purchase any products from local manufacturers until you have already made sales abroad. Unlike a wholesaler, you will not have to hold any goods in a warehouse, thereby incurring large inventory costs.

Exporters typically use one of these sales systems:

1. *Direct sales* involve dealing with the end user of a product. To maintain a closer relationship with buyers or to reduce costs, some companies prefer to do their own exporting and not use an export agent or company.

2. *Commission agents* are buying agents for foreign firms; they search for specific products for which they are paid a commission by their foreign clients.

3. *Export management companies* (EMCs) transact business on behalf of a producer for a commission, salary, or retainer plus commission. EMCs usually specialize by product, by foreign market, or by both. Export trading companies (ETCs) are similar in function.

4. *Export agents*, export merchants, or remarketers purchase products directly from a manufacturer and repackage and market the products in foreign countries.

Chapter 3 discusses current trade agreements and treaties, such as NAFTA and GATT (General Agreement on Tariffs and Trade), that regulate the import/export business.

INTERNATIONAL TRADE TODAY

The markets of the world are constantly changing. Governments come in and out of power, and trade policies shift back and forth from economic protectionism to outward-oriented free trade economies. Some regions and governments are more predictable and offer more opportunities than others. In general, though, the world seems to be heading toward a trend of more open trading policies and fewer restrictions.

For the United States, the top ten export markets for manufactured goods, in order of their amount of trade, are Canada, Japan, Mexico, United Kingdom, Germany, France, South Korea, Netherlands, Taiwan, and Singapore. Russia, Hong Kong, Southeast Asia, and Australia offer increased opportunities for import and export businesses over the next decade. Following are trade summaries for each of these important countries and regions of the world.

Canada

Canada and the United States have been close friends—geographically and economically—for most of their common history. More than 80% of all Canadians live within 100 miles of the U.S. border, and trade across the border has increased with the Canada–U.S. Free Trade Agreement of 1989 and the newer North American Free Trade Agreement (NAFTA).

Canada ranks seventh in the world in gross domestic product and is one of the world's largest producers of minerals. Canada is also the United States' largest trading partner. Total U.S.–Canada trade is currently $234 billion (U.S. dollars) and is increasing 15–20% per year, according to the U.S. Department of Commerce. Figure 1–3 provides trade details.

Japan

The Japanese economy, with a gross national product of more than $4.3 trillion (U.S. dollars), is now the second largest in the world. Although

Figure 1–3   Import/Export Comparison for Canada

	Millions of Dollars
Exports	
Newsprint	
Wood Pulp	
Timber	
Crude Petroleum	
Machinery	
Natural Gas	
Aluminum	
Motor Vehicles & Parts	
Telecommunications Equipment	
Total	**$100,177**
Major Trading Partners	U.S., Japan, U.K., Germany, South Korea, Netherlands, China
Imports	
Crude Oil	
Chemicals	
Motor Vehicles & Parts	
Durable Consumer Goods	
Electronic Computers	
Telecommunications Equipment & Parts	
Total	**$110,922**
Major Trading Partners	U.S., Japan, U.K., Germany, France, Mexico, Taiwan, South Korea
Trade Balance	**$-10,745**

Source: U.S. Bureau of the Census, *U.S. Merchandise Trade,* 1993 data.

the country has few natural resources, it has become an economic powerhouse built on its well-educated workforce. Economic downturns in recent years have cut into Japan's growth, but it is still a strong trade partner with the United States and other countries. Japan exports $150 billion more to the United States than it imports in return, according to the U.S. Department of Commerce. This trade deficit has caused some friction between the two countries. Recent negotiations have opened up some of the formerly closed Japanese markets to U.S. imports, notably medical and telecommunications products.

The economy and politics in Japan are having problems stabilizing. Once they do, Japan will again offer growing opportunities for those who know the needs of the U.S. or Japanese markets. Figure 1–4 provides trade details.

Mexico

Mexico has always been an important trade partner for the United States and Canada. The opportunities will expand as the North American Free Trade Agreement (NAFTA) works its way through the Mexican economy. Recently, manufacturing exports from Mexico expanded by over 23%, and imports grew by nearly 19%, according to the U.S. Department of Commerce. Mexico may soon replace Japan as the second largest consumer of U.S. goods and services, behind Canada.

Figure 1–4   Import/Export Comparison for Japan

	Millions of Dollars
Exports	
Machinery	
Motor Vehicles	
Consumer Electronics	
Total	**$47,950**
Major Trading Partners	Southeast Asia, U.S., Western Europe, Middle East
Imports	
Manufactured Goods	
Fossil Fuels	
Foodstuffs	
Raw Materials	
Total	**$107,268**
Major Trading Partners	China, Southeast Asia, U.S., Western Europe, Middle East,
Trade Balance	**$-59,318**

Source: U.S. Bureau of the Census, *U.S. Merchandise Trade,* 1993 data.

Mexico's 90 million people offer a new market for many U.S. exporters as well as a low-cost labor market. President Ernesto Zedillo and his party have won a majority in the legislature and, with the help of NAFTA, expect to reform and expand the Mexican economy over the next few years. Trade across the border will increase opportunities for U.S. importers and exporters. Figure 1–5 provides trade details.

Figure 1–5   Import/Export Comparison for Mexico

	Millions of Dollars
Exports	
Crude Oil	
Oil Products	
Coffee	
Shrimp	
Engines	
Motor Vehicles	
Cotton	
Consumer Electronics	
Total	$41,636
Major Trading Partners	U.S., Japan, European Community
Imports	
Metal Working Machines	
Steel Mill Products	
Agricultural Machinery	
Electrical Equipment	
Car Parts for Assembly	
Repair Parts for Motor Vehicles	
Aircraft	
Aircraft Parts	
Total	$39,930
Major Trading Partners	U.S., Japan, European Community
Trade Balance	$1,706

Source: U.S. Bureau of the Census, *U.S. Merchandise Trade,* 1993 data.

United Kingdom

The United Kingdom (England, Scotland, Wales, Northern Ireland) is exiting a painful recession that has forced it to trim its economy. This action has made it more competitive and more ready to export to other countries. More than half of the U.K.'s trade is with members of the 12-member European Union (EU)—also exiting a recession—so it has recently attempted to expand trade with North America and with former British colonies.

The U.K.'s 58 million people are a valuable resource to trade. Their relatively high earning power and production of profitable technologies make the U.K. competitive with other countries. Its economy is the fourth largest in Europe, and it is the fourth largest trading partner of the United States. As unemployment decreases, the U.K.

Figure 1-6   Import/Export Comparison for the United Kingdom

	Millions of Dollars
Exports	
Manufactured Goods	
Machinery	
Fuels	
Chemicals	
Semifinished Goods	
Transport Equipment	
Total	**$26,376**
Major Trading Partners	European Community, U.S.
Imports	
Manufactured Goods	
Machinery	
Semifinished Goods	
Foodstuffs	
Consumer Goods	
Total	**$21,736**
Major Trading Partners	European Community, U.S.
Trade Balance	**$4,640**

Source: U.S. Bureau of the Census, *U.S. Merchandise Trade*, 1993 data.

will expand as a market for U.S. goods and services. Figure 1–6 provides trade details.

Germany

As with many European countries, Germany has seen only slight economic growth over the past few years. Many feel that it is poised for economic expansion. Much of the small growth has come from the

Figure 1–7   Import/Export Comparison for Germany

	Millions of Dollars
Exports	
Machines	
Machine Tools	
Chemicals	
Motor Vehicles	
Iron & Steel Products	
Agricultural Products	
Raw Materials	
Fuels	
Total	**$18,957**
Major Trading Partners	European Community, Netherlands, Italy, United Kingdom, Belgium-Luxembourg, Western Europe, U.S., Eastern Europe
Imports	
Manufactured Products	
Agricultural Products	
Fuels	
Raw Materials	
Total	**$28,605**
Major Trading Partners	European Community, Netherlands, Italy, United Kingdom, Belgium-Luxembourg, Western Europe, U.S., Eastern Europe
Trade Balance	**$ -9,648**

Source: U.S. Bureau of the Census, *U.S. Merchandise Trade,* 1993 data.

region that was formerly East Germany, where labor costs are lower and industrial resources are available. Unemployment is high in the unified Germany.

Even so, Germany offers many import and export trade opportunities to the United States. Larger manufacturers, such as Bavarian Motor Works (BMW), are shifting some production outside of Germany. Smaller businesses are looking to use technology to compete economically with countries that have lower labor costs. Technology

Figure 1–8   Import/Export Comparison for France

Exports	Millions of Dollars
Machinery & Transportation Equipment	
Chemicals	
Foodstuffs	
Agricultural Products	
Iron & Steel Products	
Textiles	
Clothing	
Total	**$13,267**
Major Trading Partners	German, Italy, Spain, Belgium-Luxembourg, United Kingdom, Netherlands, U.S., Japan, Russia
Imports	
Crude Oil	
Machinery & Equipment	
Agricultural Products	
Chemicals	
Iron & Steel Products	
Total	**$15,244**
Major Trading Partners	Germany, Italy, U.S., Netherlands, Spain, Belgium-Luxembourg, United Kingdom, Japan, Russia
Trade Balance	**$ -1,977**

Source: U.S. Bureau of the Census, *U.S. Merchandise Trade,* 1993 data.

companies in the United States have opportunities to export products to Germany and to other European countries. About 6.5% of Germany's national products are exported to the United States. An equal amount of U.S. goods, roughly $23 billion (U.S. dollars), is imported by Germany, according to the U.S. Department of Commerce. Figure 1–7 provides trade details.

France

France is the United States' sixth trading partner, just slightly behind Germany. France has substantial agricultural resources and a highly diversified industrial sector. Though the unemployment rate is currently high, a strong franc has lowered the cost of imports and keeps inflation and wage increases low. Like other European countries, France is attempting to privatize many ventures previously owned and managed by the state. This move has increased opportunities for smaller U.S. firms to export products and services to France.

France exports machinery and transportation equipment, chemicals, foodstuffs, agricultural products, iron and steel, textiles, and clothing. It primarily imports crude oil, machinery and equipment, agricultural products, and chemicals. Figure 1–8 provides trade details.

South Korea

South Korea, until recently one of the fastest growing economies in the world, is the seventh largest trading partner of the United States. The primary reason is that the Korean government has pushed the economy toward export. Nearly a quarter of Korea's exports go to the United States—twice as much as the amount sent to neighboring Japan. Conversely, about 22% of Korea's imports are from the United States.

Korean exports include textiles, clothing, electronics, and automobiles. It primarily imports machinery, electronics, oil, steel, textiles, and grains. Figure 1–9 provides trade details.

Netherlands

The Netherlands has an advanced economy with four decades of prosperity behind it. The economy is based on private enterprise. Primary

Figure 1–9   Import/Export Comparison for South Korea

	Millions of Dollars
Exports	
Textiles	
Clothing	
Electronic & Electrical Equipment	
Footwear	
Machinery	
Steel	
Automobiles	
Ships	
Fish	
Total	$14,776
Major Trading Partners	U.S., Japan
Imports	
Machinery	
Electronics & Electronic Equipment	
Oil	
Steel	
Transport Equipment	
Textiles	
Organic Chemicals	
Grains	
Total	$17,123
Major Trading Partners	U.S., Japan
Trade Balance	$-2,347

Source: U.S. Bureau of the Census, *U.S. Merchandise Trade,* 1993 data.

exports are agricultural products, processed foods, natural gas, and chemicals. It imports raw materials, consumer goods, and crude oil. Most of its trade is within the European Union—primarily with Germany. The Netherlands imports nearly twice as much from the United States as it exports to it. Figure 1–10 provides trade details.

Figure 1–10   Import/Export Comparison for the Netherlands

	Millions
Exports	**of Dollars**
Agricultural Products	
Processed Foods & Tobacco	
Natural Gas	
Chemicals	
Metal Products	
Textiles	
Clothing	
Total	**$12,839**
Major Trading	
Partners	Germany, Belgium-Luxembourg, U.S., U.K.
Imports	
Raw Materials	
Semi-finished Products	
Consumer Goods	
Transportation Equipment	
Crude Oil	
Food Products	
Total	**$5,451**
Major Trading	
Partners	Germany, Belgium-Luxembourg, U.S., U.K.
Trade Balance	**$7,388**

Source: U.S. Bureau of the Census, *U.S. Merchandise Trade,* 1993 data.

Taiwan

With just 21 million people and few natural resources, Taiwan is a surprisingly significant U.S. trade partner. Taiwan's annual economic growth has been nearly 9% annually for over 40 years. Export growth has risen even faster; the United States is its primary market. Taiwan exports machinery, textiles, and other consumer goods. It primarily imports machinery, chemicals, crude oil, and food.

The Taiwanese government is closely involved with business. Though Mandarin Chinese is the official language, English is the language of business. Figure 1–11 provides trade details.

Figure 1–11 Import/Export Comparison for Taiwan

	Millions of Dollars
Exports	
Electrical Machinery	
Textiles	
General Machinery & Equipment	
Footwear	
Foodstuffs	
Plywood & Wood Products	
Total	**$15,205**
Major Trading Partners	**U.S., Hong Kong, European Community**
Imports	
Machinery & Equipment	
Chemicals	
Crude Oil	
Foodstuffs	
Total	**$24,601**
Major Trading Partners	**Japan, U.S., European Community**
Trade Balance	**$-9,396**

Source: U.S. Bureau of the Census, *U.S. Merchandise Trade,* 1992 data.

Singapore

Singapore is a small island-nation of 3 million people. It has a developed harbor and a skilled labor force. A former British colony, Singapore has strong service and manufacturing sectors that offer many opportunities for entrepreneurship. Though it is the tenth largest trading partner of the United States, Singapore exports more of its products to the United States than to any other country. Exports include computer equipment, rubber, and petroleum products. Singapore imports aircraft, petroleum, and chemicals, primarily from Japan and the United States. With an economy that is currently strong, Singapore is expected to become a significant trading partner. Figure 1–12 provides trade details.

Figure 1–12   Import/Export Comparison for Singapore

	Millions of Dollars
Exports	
Computer Equipment	
Rubber & Rubber Products	
Petroleum Products	
Telecommunications Equipment	
Total	**$11,676**
Major Trading Partners	U.S., Malaysia, Hong Kong, Japan, Thailand
Imports	
Aircraft	
Petroleum	
Chemicals	
Foodstuffs	
Total	**$12,796**
Major Trading Partners	Japan, U.S., Malaysia, Taiwan
Trade Balance	**$-1,120**

Source: U.S. Bureau of the Census, *U.S. Merchandise Trade,* 1993 data.

In the future, other countries and economies will challenge and replace the top ten U.S. trading partners. Contenders include Russia, Hong Kong, Southeast Asia, and Australia.

Russia

Many opportunities have opened up in world trade since the breakup of the former Soviet Union. The Russian government and economy are under tremendous pressure to change and to improve. Inflation is stabilizing. Foreign investment is expanding, especially from American manufacturers who want to take advantage of the lower labor costs. Russia already has privatized more than 100,000 state companies, accounting for more than 50% of the gross domestic product. Russia is also modernizing its telecommunications system. The door is opening, slowly, to both import and export opportunities.

Computer software is one of the areas in which Russian trade is being developed. The Russians have numerous software companies

Figure 1–13 Import/Export Comparison for Russia

Exports	**Millions of Dollars**
Petroleum & Petroleum Products	
Natural Gas	
Wood & Wood Products	
Metals	
Chemicals	
Miscellaneous Civilian & Military Products	
Total	**$2,967**
Major Trading Partners	**Europe**
Imports	
Machinery & Equipment	
Chemicals	
Consumer Goods	
Grain	
Meat	
Sugar	
Semi-finished Metal Products	
Total	**$1,744**
Major Trading Partners	**Europe, North America, Japan, Third World Countries, Cuba**
Trade Balance	**$ 1,223**

Source: U.S. Bureau of the Census, *U.S. Merchandise Trade,* 1993 data.

producing quality games and business systems. Tetris is a computer game designed ten years ago by Alexi Pazhitnov. Today, it is an international success. Russian programmers are now working on components to software distributed by Microsoft and Corel. Figure 1–13 provides trade details.

Hong Kong

In 1997, Hong Kong will revert to rule by China after 99 years as a British colony. With about 6 million people in an area of 400 square miles, Hong Kong is one of the most densely populated regions in the world. Because there is little space for growing crops or manufacturing larger machinery, Hong Kong depends on imports to supply its needs. It exports clothing, electronics, and data processing equipment, but it imports nearly $5 billion more in goods than it exports. Trade is not expected to slow down after the 1997 transfer of power. In fact, Hong Kong is now constructing a $21 billion airport and related facilities to keep up with the demands of trade. Figure 1–14 provides trade details.

Southeast Asia

Countries of southeast Asia are stepping up plans to develop a free trade area with lower tariffs among member countries, thus increasing trade. The Asian Free Trade Area members are Thailand, Singapore,

Figure 1–14   Import/Export Comparison for Hong Kong

	Millions of Dollars
Exports	
Clothing	
Textiles	
Yarn & Fabric	
Footwear	
Electrical Appliances	
Watches & Clocks	
Toys	
Total	**$9,873**
Major Trading Partners	**U.S., China, Germany, United Kingdom, Japan**
Imports	
Foodstuffs	
Transport Equipment	
Raw Materials	
Semi-manufactured Products	
Petroleum	
Total	**$9,558**
Major Trading Partners	**China, Japan, Taiwan, U.S.**
Trade Balance	**$315**

Source: U.S. Bureau of the Census, *U.S. Merchandise Trade,* 1993 data.

Malaysia, Indonesia, Brunei, and the Philippines. The plan would cut tariffs on trade within the area over the next eight years. Figures 1–15 through 1–18 provide trade details for Thailand, Malaysia, the Philippines, and Indonesia.

Australia

Though roughly the size of the continental United States, Australia's population is less than 7% of the U.S. population. Even so, the United States exports more than $9 billion (U.S. dollars) in manufactured goods "down under" each year, according to the U.S. Department of

Figure 1–15   Import/Export Comparison for Thailand

Exports	**Millions of Dollars**
Machinery & Manufactured Goods	
Agricultural Products	
Fishery Products	
Total	**$3,769**
Major Trading Partners	**U.S., Japan, Singapore, Hong Kong, Germany, Netherlands, United Kingdom, Malaysia, France, China**
Imports	
Capital Goods	
Intermediate Goods	
Raw Materials	
Consumer Goods	
Oil	
Total	**$8,542**
Major Trading Partners	**Japan, U.S., Singapore, Taiwan, Germany, South Korea, Malaysia, China, Hong Kong, United Kingdom**
Trade Balance	**$-4,773**

Source: U.S. Bureau of the Census, *U.S. Merchandise Trade,* 1993 data.

Figure 1–16   Import/Export Comparison for Malaysia

	Millions of Dollars
Exports	
Electronic Equipment	
Palm Oil	
Petroleum & Petroleum Products	
Wood & Wood Products	
Rubber	
Textiles	
Total	**$6,065**
Major Trading Partners	Singapore, U.S., Japan, United Kingdom, Germany
Imports	
Food	
Consumer Goods	
Petroleum Products	
Chemicals	
Capital Equipment	
Total	**$10,568**
Major Trading Partners	Japan, U.S., Singapore, Taiwan, Germany
Trade Balance	**$-4,503**

Source: U.S. Bureau of the Census, *U.S. Merchandise Trade,* 1993 data.

Commerce. Australian exports are not as high, but are still significant. Figure 1–19 provides trade details.

CONCLUSION

To learn more about specific countries, call the Export Hotline (1-800-760-1111 or 617-248-9393). Once you register for this free service, you can have reports faxed to you on a variety of topics. General topics include how to export, government programs, trade shows, customs, how to import, importing by industry, and information on trade agreements. You can also request comprehensive market information reports by country—from Argentina to Zimbabwe. The Export Hotline also offers industry closeups and marketing strategies.

Figure 1–17 Import/Export Comparison for the Phillipines

Exports	Millions of Dollars
Electronics	
Textiles	
Coconut Oil	
Copper	
Total	**$3,529**
Major Trading Partners	**U.S., European Community, Japan, ASEAN**
Imports	
Raw Materials	
Capital Goods	
Petroleum Products	
Total	**$4,896**
Major Trading Partners	**U.S., Japan, Taiwan, Saudi Arabia**
Trade Balance	**$-1,367**

Source: U.S. Bureau of the Census, *U.S. Merchandise Trade,* 1993 data.

Figure 1–18 Import/Export Comparison for Indonesia

Exports	Millions of Dollars
Petroleum & Liquefied Natural Gas	
Timber	
Textiles	
Rubber	
Coffee	
Total	**$2,770**
Major Trading Partners	**Japan, Europe, U.S., Singapore**
Imports	
Machinery	
Chemical Products	
Manufactured Goods	
Total	**$5,439**
Major Trading Partners	**Japan, Europe, U.S., Singapore**
Trade Balance	**$-2,669**

Source: U.S. Bureau of the Census, *U.S. Merchandise Trade,* 1993 data.

Figure 1–19   Import/Export Comparison for Australia

	Millions of Dollars
Exports	
Textiles	
Garments	
Telecommunications	
Recording Equipment	
Petroleum	
Minerals	
Total	**$8,272**
Major Trading Partners	Hong Kong, Macau, Japan, U.S., Germany, South Korea, Russia
Imports	
Specialized Industrial Machinery	
Chemicals	
Manufactured Goods	
Steel	
Textile & Yarn	
Fertilizer	
Total	**$3,294**
Major Trading Partners	Hong Kong, Macau, Japan, U.S., Taiwan, Germany, Russia
Trade Balance	**$4,978**

Source: U.S. Bureau of the Census, *U.S. Merchandise Trade,* 1993 data.

2

FORMING YOUR IMPORT/EXPORT SERVICE

When starting your import/export company, you can enter the business in a number of ways, depending on the aspects of foreign trade in which you are most interested. Some companies involved in foreign trade offer more services than others. Some import/export companies, for example, act only as sales agents: they find buyers and take a commission, but do not help with the actual shipping, documentation, or financing of the sale. Others offer full-service importing or exporting: they buy directly from the manufacturer and take care of all import and export responsibilities, including marketing. These companies often specialize in either import or export, and stay within one industry.

If you are interested in entering the import/export business, perhaps the best way to start is as a sales agent for either a domestic company wishing to export or a foreign firm that wants to tap the U.S. market. You can familiarize yourself with the various markets, industries, and international trade regulations, as well as assess your opportunities and limitations—without the risk and expense of starting up a full-scale company. As you gain valuable experience and build up your business, you may then decide to expand your role in the import/export trade by seeking larger markets and offering a broader range of services to your clients.

THE FUNCTION OF IMPORT SERVICES

Even though your import business might be located in the United States, importing can be as complex a business as exporting. In some instances, particularly when dealing with emerging economies, an importing business may require even more careful monitoring of records, timetables, and political events abroad. In many transactions, you'll take title of the product and handle all documentation, including customs requirements, warehousing, and shipping, once the delivery arrives in the United States. In addition, you will be in charge of sales within the United States after the product passes through customs. This means finding U.S. reps, distributors, and retailers who will buy the product. As an additional opportunity, you might consider marketing the product through mail order, one of the highest retail growth industries.

The prime objective when acting as the importer for a foreign manufacturer is to reach your targeted market. You should have a clear definition of the trade channel through which the product will travel to reach the market, and your role within that channel. A *trade channel* is the method by which products or services are distributed from the manufacturer to end users. A manufacturer using an intermediary who resells to users operates in a three-level channel of distribution. The intermediary can be a merchant who purchases the merchandise and resells it, or an agent who acts as a broker but doesn't take title to the merchandise.

Your choice of trade channel will be dictated by your market research and, as in exporting, formulated in a marketing plan that encompasses selling and distribution strategies. It is important to understand how your particular channel of trade operates because each participant adds costs—but not always value—to your product. Know your position in the channel of trade, and who your partners are in that channel. Efficiencies achieved in any one stage can be canceled by the inefficiencies of weak partners in another. Be aware of who adds costs to the product you are selling. Is that cost commensurate with the value added to the product? If not, the net result is a poor perception of value by the customer and, consequently, lower sales. Efficiency, or the reduction of cost, can lower sales prices and thereby help obtain a competitive edge. If the efficiencies you achieve are matched by efficient trade-channel affiliates, the result is likely to be higher sales for you and your foreign client. Always target higher sales as the goal of your business.

Depending on how you position yourself in the channel of trade, you will be dealing with the following:

1. *Manufacturer's representatives.* One of the best ways to distribute a product is through these independent salespeople who operate out of agencies that handle an assortment of complementary products. Each representative allocates his or her selling time to the various products promoted through the agency. Most reps work on commission, thereby allowing you to field a sales force, either regionally or nationally, without the capital expenditure otherwise required. The downside is that, because reps carry different product lines, yours may be placed far down on the priority list. With commission reps and agents in exporting, you should formalize any relationship by signing an agreement stipulating sales territory, terms of sale, method of compensation, and whether the work is on an exclusive or nonexclusive basis.

2. *Wholesale distributors.* Using this channel, you import a product and sell it to a wholesaler, who in turn sells it to a retailer or other agent for further distribution through the channel until it reaches the end users. If possible, wholesalers should be placed under contract, and you should make sure they maintain adequate facilities and personnel for normal servicing operations.

3. *Retailers.* These distributors are positioned at the end of the trade channel, where the product reaches the end users. If the end users of the product you are importing are in the general consuming public, you can sell directly to the retailer. (If the end user of the product you are importing is an original equipment manufacturer (OEM), you won't need to worry about the retailer.)

To find reps, distributors, and retailers that will be suitable for handling your imported product, refer to the following sources (consult Appendixes D and E of this book for further details):

- Publications of the Manufacturer's Agents National Association (MANA), particularly *The Directory of Manufacturer's Sales Agencies* and *Agency Sales Magazine.*

- Lists of attendees and exhibitors at trade shows that are applicable to the product you are handling.

- Trade associations, publications, and journals that cover the industry in which you are interested.

- The International Union of Commercial Agents & Brokers.

- U.S. and State trade centers.
- Your bank.
- Your local business telephone directory.

Whether importing or exporting, you should screen all prospective reps or distributors. You can do this by having them fill out a credit application and checking all their trade references, as well as their bank, to obtain a credit rating. You might also obtain membership in your local credit bureau and draw reports on each account, or utilize one of the financial rating services for business such as Dun & Bradstreet (D&B) or the National Credit Office (NCO).

THE FUNCTION OF EXPORT SERVICES

Exporting is often considered the best strategy for entering into international trade. As noted earlier, 85% of exports from the United States originate from just 250 large manufacturing companies. That leaves a large number of U.S. companies that *should* be exporting but lack the knowledge and resources to do so. That's where you come in.

As an export management company (EMC), you'll provide these U.S. producers with the exporting expertise that they lack. Your responsibilities will include finding, evaluating, and appointing dealers, distributors, and commission representatives in foreign markets, and providing promotional support such as advertising and trade show exhibitions. As you grow beyond a sales capacity, you may also handle duties such as translation of important documents and correspondence, preparation of all agreements with foreign distributors, keyboarding of all acceptances and approvals, arrangement of financing, handling of all correspondence dealing with order processing, management of all documentation and shipping, and provision of all aftermarket assistance. In some cases, whether you offer limited services or run a full-service management company, you may even take title of the goods you are exporting and thereby act as a distributor for your client.

When first starting out, however, your main function will be to sell your clients' products in foreign markets. Frequently, you will be required to act as their agent, transacting business in their name for a commission, a salary, or a retainer and commission. To do this, you will have to perform market research to determine what foreign markets are the most appropriate, and write a marketing plan to chart your strategy.

Next, you must match your clients' products with specific buyers in foreign markets. There are several avenues you can pursue when seeking buyers for your client. They include:

- *Commission agents*—intermediaries commissioned by foreign firms searching for U.S. products to purchase.
- *Country-controlled buying agents*—foreign government agencies or quasi-governmental firms charged with the responsibility of locating and purchasing desired products.
- *Commission representatives*—foreign counterparts to independent sales representatives in the United States; they usually work on a commission basis, assume no risk or responsibility, and should be placed under contract for a specific period of time. The contract should stipulate sales territory, terms of sale, method of compensation, and whether they will work on an exclusive or nonexclusive basis.
- *Foreign distributors*—similar to U.S. wholesale distributors in that these merchants buy for their own account. They actually take title to the products being exported. To ensure proper protection for your clients, you should place these buyers under contract as well, making sure they maintain adequate facilities and personnel for normal servicing operations.
- *State-controlled trading companies*—in some foreign countries, government-sanctioned and controlled trading entities. These agencies often deal in raw materials, agricultural machinery, manufacturing equipment, and technical instruments.

How do you find buyers in foreign markets for your clients? There are several ways. Perhaps the largest U.S. clearinghouse of information for finding foreign buyers is the International Trade Administration (ITA), a division of the Department of Commerce. Through the ITA's U.S. & Foreign Commercial Service (US&FCS), several resources are available for locating foreign buyers. You can contact the department's industry desk officers and country desk officers, participate in trade missions and catalog/video catalog shows, and make sure your client is on all export mailing lists and trade lists. In addition, the US&FCS maintains several invaluable tools to find foreign buyers.

If at least 51% of the content of your client's product is of U.S. origin, the US&FCS will evaluate the potential of the product and match it against a list of potential buyers. The US&FCS will perform all the background work, including screening of all possible contacts, and will narrow the field of buyers to the major markets in two countries and arrange face-to-face meetings for you through the U.S. embassy or consulate. You will then join a trade delegation to those countries for meetings that are similar to business conferences, but are held in a foreign country and have a specific theme. Every month or so, the Department of Commerce holds a Matchmaker conference in a different part of the world, and each of these conferences is geared specifically toward matching companies in a specific field. Interpreter services are provided during the meetings. For the latest schedule of Matchmaker events, contact the Department of Commerce at (202) 377-0592.

A less costly alternative to the Matchmaker Trade Delegation is the Trade Opportunities Program (TOP). By subscribing to TOP, you can receive up-to-the-minute leads from around the world electronically, every workday, through the Commercial Information Management System (CIMS). These leads include direct sale requests, representation offers, and foreign government tenders, as well as investment opportunities. Names and contact information are included, so you can respond to these leads directly.

Another excellent source of leads is the Export Contact List, a database containing the names and brief profiles of thousands of companies soliciting international business contacts. Through this service, you can view business profiles of possible foreign buyers, which allows you to prescreen prospects before contacting them. Agents, distributors, marketing firms, banks, state trading and procurement agencies, and other firms that may be of interest, are included on the list.

Perhaps the best matchmaking service available to you, the Agent/Distributor Service matches your client's product with potential agents and distributors worldwide. Commercial specialists in the country you've targeted will then assess these contacts, evaluating them in terms of their interest and capability. When their evaluation is accomplished, you receive a list of the six most qualified leads. In addition, you can receive guidance in writing correspondence, formulating agreements, obtaining local business practice information, and requesting background reports.

World Traders Data Reports provide background on potential trading partners in foreign markets. You can determine the primary business activity of the firm in question, its standing in the local business community, its creditworthiness and overall reliability, and its suitability in regard to a particular product you are exporting.

Commercial News USA has a circulation of more than 100,000 business readers worldwide. By placing an ad, you can locate sales representatives and buyers for a planned export.

Other avenues for finding foreign buyers include:

- Annual reports of your client's competitors.
- Directories of conventions in the country you are targeting.

- A list of trade show attendees and exhibitors in the country you are targeting.
- Your bank or your client's bank if it has international offices.
- U.S. embassies or consulates (or obtain a booklet entitled *Guide for Business Representatives,* publication 7877, available from the Government Printing Office).
- Commercial organizations in the country you are targeting.
- The U.S. Department of Agriculture's Foreign Agriculture Service, located in Washington, DC (among its several programs are *Trade Leads, Foreign Importer Listings, Buyer Alert, Export Briefs,* and *Contacts*).
- The International Union of Commercial Agents & Brokers.
- Foreign consulates, embassies, and trade offices.
- International telephone, telex, and facsimile directories.
- American Chambers of Commerce abroad.
- Freight forwarders and customs brokers.

When searching for foreign buyers, take special care in screening each prospect. Remember, they will be representing your client. If you contract with a representative who doesn't perform well, this will reflect on you as the exporting agent of your client. If you obtain leads through the Matchmaker Trade Delegation or the Agent/Distributor Service of the US&FCS, the contacts will be screened for you. That is not the case with random inquiries or those generated through trade shows. You will have to screen these leads yourself.

Most exporters use what is called the Package 39 screening method, which employs a three-part package consisting of a one-page fact sheet, product literature, and a questionnaire. You should develop a Package 39 in conjunction with your client and have it printed in sufficient quantity for anticipated mailings and responses to random inquiries.

The fact sheet should outline your client's commission structure, agreement policies, and company information, to give prospective buyers a snapshot of who they will be dealing with and what they can expect to receive. The questionnaire, fully filled out, should be sent back to you for evaluation before you consider any buyer.

Your questionnaire should ask each company for the following information:

- What products are handled, both in import and export? (Are the products similar to yours?)
- Where it makes the majority of its sales.

- How it functions in terms of distributors, salespeople, agents, and so on.
- What territory it covers (the entire country? other countries?).
- What commission is expected.
- How many branches or agents/salespeople it has.
- Bank and commercial references.
- Company details, such as size, duration of association, annual sales, assets, liabilities, and so on.

If a prospective buyer doesn't send back the questionnaire, send one reminder letter. If it still doesn't arrive, move on to other leads that exhibit more interest.

Once you get a questionnaire back, be sure to check the references. Find out whether other companies that deal with this representative are satisfied with their working relationship. Try to determine what areas the representative is most capable of covering. He or she may ask for a larger territory than can be effectively covered.

In many instances, when dealing with export contacts overseas, you will encounter import opportunities as well. Buyers you work with may want you to handle a product they wish to export into the United States, or you may run across a product, when you are traveling, that you feel will be a sure hit in the American market. On these occasions, you will then manage the importation and distribution of these products in the United States.

DECIDING WHETHER TO BE A GENERALIST OR A SPECIALIST

Whether you are acting only in a sales capacity or offering your clients a full range of services, your import/export company will manage the distribution of your client's product into another country or into the United States. This is a big job, and you'll need to decide early whether you want to handle imports or exports or both. Offering both import and export services can be profitable if you find clients who want you to perform both services for them. Otherwise, you may find yourself overwhelmed by the requirements of developing two sets of clients for separate services.

Another choice you'll have to make is what type of products your company will specialize in. You may feel there isn't a need to limit the products you represent when it comes to importing or exporting, but your clients will definitely feel otherwise. They will evaluate your company on its ability to discuss and promote intelligently the products they offer. If you or your staff don't have the background and ability to handle their products, they will search elsewhere for a management company with the type of expertise they seek.

The products that would be best for you to handle as an importer or exporter are products that you already have a great deal of experience promoting or using. Put together a resume of your professional experience and your personal hobbies. If you've spent a great deal of time selling or using personal computers, you may want to consider handling products revolving around PC technology. For example, components used in the manufacturing of a computer, or end products like monitors, printers, or modems might be right up your alley. By concentrating on products with which you are already familiar, you will have a definite competitive advantage when marketing your service to the producers of these products, and you will ensure your ability to promote them more effectively.

You'll also have to decide at what level you will support your clients. As mentioned already, management companies vary in size and service. The extent of services you'll offer your clients will not only impact your start-up requirements, but your staffing needs as well.

If you are going to perform only a selling function, you could start your business from home, employing just yourself or perhaps one additional person. On the other hand, if you have sufficient capital and experience in the import or export industries, starting as a larger, full-service management company may be feasible. Keep in mind, however, that if you decide to start a full-service company, you'll have to consider leasing commercial office space and hiring enough people to service your clients properly. Employees may include additional account supervisors and/or administrative support personnel with backgrounds in international trade.

Realistically, starting out as a full-service management company might be beyond your means or even your aspirations. Carefully evaluate your personal financial condition to determine the amount of capital you have to invest in such a venture. If your resources are limited, start your business as a small export management company acting purely in a sales capacity, or as a small importer performing marketing tasks in the United States for a foreign exporter.

IMPORT/EXPORT MERCHANTS

Another option for an entrepreneur in the international arena is starting business as an import/export merchant. This type of international entrepreneur does not have any specific client base and does not specialize in any one industry or line of products. The merchant purchases goods directly from a domestic or foreign manufacturer and then packs, ships, and resells the goods, assuming all risks.

In many instances, the import/export merchant will already have buyers lined up domestically or in foreign countries. The merchant will usually buy and sell based on a letter of credit, thereby minimizing the risk.

This can be a very viable and profitable avenue in which to start a business in international trade, but it is often much riskier than starting as an import/export management company. There is a lack of stability in dealing with a specific foundation of exporting or importing clientele. And, though domestic and foreign exporters are hungry for sales, many like to have some control over the type of representation they receive in foreign markets. As a merchant, you would take title to the product, and the manufacturer's control over the marketing would become minimal, but the effect is to cut down the market available to you as an import/export merchant.

Merchants do have their advantages, however. Because they aren't necessarily reliant on a group of clients for the welfare of their business, import merchants can claim a greater deal of flexibility in their business relationships. Also, because they take title to the goods they trade in the international arena, their potential profile can be much greater.

For our purposes here, we will concentrate on starting a business as an import/export management company (I/EMC) rather than as a merchant, even though being an import/export merchant is a good opportunity. Much of the information in this book can be used by merchants as well as management companies. However, management companies offer an added degree of stability while still opening up the same international opportunities. The Department of Commerce recommends the use of I/EMCs and publishes a list of I/EMCs by geographic and product sector in a booklet called *Partners in Export Trade: The Directory for Export Trade Contacts.*

COMPILING AN ACCURATE MARKET SURVEY

When you first decide to start an import/export business, you may have a specific product (or service) in mind that you want to import or export, or you may just have an idea about the type of product. Market research will help you determine whether there is a demand for that product, and in which markets that demand is the strongest. Conducting thorough market surveys is the foundation of any successful business. In fact, strategies such as market segmentation (identifying specific segments within a market) and product differentiation (creating an identity for your product or service that separates it from your competitors') would be impossible to develop without market research. If you plan on introducing a product in more than one country, you will have to conduct a market survey for each country where you plan to do business.

Some of the key points you will learn from a market survey are:

- What markets are the most promising for a particular product.
- What markets are the largest and/or are growing fastest.
- How much competition your product will have and from what companies.
- The price and present sales volume of similar goods in potential target markets.
- An estimate of the total sales volume you can reasonably obtain.
- How domestic or world events may affect a market.
- The demographic characteristics of the market, such as median age, sex, income, and spending habits.
- What cultural characteristics might affect your sales (these can include regional tastes, values, and opinions).
- What international trade barriers are in place and how they will affect your ability to compete.

There are four primary research methods you'll have to choose from:

1. The historical method uses past data to define current market conditions.
2. The observational method studies current market data in order to predict future conditions.
3. The experimental method, using appropriately controlled tests, seeks to discover whether specific marketing activities will be effective.
4. The survey method, the most prevalent method, uses research on existing markets.

A thorough market survey will help determine a reasonable sales forecast for a particular product you are considering for export or import. Here are the basic steps for assessing your market and making a forecast:

1. Determine the trading area in which the exported or imported product will be distributed.
2. Determine the area's purchasing power.

3. Study the population within this area to determine its potential spending characteristics.

4. Determine the present sales volume of the type of product you will be offering. If you will be exporting or importing a product unique to a particular trading area, determine the sales volume of a similar product already present in the market.

5. Estimate what proportion of the total sales volume you can reasonably obtain. If you are basing total sales on a similar product, use that product as a model to gauge sales of the product you will be exporting or importing.

In conducting your market survey, you will be gathering two types of data: primary information that you will compile yourself or hire someone to gather, and, more likely, secondary information already compiled and organized for you. Reports and studies done by government agencies, trade associations, or other businesses within your industry are examples of the latter. Search for them, and take advantage of the information they contain.

Primary Market Research

Two types of information can be gathered through primary research:

1. *Exploratory information*—geared toward defining a problem by questioning targeted consumers, using fairly open-ended and general questions that elicit lengthy answers.

2. *Specific information*—concentrates on solving a problem that has already been defined; usually involves more in-depth questioning than exploratory research. The objective of specific research is to decide on concrete courses of action that will resolve a problem defined by exploratory research.

Most companies hire a marketing firm to acquire primary data for them, but this is not always the case. When conducting primary research using your own resources, you must first decide how you will question your target group of individuals. There are three methods you can use: (1) direct mail, (2) telemarketing polls, and (3) personal interviews.

Before conducting your market research, however, you should familiarize yourself with the numbering systems utilized in the import/export trade. These numbering systems are important because products for import and export are classified under these systems, and trade statistics are gathered from them. Therefore, when gathering information, whether primary or secondary, most agencies will require an accompanying number along with the type of product for which you are currently conducting a survey.

The numbering systems used in the import/export trade include:

- *Harmonized Tariff Schedule of the United States (HTS)*. Developed in conjunction with the Customs Cooperation Council (an international organization of 150 countries), the Harmonized System (HS) is an 11-digit number that classifies exports and imports in order to establish rates and duties (tariffs) as well as gather statistics.
- *Schedule B*. Used for classifying exports, Schedule B is a 10-digit number that exporters are required to use on their Shippers Export Declaration forms. As with the HTS, trade statistics are gathered based on the Schedule B number.
- *Standard International Trade Classification (SITC)*. Developed by the United Nations, the SITC is a 5-digit number used to classify exports and imports by commodity, country, and Customs District.

To find the preceding numbers for a product you plan on exporting or importing, consult *U.S. Foreign Trade Statistics: Classification and Cross Classification*, a booklet published by the Government Printing Office. Simply follow the listing until you find the product's SIC (Standard Industrial Classification) number, which is issued by the U.S. government. Listed with the SIC number will be the Schedule B number(s).

Secondary Market Research

As previously mentioned, most secondary research information will have been gathered for you by firms outside your company and will be fairly easy to obtain free or at a nominal cost. Secondary research is not as complicated as primary research. It doesn't require any interviews to determine problems and develop courses of action. You will need only knowledge of where to search for agencies that have already gathered the information.

General information on trade can begin with the Trade Information Center, which offers comprehensive data on federal programs that support U.S. export. Its toll-free telephone number is (800) USA-TRADE (872-8723). In addition, the U.S. Department of Commerce offers the Economic Bulletin Board, a PC-based modem service with information on domestic census, economic, labor, and monetary matters. To learn how to log on, call (202) 377-1986.

Working with the International Trade Administration

A division of the Department of Commerce, the International Trade Administration (ITA) provides a wide variety of programs and services designed to help American companies of all sizes get started in exporting. The ITA can be especially helpful to smaller firms that lack the financial and managerial resources to compete effectively against larger companies. In particular, it provides market identification, market assessment, and overseas contact assistance through its many domestic offices and overseas posts. These services are available either at no charge or for a nominal fee.

The ITA also manages the U.S. & Foreign Commercial Service. With offices in over 100 countries worldwide (countries considered to be the primary trading partners of the United States), the US&FCS is a federal trade promotion organization with a global network of trade professionals who are trained and available to assist small businesses with their exporting needs. Each US&FCS post, for example, develops a country marketing strategy and action plan. The plan allots time and resources for active assistance in response to U.S. business requests, and for identification of local trade and investment opportunities.

Helping American companies with major contracts is another top priority. The US&FCS posts are also continually alert to spot trade and investment opportunities. In addition, they gather data on country trends affecting trade and investment, analyze industry sector prospects, and identify and evaluate importers, buyers, agents, distributors, and joint venture partners for U.S. firms.

The US&FCS offers free counseling by trade specialists to assist business owners with exporting questions and problems, and a variety of other services such as market research, help in finding foreign contacts, and product promotion. The market research services include a comparison shopping service and foreign market research. In addition, the US&FCS provides the following market research services:

- *Trade Statistics*—up-to-date statistics available electronically from information gathered by the United Nations and the U.S. Bureau of the Census. Statistics date back to 1962 and can be provided in dollar value, quantity, unit value, growth rate, market-share percentage, and a variety of other forms for periods of a month, quarter, or year, or for a five-year grouping. (This is especially helpful when developing a marketing plan for a product.)

- *World Traders Data Reports*—background reports on potential trading partners in foreign markets; described earlier in this chapter.

In addition, the US&FCS has several references available to U.S. exporters, including:

- Export statistics profiles (ESP).
- Overseas business reports.
- Foreign economic trends.
- *The BNA Export Reference Manual.*
- *The Exporters' Encyclopedia for Foreign Markets.*
- Country files.

When contacting the ITA, be sure to convert the SIC number for the product you are handling to a Schedule B number.

Working with the U.S. Department of Commerce

The U.S. Department of Commerce can provide a wealth of information to exporters and importers. There are 68 Department of Commerce district and branch offices in cities throughout the United States and Puerto Rico. Their function is to provide information and professional export counseling to businesspeople. The U.S. Department of Commerce is headquartered at 14th Street and Constitution Avenue, N.W., Washington, DC 20230.

The U.S. Bureau of the Census, a component within the Department of Commerce, gathers and publishes data on imports and exports. Its detailed reports include:

- *Highlights of U.S. Export and Import Trade* (monthly).
- *Summary of Export and Import Merchandise Trade.*
- *Vessel Entrances and Clearances.*
- *Waterborne Exports and General Imports.*
- *General Imports of Cotton Manufacturers.*
- *General Imports, Schedule A, Commodity by Country.*
- *Exports, Schedule E, Commodity by Country.*

- *General Imports, Commodity Groupings by World Area.*
- *General Imports, World Area by Commodity Groupings.*
- *Exports, Commodity Groupings by World Area.*
- *Exports, Schedule B, Commodity by Country.*

You can pick up reference copies of these reports at local U.S. Department of Commerce district offices or obtain them on a subscription basis.

In addition to its reference booklets, the Census Bureau provides information on a subscription basis through Customer Services and the Foreign Trade Division.

Through Customer Services, you can subscribe to the National Trade Data Bank on an annual basis. Information from the National Trade Data Bank is available in CD-ROM form under the titles *U.S. Imports of Merchandise* and *U.S. Exports of Merchandise.* The database for imports includes quantity, value for all methods of transportation, and value of commodity by country of origin; customs district of entry, customs district of unloading, and rate provision. The database for exports provides information on quantity, value, and shipping weight by country of destination, customs district of exportation, and method of transportation.

You can also purchase individual disks for a specific year and month. Because most disks are updated on a monthly basis to reflect the most current information, by purchasing the December disk of a specific year you will have all available statistics for that year. If you are tight on cash, these CD-ROM disks are available for viewing at any Government Depository Library. Usually, a Government Depository Library is located in every congressional district. Consult your local telephone directory for the one closest to you.

The Foreign Trade Division of the Bureau of the Census also maintains databases on imports and exports that are available in CD-ROM format. Most of the information contained in these databases is similar to information in the National Trade Data Bank.

Associations

You can find several helpful sources of information through an industry association. Most associations can offer nonmembers a reason to join because of the wealth of information they have accumulated on a particular industry—market statistics, lists of members, books and reference material lists, and discounts with certain suppliers. The Direct Marketing Association, for example, prepares a yearly report on the association and the industry.

Census Tracts

Valuable information for importers can be obtained from census tracts. Almost every county government publishes population density and distribution figures in easily available census tracts. They indicate the number of people living in specific areas such as precincts, water districts, or perhaps, 10-block neighborhoods. Some counties publish reports that show the population 10 years ago, 5 years ago, and currently, thus indicating population trends.

Maps

Maps of major trading areas in counties and states are also useful to importers and are available from chambers of commerce, industrial development boards, trade development commissions, and city newspaper offices. These maps show where the major business of the subject area is conducted and reflect the population's spending habits.

Look at road maps of any area for information on the ease of access to specific sites. Access is an important consideration in determining market area limits, especially if you are distributing imports yourself.

Domestic Market Research

Companies importing goods are located in or near potential markets. Primary research is therefore easier for them than it is for exporters. Your research may target wholesale buyers, retailers, or the general public, depending on how you plan to distribute your products and what questions you want answered. If you choose a direct mail questionnaire, make sure your questions are short and to the point. Most people don't like to be bothered with direct mail questionnaires. If yours is lengthy, your chances of receiving a significant response rate will drop.

The same is true of telemarketing. Most people are bombarded with phone solicitations these days and have become wary of unfamiliar voices over the phone. This overkill, combined with the fact that you are invading their free time at home, makes you an unwelcome intruder. Many people, however, will grant you a small amount of their time to answer a few questions. If you get too verbose, they'll hang up on you.

The best way to obtain primary data is to conduct person-to-person interviews. Once you've gained the attention of an individual who agrees to an interview, it is easy to sit down and ask questions that will take an hour or more to complete. The advantage of personal interviews over direct mail and telemarketing is that you're probably not invading the individual's personal territory or time. Interviews are usually conducted at a prearranged time that is convenient for the interviewee. Many interviewers offer an incentive—a small payment such as $10 or a free gift—for agreeing to an interview. It is important for you to be dealing with a willing candidate.

Foreign Market Research

For exporters, primary research is expensive and difficult to conduct because the market is so far away. Most exporters rely on secondary research—data compiled from existing sources such as trade statistics.

Companies that require primary data often find it is easier to hire a market research company in the targeted country than to perform the survey themselves. The US&FCS offers several market research services, including a Comparison Shopping Service. This service prepares a detailed, customized report that answers the following questions concerning a specific product:

1. Does the product have sales potential in the market?
2. Who is supplying a comparable product locally?
3. What is the usual sales channel for distribution of this type of product into the target market?
4. What is the current price for a comparable product in this market?
5. Are purchases of such products primarily influenced by price or other competitive factors, such as quality, delivery, service, promotion, brand, and so on?
6. What is the best way to obtain sales exposure in the market for this type of product?
7. Are there any obstacles to sales of this type of product in this market, such as quotas, duties, or local regulations that might impede performance?
8. Who might be interested and qualified to represent or purchase this company's product in this market?
9. If a licensing or joint venture strategy seems desirable for this market, who might be an interested and qualified partner for the U.S. company?

The reports are available for 52 countries and cost only $500 to $1,500, depending on the country. They include an extensive amount of valuable information and are well worth the cost for most companies considering exporting.

Another valuable service that the US&FCS offers is its Foreign Market Research. Through an international computerized Commercial Information Management System (CIMS), the US&FCS can compile information for customized reports, based on the type of product or industry, that profile the export markets of interest. Based on your needs, a report can include the following country-specific facts:

- Best-selling products.
- Market access.
- Top imports.
- End users.
- Trade barriers.
- Market size.
- Market characteristics.
- Competitive analyses.
- Market forecasts.
- Industry forecasts.
- Economic trends.
- Trade events.
- Government regulations.

These reports can be prepared on either hard copy or diskette. The Foreign Market Research service is valuable for small I/EMCs that do not have the resources to conduct thorough primary research themselves. The reports generated from this service will help you select new markets that are experiencing high growth levels, evaluate conditions that affect your entry and performance in the market, and develop selling strategies that will help maximize your effectiveness in that market.

USING IMPORT/EXPORT CONSULTANTS

Most people jump headlong into a business venture, often pouring in their life savings without a thought toward submitting their business plan (if they even have one) to a competent business consultant for analysis.

Careful planning is necessary in any business venture. Your planning should be based on an unbiased analysis designed to uncover potential failure factors. Keep your enthusiasm in check and follow a cautious, rational path.

Successful entrepreneurs seek qualified outside opinions and demand that their consultants tear apart their business plan in every possible way. Only then can entrepreneurs see, from an objective standpoint, both the pitfalls and the promises in their business ideas.

Finding a Qualified Consultant

Demand proof of a consultant's expertise before retaining his or her services. Request professional and bank references, and check them out. Make sure the consultant can prove practical experience in managing and operating businesses—the more varied, the better.

The Business Counseling Section of the International Trade Administration (ITA) can be extremely helpful in arranging counseling for your new import/export venture. Specialists in trade, working for the ITA, offer in-depth counseling on all phases of international trade. In addition, they will schedule appointments with officials in the ITA and in other agencies, so you can obtain from the best source the information you require. The Business Counseling Section also maintains an Export Information Reference Room in Washington, DC, where interested individuals can review a wide range of information on importing and exporting.

You should also look into the seminar and educational programs offered by the ITA through the US&FCS. Fees to attend these seminars and educational classes are very reasonable, and you'll be able to obtain a copy of *A Basic Guide to Exporting*, a Department of Commerce publication that lists hundreds of resources for exporters. (It can also be purchased through federal bookstores for less than $10.)

Although highly paid consultants are available in many fields relating to specific areas that affect your business, the consultant best able to advise you is probably someone who is already successful in the same business. Look in another part of town or a nearby city for an established business that will not be in direct competition with you, and ask the owner or manager to analyze your plans.

Because poor location and ineffective advertising are among the most common reasons for business failure, you will want these aspects of your plans addressed with particular care. Offer a good fee—an amount in keeping with your geographic area, the experience of the consultant, and the complexity of the problems you are asking him or her to study.

Consulting fees range from $45 to $175 per hour. Some consultants contract by the hour, others by the day. In addition, you can expect to pay out-of-pocket costs, such as travel or telephone bills, related to the work you're having the consultant do. Less than 20% of professional consultants in the nation report they are fully booked. That means the field is competitive, so keep looking until you are satisfied the consultant you choose can do the job for you at a reasonable cost.

Whatever this cost turns out to be, it is definitely worth paying. Don't hesitate to take this important step before you start any business. Remember to ask for a negatively stressed analysis with key success factors clearly stated.

WRITING YOUR BUSINESS PLAN

By now you may have decided whether you want to import or export, and what type of products you will represent. You should have some broad ideas on how you will set up and run your business. The process of creating a business plan forces you to take a realistic, objective look at your proposed business in its entirety. Why is it so important to see your venture as a whole? Most people who have business ideas deal with them haphazardly. Putting a business plan together and writing down specifics not only gives you a chance to see your business as its creator, but also allows you to step outside it and take a levelheaded approach to implementing your creation.

A finished business plan becomes an operating tool that will help you manage your business and work toward its success. The final, completed plan is the chief instrument for communicating your ideas to others—businesspeople, bankers, and partners. If you seek financing for your business, the plan will become the basis for your loan proposal.

A strong business plan holds few surprises for its target. It conforms to generally accepted guidelines of form and content. Aside from introductory material, a business plan typically has as many as 13 sections. Each section should include specific elements that will clarify your business goals. The typical business plan is structured like this:

    a. Cover.

    b. Title page.

    1. Statement of purpose and summary.

    c. Table of contents.

    2. Description of business.

    3. Market analysis.

    4. Market strategy.

    5. Design and development plans.

6. Operations plan.
7. Management structure.
8. Timetables and schedules.
9. Potential pitfalls.
10. Community benefits.
11. Financial data.
12. Supporting information.
13. SBA materials (if applicable).

An important fact to keep in mind when preparing your plan is that you will not be creating it in the same order that it is *presented*. Following are some tips on how to prepare each section of your business plan.

Cover

A business plan should have a wraparound cover. There is no reason to have your plan bound in leather. What is required is that the binding be neat and of adequate size to hold your material. Buy small packages of blue, black, or brown covers with inside-edge grippers at a stationery or office supply store. A lender is more likely to think well of you if you remain conservative in this regard, so don't spend money on unnecessary show. Subtle factors like this reflect your business judgment. In some respects, the way a person reacts to your business plan will affect his or her opinion of your management ability.

Title Page

Start your business plan with a title page. On this page, put the name of the business, the name(s) of the principals who own it, the complete business address, and the telephone, telex, and fax numbers. If you have a professional, businesslike logo, it can be used to dress up your title page.

Statement of Purpose and Summary

Next comes a statement of purpose and summary. Use that wording as its title. The summary should tell the reader what you want. This is very important. All too often, what the business owner desires is buried in the middle of the plan. Make clear what you are asking for in this section. The statement of purpose cannot be completed with numbers until you've calculated your capital needs. Write a draft and leave the numbers blank, to be filled in later. The summary should cite the nature of the business, the legal form of operation (sole proprietorship, partnership, corporation, or limited partnership), the amount and purpose of the loan being requested, a proposed repayment schedule, the equity share of the borrower, and the equity–debt ratio after the loan, security, or collateral is offered. List the market value, estimates, or quotes on the cost of any equipment to be purchased with the loan proceeds.

Suppose you own a business and want to expand. This is how your statement of purpose might read:

> Import International, Inc., a closely held company incorporated under the laws of the State of Oregon, is seeking a loan of $75,000 to purchase equipment and inventory and upgrade a building at 520 Olive Street, Springfield, Oregon. The money will be used to perform necessary renovations and improvements, to maintain sufficient cash reserves, and provide adequate working capital to successfully expand an existing wholesale import company.
>
> The sum, together with the $20,000 equity investment of the principals, will be sufficient to finance the expansion through the transition phase so that this recently started business can operate as an ongoing, profitable enterprise.

Make it easy for the loan analysts to know your wants and capabilities. They can then say yes or no immediately and not waste your time or theirs.

Whether the plan is to be used for financial or operations purposes, its statement of purpose should be kept short and businesslike, probably no more than a half-page. It could be longer, depending on how complicated the use of funds may be, but the summary of a business plan, like the summary of a loan application, is generally no more than one page.

In financially oriented business plans, the page following might have a table that shows how the loan proceeds will be distributed, and the sources and uses of funds. You can amplify this with a small list showing what is going to be used as collateral and the conditions of the loan you propose.

Table of Contents

Following the statement of purpose comes a table of contents. You will naturally prepare this last, but be aware that you need to include one.

When you or others look over your plan, you should be able to quickly find certain information, financial data, and market information.

Description of Business

The section describing the business provides the reader with a general idea of the venture. Include any variables that provide insight into the business, the industry, and its markets.

Market Analysis

In this section, your main objective is to provide research that defines the potential customers, the size of the market, the competition, and how much of the market share you can reasonably hope to attain. This is perhaps the most important section you'll be dealing with. You'll be developing expected sales figures that define factors to be discussed later in the plan. It may be to your advantage to complete this section before attempting any others.

Market Strategy

Once you have defined your potential market and expected sales figures, you have to detail how you will reach those projections. Based on your marketing analysis, you should describe exactly what your marketing strategy will be.

Design and Development Plans

The section on design and development plans is geared toward detailing the status of the proposed product or service before it is ready to hit the market. If your product or service is already completely developed, you can forgo this section.

If you have developed the idea but not the product, or have plans to improve an existing product, or own an existing company with plans to introduce a new product, this section is extremely important to your business plan. The investor will want to know the development progress of any product or service concept, the costs associated with making it a marketable item, and the estimated period of time.

Operations Plan

In the operations section, you'll want to describe your facility requirements, plus any production or inventory purchasing plans. It is essential to present any costs the business will acquire in the production and
inventory cycle.

Management Structure

Investors will be interested in the management structure of the organization. Who will run the business? What type of support personnel
will there be? They will also want to know what kind of compensation
any management personnel will receive, as well as any equity positions
that may be given in order to attract key individuals.

Timetables and Schedules

After the management section, coordinate all the preceding information into a timetable that will chart the development of the company
from start-up to a projected break-even date and beyond. This is an integral step to raising money. Your main task in this section is to inter-
relate all the major events involved in your company's growth to
projected deadlines for the completion of those items.

Potential Pitfalls

The pitfall section is included to show that you have thought of all the
potential difficulties you might encounter when starting this venture.
This type of information lends credibility to your ability to manage
and conceptualize the various risks involved in business.

Community Benefits

Aside from the pitfalls, you also want to show potential investors the
community benefits that will be derived from your business: the economic impact of your business on the community in the form of jobs, increased money circulated through the local area, living standards, and
so on. In addition, describe how your business will affect the human element as well as the community in general. If you're providing a product

or service that is unavailable in that community, this is a definite plus. If your business will increase community pride, that is another benefit.

Financial Data

The financial data in the business plan highlights the important financial points of the business including sales, profits, cash flows, and return on investment.

Supporting Information

Supporting documents follow the financial data. Some people prefer to put a half-page summary of personal information right after the summary of the business and before the table of contents. This is a matter of discretion; many advisers believe that it makes sense because lenders are investing in the individual as much as or more than they are investing in a business. Frequently, individual tenacity, dedication, and character are the deciding factors of success in small businesses. In any case, it's important for lenders to know that they have a person who can make a business go. A personal summary following the first summary of the business can give them this information.

Personal data might show your educational and work history in a functional way, and the things you've done that support your ability to run a business. Credit references and a summarized financial statement can be included as well; any financial statement should be no more than 60 days old. Keep this in mind if you're presenting a plan to different prospects for a longer period and update your financial statement as required.

SBA Materials

This last section is included only if the purpose of developing your business plan is to obtain SBA financing. Documents required by the SBA may be useful to you in setting up your business.

WRITING YOUR MARKETING PLAN

Once you have obtained information on your potential markets, the next step is to organize that knowledge into a plan to direct your marketing efforts. Your market research will enable you to determine which markets are viable for the products you'll be importing or exporting, and your marketing plan will help you organize the process and develop strategies concerning pricing, shipping, and making sales.

For an exporter, a marketing plan would look similar to the outline shown in Figure 2–1.

When you put together your marketing plan, make sure to write down all of the questions that you will need answered. Besides helping you organize your research, a marketing plan will prompt you to think

Figure 2–1   Sample Marketing Plan

I. Summary
II. Product Analysis
1. Where can I buy these products?
2. What is the local cost of these products?
3. What are their selling features?
III. Foreign Market Analysis
1. What countries have the greatest potential?
2. What types of people will purchase these products? What do they like about the products?
3. What is the best way to distribute the products in each market?
4. If I decide to use a foreign distribution company, how will I find one?
5. Will I need to travel abroad to find markets or distributors or to conduct research? Can I find a reliable distributor that will do this through the mail for me?
IV. Pricing/Terms
1. What variables will affect pricing? (Domestic cost, shipping costs, overhead, cost of financing, insurance, and so on)
2. What types of tariffs or trade barriers are there in each country?
3. What terms will I sell on? How will I be paid? Letter of credit from buyer?
V. Competitive Analysis
1. Can I be competitive? (Analyze the competition.)
2. How large is the market currently?
3. Can I expand this market, or will I be taking a share of the existing market?
VI. Marketing Tactics—Distribution and Sales Promotion
1. What channels will I use to distribute the product?
2. How will I time the distribution?
3. Will the distribution be intensive, selective, or exclusive?
4. What sales promotion methods and media will I use, and on what budget for each campaign?
VII. Financials & Sales Forecasts

about what needs to be done, and in what order, to get the business off the ground. Many of the questions will not relate specifically to the market, such as financing or trade barriers, but will need to be answered before you make a sale.

FUNDING YOUR BUSINESS

Raising start-up capital and financing ongoing operations is clearly a wide-ranging subject. It sometimes seems impossible to separate the myriad details you need to be aware of in order to put your business on firm financial footing. Do not worry needlessly about any bewilderment you may initially experience. Veteran financial planners are the first to admit that the question of raising money is broad and is, in large measure, a function of the sophistication and experience of the person involved.

How does the entrepreneur who has never raised capital before go about raising money? You can attempt to have others raise the capital for you, or try to raise it through your own resources. If you seek all of your capital from one large investor, you will end up with a much smaller piece of your company. If you attempt to raise the money yourself from among your own acquaintances, you can normally arrange a much better deal for yourself.

Carefully assess the proposed value of the business, determine how much capital you are going to need, in what increments, and over what time period. Then, decide about the source—a Small Business Investment Company (SBIC), a single investor, a private placement of securities with friends and relatives, a private placement through a securities firm, or a public offering either through a securities firm or through a self-issuer distribution.

Tap Yourself First

The best source of financing for starting a business is your own money. It is the easiest and quickest form of capital to acquire, there is no interest to be paid back, and you don't have to surrender any equity in your business. But getting any venture off the ground can be a very costly proposition—one that may be beyond your immediate cash reserves. If this is the case, there are several avenues you can explore in order to obtain the necessary capital. Many small businesses have been funded by early retirement funds, savings, windfalls, and even personal credit cards and small personal loans.

Friends and Relatives

After your own resources, those of your friends and relatives are the next best choices. Any money raised this way, however, should be treated as a real loan. Have a lawyer draw up loan papers for each friend or relative who contributes money to your venture. This approach to loans from friends and relatives serves two purposes: (1) it protects their loan, and (2) it prevents them from gaining equity in your business, unless you default on the loan.

Borrowing from Banks

Banks are probably the most visible source of ready financing, and you should already have contact with a few banks through your personal and business accounts. Though banks are logical places to go in order to raise capital, they are many times not the best, because they are notoriously conservative.

Most banks will require some sort of collateral as security for the loan. They will also want to know what the loan is for, so be prepared to show them your business plan. Your personal background information will have a direct bearing on how your loan applications are treated.

Depending on the size of the loan you request, there are several bank loan and collateral possibilities. If you have a *savings account* at a bank, you can use this money as collateral for a short-term loan. This is actually a very good way to get financing, because it lowers your interest rate. For instance, if you take out a loan at 10% and your savings account is earning 3%, the actual interest rate you'll be paying is 7%.

It may be possible to use your life insurance policy as collateral if it has any cash value. Loans can usually be made for up to 95% of a policy's cash value. By borrowing against your life insurance policy, you don't have to actually repay the loan; all you need to do is pay the interest charges along with your premium. However, if you don't eventually repay the amount borrowed, your policy will decrease that much in value.

Signature or *personal* loans are a possibility if your credit is good. You can usually take out a loan of this type for several thousand dollars, or even more if you have a good relationship with the bank. These loans are usually short-term and have very high interest rates.

Another short-term loan is a *commercial* loan, which is usually issued for a six-month period and can be paid in installments during that time or in one lump sum. Stocks and bonds, your life insurance policy, or your personal guarantee can be used as collateral. If the loan is exceptionally large compared to your assets, the bank may require that you post with them a cash reserve equal to 20% of the loan amount.

You can also use as collateral any *real estate* you own. Loans of this nature can be secured for up to 75% of the real estate's value and can be set up for a term of 20 years if necessary.

Other loan possibilities include *inventory, equipment,* or *accounts receivable* financing. These types of loans use the value of your inventory, equipment, or accounts receivable as security for a loan. When you use your inventory as collateral, a bank will usually loan up to 50% of its value. Equipment loans will cover 80% of the equipment's value. With accounts receivable, most banks will loan up to 80% of the receivables' value.

Another finance option from a bank is a line of credit, which is similar to a credit card. You are given a preset limit that you can draw from, and you are then charged interest on whatever amount you use. Interest rates for this type of account are higher than those for an ordinary loan, but it can end up costing less if you use less money. For example, if you get a $50,000 loan and end up using only $30,000, you still pay interest on the full $50,000. If you have a $50,000 line of credit, you can take out up to that amount, but if you use only $30,000, that is all you will have to pay interest on.

Some banks offer a line of credit valued at the difference between 80% of your home's value and your current first mortgage. For example, a home valued at $100,000 can secure a line of credit of $80,000 less any mortgages. If the mortgage is $50,000, the line of credit may be up to $30,000.

Finance Companies

Geared mostly toward active investors, finance companies will allow for a greater amount of risk in a loan than will banks, but they charge a higher interest rate. Generally, finance companies will be more interested in your collateral, your past track record, and the potential of your new business, rather than in the strength of your credit.

Using Your Credit Cards

One of the most overlooked avenues for obtaining start-up capital is your credit cards. Most charge extremely high interest rates, but it is a way to get several thousand dollars quickly without the hassle of dealing with paperwork, as long as you don't go above your specified credit amount.

One successful entrepreneur had three credit cards with a credit line of $3,000 on each card. Using his credit cards, he cashed each in for the full amount and started his business. Within six months, he had built up a very good business and approached his bank for a loan of $10,000. He received the loan for a three-year term at 12%. With the $10,000, he paid off his credit card balances, which were incurring a 20% annual rate. After another six months, he paid off the bank loan of $10,000. It doesn't always happen this smoothly, but credit cards have started many small businesses.

Small Business Administration

The Small Business Administration (SBA) is not in the lending business. It's in the loan guarantee business. It may not make or guarantee a loan if a business can obtain funds on reasonable terms from some other source. Borrowers must first seek private financing before applying to the SBA. The SBA considers itself to be a lender of last resort.

To qualify for an SBA loan, your loan application must be for financing of an independently owned and operated business. Loans cannot be made to speculative businesses, newspapers, or businesses engaged in gambling; nor can loans be made to pay off a creditor who is adequately secured and in a position to sustain loss, provide funds for distribution to the principals of the applicant, or replenish funds previously used for such purposes.

Be fully prepared to prove to the SBA that your proposed company has the ability to compete and be successful in its particular field. Whether you're seeking a loan for a new concept or an established one, don't underestimate the importance of the category into which the SBA groups it. The success or failure of your application may rest on the classification the SBA assigns it. Determine which field or area your business can best compete in, state this in your application, and be prepared to back it up.

To help you prepare for this question, you should be aware of how the SBA formulates its guidelines. A key publication it relies on is the *Standard Industrial Classification (SIC) Manual,* published by the federal Bureau of the Budget. The SBA also uses published information concerning the nature of similar companies, as well as your description of your proposed business. The SBA will not intentionally work against you; therefore, it is up to you to steer the agency in the direction most beneficial to you.

Although loans are available for just 1 or 2 years and for as long as 25 years (for construction and real estate purposes), the vast majority run for 5- to 8-year terms, with 10 years being the limit (except for working-capital loans, which are limited to 7 years).

As collateral for an SBA loan, you can use certain assets as security:

- Land and/or buildings.
- Machinery and/or equipment.
- Real estate and/or chattel mortgages.
- Warehouse receipts for marketable merchandise.
- Personal endorsement of a guarantor (a friend who is able and willing to pay off the loan if you fail).

Another popular service is SBA On-Line, a computer bulletin board operated by the Small Business Administration. It receives more than 1,000 calls a day and has handled over a million calls since it opened in 1992. Once you're familiar with computers and modems, you can access this resource by having your system call (900) 463-4636. There is a small fee for its use, currently about $6 an hour. The bulletin board includes extensive resources for small businesses and access to other government agencies. One of the resources is Reach Strategic Venture Partners (RSVP), a database that lets companies list their interest in a joint-venture partner for an overseas project. The agency sends its materials to hundreds of trade-related organizations around the world.

Some of the SBA's other programs to encourage international trade are profiled in the sidebar, "Export Help." For further information, contact the SBA Office of International Trade, 409 Third Street, S.W., 6th Floor, Washington, DC 20416, or call (202) 205-6720.

The LowDoc Loan Program

The Small Business Administration has adopted a program that makes applying for a loan somewhat easier. Called the LowDoc Loan Program, it combines a simplified application process with a more rapid response (up to two weeks) from SBA loan officers, slashing pages of documents and red tape out of the loan process.

The LowDoc program was created in response to complaints that the SBA's loan application process for smaller loans was needlessly cumbersome for borrowers and for lenders that participate in the SBA's 7(a) General Business Loan Guarantee Program ("7(a) loan program").

Nothing—not currency fluctuations, not tariffs, not expensive shipping—has inhibited the growth of American small businesses trying to sell their products and services overseas as much as the lack of reliable sources of working capital.

You may have an export order, and your banker may be somewhat interested, but that's not necessarily going to get working capital working for you in time to keep your potential buyer from giving up and handing the sale to a big foreign competitor. Businesses whose capital assets and machinery are tied up as collateral for long-term loans can't move quickly to nail down working capital. And lenders often consider export working capital loan requests too small and risky when compared with longer-term domestic loans.

That's where the SBA comes in. Our new Export Working Capital Program (EWCP), which replaces the SBA's Export Revolving Line of Credit, can support single transactions or multiple sales. Under the program, the SBA guarantees up to 90% (as high as $750,000) of a private-sector loan.

Guarantees can be extended for preshipment working capital or a combination of the two. A preshipment guarantee is used to finance the production or acquisition of goods and services for export; a postshipment guarantee is used to finance receivables resulting from export sales.

EWCP loans are generally for a 12-month term but may be renewed twice, up to a total of 36 months. Collateral can include export inventory, foreign receivables, assignments of contract or letter-of-credit proceeds, domestic receivables, and, in some cases, personal guarantees.

The SBA offers a range of assistance for small exporters. Our free publication *Bankable Deals: A Question & Answer Guide to Trade Finance for U.S. Small Business* helps take the mystery out of export financing; it provides answers to the questions we're asked the most. Companies new to exporting can take advantage of counseling and training programs offered through our resource partners, the Service Corps of Retired Executives and Small Business Development Centers, nationwide. And our International Trade Loan Program provides a combination of fixed-asset financing and short-term working capital.

For more information on the EWCP or any of the SBA's export programs or publications, call the Office of International Trade at (202) 205-6720 or (800) U-ASK-SBA.

Erskine Bowles, "Export Help," *Entrepreneur*, November 1994, p. 202.

The process tended to discourage borrowers from applying for (and lenders from making) loans of less than $100,000.

LowDoc streamlines the loan application process for guaranteed loans under $100,000. The approval process relies heavily on a lender's experience with and judgment of a borrower's credit history and character. The primary considerations are the borrower's willingness and ability to repay debts, as shown by his or her personal and business credit history and past or projected cash flow. No predetermined percentage of equity is required, and lack of full collateral is not necessarily a determining factor.

The application form for loans under $50,000 consists of a single page. Applications for loans from $50,000 to $100,000 include that short form application plus the applicant's income tax returns for the previous three years and personal financial statements from all other guarantors and co-owners of the business. Commercial lenders are likely to require additional paperwork to satisfy their own requirements. Other documents required by legislation, regulation, and executive order are dealt with at the loan closing.

Any small business eligible under the regular 7(a) loan program can apply under LowDoc if its average annual sales for the previous three years are $5 million or less and it employs 100 or fewer individuals, including the owner, partners, or principals.

THE AGENCY FOR INTERNATIONAL DEVELOPMENT

The Agency for International Development (AID) is a financial guarantee program for U.S. firms needing financing to export manufactured goods to AID-assisted developing countries. For more information, call the AID Office of Investment at (202) 647-1805.

Eximbank

The Export-Import Bank of the United States (Eximbank) was established in 1934 to encourage U.S. exports and to aid in their financing. It extends long-term loans to borrowers outside the United States who want to purchase U.S. goods; guarantees export credits offered by U.S. commercial banks; and ensures certain losses by U.S. exporters.

Eximbank provides services similar to those of the SBA but is geared specifically toward companies that export and import. Eximbank provides loan guarantees in much the same way as the SBA. The program is called the Commercial Bank Guarantee Program. If an importing or exporting company is approved for the loan guarantee program, Eximbank will help it get a medium-term loan (181 days to 5 years) from a commercial bank by guaranteeing to pay back the bulk of the loan upon default. The loan must be collateralized, but the Eximbank will accept as collateral second mortgages on plants, equipment, inventory, and accounts receivable. This makes the program a good way to expand existing operations, but is not of much help for entrepreneurs who have no collateral. The guarantees are primarily designed for domestic manufacturing businesses that want to expand to export production.

A similar service, called the Working Capital Guarantee Program, helps small to medium size businesses find export-related working capital loans from financial institutions.

Other services available through the Eximbank are:

- *Long-term loans.* For architectural and engineering projects, long-term loans of up to 15 years are available, but a project must be capable of generating at least $10 million in additional exports to qualify for the loan.

- *Foreign credit insurance.* The Foreign Credit Insurance Association (FCIA) offers credit risk protection for export credit sales. This insurance is for exporters that extend credit to foreign buyers. The policy protects the seller in case the buyer fails to pay its bills. A number of different policies are available for large or small companies, including a policy for companies that are new to exporting. For any company extending credit, this type of policy can be a lifesaver, especially if unforeseen and uncontrollable political and economic events or unfamiliar legal systems make collecting a debt impossible.

For more information on all of its programs, contact the Export-Import Bank of the United States, 811 Vermont Avenue, N.W., Washington, DC 20571; (202) 566-8860, or, from the continental United States, call the toll-free Eximbank Hotline with any questions: (800) 424-5201. For more information on the Eximbank, see the sidebar, "Bank on It."

Using Suppliers as Loan Sources

You won't be able to finance your complete start-up through suppliers, but you may be able to offset the cost of the merchandise during your start-up period by obtaining a lengthy payment period, or *trade credit*. When you're first starting your business, suppliers usually will not extend trade credit. They're going to want to make only COD deals, but

BANK ON IT

The Ex-Im Bank, created by Congress in 1934, makes working capital guarantees to small and medium-sized companies to cover up to 90% of the principal and interest on commercial loans. The guarantee can apply to a single loan or a revolving line of credit and generally must be repaid in one year.

Louisiana entrepreneur Michael Rongey has used the Ex-Im Bank working capital guarantee program for about six years. Rongey is co-owner with his brother of Reliable Industries Inc. of New Orleans, a $10 million company that supplies spare parts for American-made heavy equipment overseas.

"Were it not for the [Ex-Im Bank] backing our receivables," says Rongey, "I don't think my bank would have stepped up to the plate until we had sufficient inventory and net worth." Rongey, who started his business in 1981, first received support from Ex-Im Bank in 1988.

To be eligible for the working capital guarantee, entrepreneurs must have been in business at least one year, have a strong business plan indicating growth potential, and be able to collateralize the loan. Additional keys, Rongey says, are having a bank willing to go to bat for you during negotiations, and finding a financial institution with a good Ex-Im Bank master policy (allowing commercial banks to approve loans themselves).

In addition to working capital guarantees, Ex-Im Bank offers short-, medium-, and long-term insurance programs. Most small businesses use the short-term program, which insures transactions involving low-cost products such as spare parts. The entrepreneur pays an insurance premium, and the foreign buyer is given up to six months to pay for the products. If the buyer fails to pay, Ex-Im Bank reimburses the entrepreneur.

The Ex-Im Bank's Small Business and Umbrella insurance programs are geared to small companies new to exporting. Each provides a one-year blanket policy insuring export credit sales of products. Eligible companies cannot have more than $2 million in net annual export credit sales. Project Financing is a new Ex-Im program that allows the receivables proceeds of a project to repay the financing.

Business owners can approach Ex-Im Bank directly or through any commercial bank that deals with the agency. In addition to its Washington, DC, headquarters, Ex-Im Bank operates five full-service regional offices: Chicago, New York City, Miami, Houston, and El Segundo, California. Ex-Im Bank also has a number of other resources for small-business owners, including an information hotline ((800) 424-5201) and briefing seminars and discussions; call (202) 566-4490 for a schedule.

Cynthia E. Griffin, "Bank on It," *Entrepreneur*, August 1994, p. 56.

you should try to get on a credit basis with your suppliers immediately. One of the things you can do to make that happen is to have a properly prepared financial plan and negotiate with the owner or the chief financial officer of the supplier.

If you're successful, you may defer payment for supplies from the time of delivery to 30, 60, or even 90 days, interest-free. This is not specifically a loan, but you don't have to pay for the goods right away, and the money needed for those supplies is kept in your pocket during the crucial start-up period.

Selling Equity

Sometimes, raising start-up capital requires giving up a portion of your business to private investors. Such money is called *equity capital*. Equity financing means dividing your business ownership among investors who contribute capital but may or may not participate in the operation of the business itself. No loans are associated with equity capital, and no legal obligation is placed on you to pay back the amount invested. All the investor gets in exchange for the money is a percentage of the business and of the losses and profits associated with it.

Equity capital may, at first glance, seem like the best way to raise start-up capital, but many drawbacks are associated with this method. First, you give up a portion of your business and, with it, some control. That means you have to share your profits with your new partners, and, depending on how you set up the company (partnership, limited partnership, or corporation), you could become responsible for the actions of your partner(s). If your partners go into debt, you and your company may also.

Second, with some types of equity financing, you might relinquish control of your company. Have your lawyer draw up documents for equity investors to sign, stating the amount and value of the equity being offered. The individual with the idea will usually retain 50% of the equity in the company, and the other 50% will be sold to investors. The 50–50 rule is fairly common, but everything is negotiable in a deal such as this.

Venture Capital

Obtaining start-up money from venture capitalists is a very difficult and potentially detrimental avenue to take. Although professional venture capitalists invest over $3 billion annually in new and growing businesses, it is in only about 3% of the deals they see each year.

Venture capitalists like to invest in relatively new businesses that are risky but have a successful track record and a potential for relatively high profit and growth.

Who are the venture capitalists? There are approximately 400 venture capital firms throughout the United States, about half of which are private partnerships that have been funded by corporate and institutional investors. They are a diverse group of investors with different investment interests, skills, and objectives. Venture capitalists differ in the industries they will finance and the stages of development of the companies they will fund. Some prefer to provide seed money for start-ups; some only do later rounds of financing or leveraged buy-outs; some may specialize in a particular geographic area. They have differing parameters on the minimum amount of money they will invest. Some may invest in $50,000 to $100,000 minimums; others will not invest less than $200,000 to $500,000.

Venture capitalists expect two things from the companies they finance: (1) high returns and (2) a method of exit. Because venture capitalists hit the jackpot with only a small percentage of the companies they back, they must go into each deal with the possibility of a return of 5 to 10 times their investment in 3 to 5 years if the company is successful. This may mean that they will own anywhere from 20% to 70% or more of your company. Each situation is different, and the amount of equity the venture capitalist will hold depends on the stage of the company's development at the time of the investment, the risk perceived, the amount of capital required, and the background of the entrepreneur.

The key to attracting venture capital is the potential growth prospect for the company. If your company does not have the potential to be a $30 million to $50 million company in 5 to 7 years, you are going to have a difficult time obtaining money from most venture capitalists. They do not invest in small businesses. They invest in large businesses that are just getting started. There are some venture firms that may have an interest in financing your new import/export business even if your growth prospects are not that high, but they are difficult to find.

However, if you're willing to give a venture capitalist a piece of the action, and if you're prepared to accept the venture capitalist as a partner in your business, you might be a candidate for venture financing. The best way to begin your search for funds is to obtain a comprehensive list of venture capital companies. Contact the National Association of Small Business Investment Companies (NASBIC), 1156 15th Street, N.W., Room 1101, Washington, DC 20005; (202) 833-8230. Its membership directory, available for $5, lists, by state, all Small Business Investment Companies (SBICs) that belong to the Association. The directory provides information about the contact person, investment policies, industry preferences, and preferred investment or loan limits of each individual investment company.

HIRING EFFECTIVE EMPLOYEES

Until you get more business than you can handle by yourself, it will be cost-efficient to operate on your own from your home or a small commercial office. The import/export business is one of the few with great potential that can be realized without the substantial costs of hiring employees.

This does not mean, however, that you should eliminate the idea of having someone work with you, particularly once you have achieved a consistent level of business. At first, you may decide you need someone else around to help answer the phones and type up correspondence. Over time, as your client base increases and you expand on services provided, you may find you need to hire more people to handle various aspects of the business. Keep in mind that there are many large I/EMCs in the United States that now have extensive staffs, but most of them have one thing in common: they started with just one person and a very low budget.

Any successful company, it's often said, is only as good as its employees. Finding the right staff to maintain and increase your growth is crucial. How does one go about finding the right people? For the import/export businessperson, there may be several considerations that go beyond the normal hiring procedures for qualified staff. A good question to ask might be: Are there any other qualifications or cultural requirements that might add extra value to my business? If you're conducting business with non-English-speaking countries or communities, for instance, hiring employees who speak the language fluently might have a huge positive impact on your business. Perhaps you're an exporter in Texas selling goods to companies in Mexico. If you don't speak Spanish yourself, having a Spanish-speaking employee on staff would be an enormous benefit. Whether in sales or administration, having someone well-versed in the target country's culture or fluent in its language not only increases your profile with your clients, but also reduces the chances for the misunderstanding or confusion that sometimes occurs in international business.

As an extreme example of business colliding with culture, take the case of one import merchant from Los Angeles who was beginning to import goods from China. In early January of 1994, he had closed a big sale with a Phoenix-based buyer for his products. The agreement stated that the order would be delivered in 60 days, with an ETA of early March. The importer's normal lead time was usually less than 45 days, so he felt he had more than enough time in which to fill the order.

Although his import focus was China and Hong Kong, the importer was not aware of some of the cultural differences that demarcate the Chinese manufacturing sector from the West's. In this case, he did not take into account the factory work stoppages for the most important holiday in China: the Lunar New Year at the end of January. Throughout China, many factories close down for one week, or even a full month or more, for the Lunar New Year holidays. The importer simply assumed that China's manufacturing sector, one of the leading sectors fueling China's explosive growth, operated under the same guidelines as those in Europe or the United States. Had the importer, or someone in his office, been more familiar with China, he might have been able to take the holiday work stoppage into account and provide a more accurate ETA for his goods. Fortunately, the importer was able to ship in time for a late March delivery, but the change in schedule very nearly cost him his prize account.

This example is an extreme case of cultural differences affecting the importer or exporter, but keep in mind that these types of situations *do* come up, especially when dealing with countries with emerging economies. Be aware. As your company begins to experience real growth, keep in mind some of the important hiring questions you must consider. The importers or exporters best poised to profit from the increasing globalization of business will be those that not only provide the best price and sales, but also offer a commensurate level of customer service.

Administrative Assistants

As you grow, one of the first areas you'll need help in is administration. A great deal of importing/exporting involves correspondence work, invoicing, and the preparation of documents. This work is important, but it can detract from the performance of more important duties that you should handle personally, such as marketing your services to clients in the United States or abroad, arranging deals with representatives and distributors, and promoting your clients' products in order to increase their visibility in selected markets.

When you reach a point where the paperwork and other daily tasks start to drastically cut into your marketing and customer service time, you should hire an administrative assistant on a full- or part-time basis. Look for an organized and detail-oriented individual who has pleasant phone manners and good communication skills.

Account Supervisors

Depending on the size of each account, a person with extensive experience in international trade may be able to handle.from three to five accounts in a given year. If the accounts are small and don't require much support, more than five may be serviced properly. However, when you reach a level that is beyond your ability to service by yourself, you are going to have to hire another person to begin recruiting and servicing accounts.

Ideally, this person should have some knowledge of international trade, coupled with an enthusiastic outlook regarding sales and the services offered by your company. This is important because he or she will be selling those services to other companies wishing to export their products. While you'll be able to initially assign the newcomer an account to service, he or she will eventually have to market the service in order to recruit his or her own accounts.

In order for an employee to be enthusiastic about sales and provide quality service, you'll have to make a worthwhile offer. Your company will be receiving a commission on the volume of sales imported or exported for clients, so you should provide your account supervisor with either a draw versus commission or salary and commission on each account.

A draw versus commission is the best vehicle for motivating an account supervisor to perform at peak efficiency. Salary and commission are nice, but they don't tend to motivate someone as much as the draw versus commission. This arrangement, of course, depends greatly on the individual. You may have a very valuable person whom you want to hold onto, and offering a salary plus commission expresses your satisfaction with his or her performance. The offer is also an excellent way to make sure your account supervisor stays with you instead of going into business as your competition and taking away your accounts.

To protect yourself against pirating, have every account supervisor you hire sign a written employment contract that contains a noncompete provision. You should consult with your attorney regarding the state laws that may affect a noncompete provision, but usually you can limit the competition from a former employee by geographic area as well as time period.

Other Concerns

In addition to administrative help and recruitment of good account supervisors, you may reach a point when you can hire your own counsel on international laws and customs, as well as someone who is conversant in several different languages of countries where you conduct business. For the most part, however, these are very specialized fields and can be contracted on an as-needed basis through a legal firm and a language translation service. For an in-depth discussion of personnel issues, consult *The Entrepreneur Magazine Small Business Advisor* (John Wiley & Sons, 1995).

3

UNDERSTANDING IMPORT/EXPORT REGULATIONS

In the import/export business, you are paid for what you know about people, products, and laws. Knowledge and understanding of world trade laws are vital to your success. This chapter offers an overview of import/export laws and regulations.

It will be up to you to keep up with the latest changes in laws and regulations impacting your clients and your products. Fortunately, there are many ways to do so. First, let's review the basics.

EXPORT LAWS AND REGULATIONS

In most transactions, you will use an international freight forwarder or customs broker to handle the shipping requirements and documentation. These agents are familiar with the import rules and regulations of foreign countries, methods of shipping, U.S. government export regulations, and documents connected with foreign trade. They can also assist with an order from the start by advising the exporter of the freight costs, port charges, consular fees, cost of special documentation, and insurance costs, as well as their handling fees—all of which are needed to prepare the quotation.

Even if a freight forwarder handles all of your licensing, documentation, and customs regulations, you should have a knowledge of the necessary forms and licenses. Shipping documents consist of export licenses and export declarations. Export licenses are either validated or general, depending on the goods.

- *Validated export licenses* are for goods that the U.S. government wants to control, such as articles of war, advanced technology, and products in short supply. Obtaining a validated license can be time-consuming and costly—and in some cases impossible—if the U.S. government does not want to ship a particular item to a particular region. A company new to the import/export business is advised not to try to ship goods requiring a validated license, at least at first. Starting your business should be enough to worry about, without these added complications. The Department of Commerce can tell you which items are on the Commodity Control List (CCL) and therefore require validated licenses.

- *General export licenses* cover most goods shipped from this country. Like validated licenses, general licenses are issued by an office within the Department of Commerce called the Bureau of Export Administration (BXA). General licenses are permits that allow your company to ship a specific type of good to a specific destination. General licenses are broken down into 18 different types. To find out which type you will need, you can talk to your freight forwarder or the BXA, or consult a copy of the Export Administration Regulations at any Department of Commerce location. You can also purchase a copy through the U.S. Government Printing Office, Washington, DC 20402; (202) 783-3238. The BXA also sponsors the Export Licensing Voice Information Service (ELVIS), an automated attendant that offers a range of licensing and emergency handling information. The ELVIS number is (202) 482-1900.

Applications for export licenses are usually acted on by the BXA within two weeks. If no special clearances are required, the license will usually be issued within three to four weeks of the date of application. Normally, a license is issued with a one-year validity period, which means that you can export the same commodity for up to one year with the license. If minor changes are necessary—for example, in the price

Figure 3–1 Shipper's Export Declaration

U.S. DEPARTMENT OF COMMERCE · BUREAU OF THE CENSUS · INTERNATIONAL TRADE ADMINISTRATION

OMB No. 0607-0018

FORM **7525-V** (1-1-88) **SHIPPER'S EXPORT DECLARATION**

1a. EXPORTER (*Name and address including ZIP code*)

ZIP CODE

2. DATE OF EXPORTATION

3. BILL OF LADING/AIR WAYBILL NO.

b. EXPORTER'S EIN (IRS) NUMBER

c. PARTIES TO TRANSACTION

☐ Related ☐ Non-related

4a. ULTIMATE CONSIGNEE

b. INTERMEDIATE CONSIGNEE

5. FORWARDING AGENT

6. POINT (STATE) OR ORIGIN OR FTZ NO.

7. COUNTRY OF ULTIMATE DESTINATION

8. LOADING PIER (*Vessel only*)

9. mode of transport

10. EXPORTING CARRIER

11. PORT OF EXPORT

12. PORT OF UNLOADING (*Vessel and air only*)

13. CONTAINERIZED (*Vessel only*)

☐ Yes ☐ No

14. SCHEDULE B DESCRIPTION OF COMMODITIES
15. MARKS. NOS. AND KINDS OF PACKAGES
} (*Use columns 17-19*)

D/F (16)	SCHEDULE B NUMBER (17)	CHECK DIGIT	QUANTITY-SCHEDULE B UNIT(S) (18)	SHIPPING WEIGHT (*Kilos*) (19)	VALUE (U.S. dollars, omit cents) (Selling price or cost if not sold) (20)

21. VALIDATED LICENSE NO./GENERAL LICENSE SYMBOL

22. ECCN (*When required*)

23. Duly Authorized officer or employee

The exporter authorizes the forwarder named above to act as forwarding agent for export control and customs purposes

24. I certify that all statements made and all information contained herein are true and correct and that I have read and understand the instructions for preparation of this document, set forth in the "**Correct Way to Fill Out the Shipper's Export Declaration.**" I understand that civil and criminal penalties, including forfeiture and sale, may be imposed for making false or fraudulent statements herein, failing to provide the requested information or for violation of U.S. laws on exportation (13U.S.C. Sec. 305; 22 U.S.C. Sec. 401; 18 U.S.C. Sec. 1001; 50 U.S.C. App. 24 10).

Signature

Confidential - For use solely for official purposes authorized by the Secretary of Commerce (13U.S.C.301(g).

Title

Export shipments are subject to inspection by U.S. Customs Service and/or Office of Export Enforcement

Date

25. AUTHENTICATION (*When required*)

The "Correct Way to fill Out the Shipper's Export Declaration" is available from the Burea of the Census, Washington, D.C. 20233.

FedEx M-1086 6/91 LOGOS # 103369

of goods—you will have to have the license amended. Major changes (such as a different commodity or buyer) require a new license.

A *shipper's export declaration* (Figure 3–1) is an additional form, required for any shipment from the United States worth more than $500, which goes along with the license to help move the goods through customs. The declaration contains shipping information, a description of the merchandise, and authorization for shipment. It is deposited with the exporting carrier, and two copies must go to U.S. Customs. Many shipping companies include the export declaration with the bill of lading, so both are filled out at the same time.

The Trade Act of 1974 offers provisions for legally responding to violations of trade agreements and unfair foreign trading practices. Through a U.S. Department of Commerce Trade Representative, a U.S. importer or exporter can file a petition for an investigation. If it is determined that a trading partner has violated a trade agreement, the U.S. government will attempt to enforce the agreement under Section 301 of the Trade Act. If you feel that a trader or a country is not following the terms of a trade agreement, you can petition the Department of Commerce to take action.

WORKING WITH THE U.S. CUSTOMS SERVICE

It is the importer's job to clear items through customs and pay all applicable tariffs. The paperwork required to pass goods through customs will be some combination of the collection documents that we will discuss in Chapter 5. As an exporter, your only job (if you don't use a forwarder) will be to find out what documents are necessary with the shipment and to provide them. As an importer, you will have to clear your incoming goods, but have no fear, it really isn't as difficult as most people make it out to be. If you hire a customs broker, the broker will take care of all of the details for you.

When goods arrive at the dock in the United States, the customs office will notify you (or your customs broker) and will give you five days to provide the necessary documents, pay the duty, and collect the goods. You should have a good idea when the products are due because the exporter or manufacturer will notify you what ship they are on and when it is expected to arrive. If it takes you longer than five days to claim the goods, the Customs Service will move the goods to a warehouse and charge you storage fees for each day the goods are there.

The overseas exporter will send you the documents you need to pick up your goods at the pier. There are four steps involved in processing imports:

1. Entry—the filing of documents.
2. Appraisal and valuation—the inspection and appraisal of the shipment.
3. Classification—the determination of the duty rate.
4. Liquidation—the calculation of the actual amount of duty due.

This whole process usually takes less than one week.

Entry

The overseas exporter will send the commercial invoice and bill of lading to you, the importer, once you have paid for the goods. If you use a commercial letter of credit, you will have to pay your bank, which will then release the documents to you.

As an importer, you will then have to fill out a customs entry form. On this form, you will estimate the duty that you have to pay. You can then either pay the collector of customs immediately, or post a customs bond (Figure 3–2) guaranteeing your ability to pay. If you use a customhouse broker, the broker should have a bond that can cover you until the actual duty has been set and you have paid it.

In special cases, such as with perishable items, the Customs Service will issue a permit for immediate release of goods. You must apply for the permit before the goods arrive.

There are actually 22 different types of entry, covering everything from checking personal baggage to large commercial shipments. The three types of entry you will most likely see as an importer are:

1. Consumption entry—used when goods are intended for resale; the most common type of entry.
2. Immediate transport entry—when the importer wants the goods immediately transported to another location within the United States for customs clearance.
3. Warehouse withdrawal for consumption entry—deposit of goods in a customs-bonded warehouse, to be withdrawn in portions. Each time the importer withdraws part of the shipment, duty must be paid on that part.

Firms that import into the United States materials or components that they process or assemble for re-export may obtain "drawback refunds" of all duties paid on the imported merchandise, less 1% to cover Customs costs. This practice benefits U.S. exporters competing in foreign markets.

Figure 3–2   U.S. Customs Bond

Approved through 10/25/93; OMB No. 1515-0144
See back of form for Paperwork Reduction Act Notice

DEPARTMENT OF THE TREASURY
UNITED STATES CUSTOMS SERVICE

CUSTOMS BOND
19 CFR Part 113

| CUSTOMS USE ONLY | BOND NUMBER₁ (Assigned by Customs) |
| | FILE REFERENCE |

In order to secure payment of any duty, tax or charge and compliance with law or regulation as a result of activity covered by any condition referenced below, we, the below named principal(s) and surety(ies), bind ourselves to the United States in the amount or amounts, as set forth below

Execution Date

SECTION I — Select Single Transaction OR Continuous Bond (not both) and fill in the applicable blank spaces.

| ☐ SINGLE TRANSACTION BOND | Identification of transaction secured by this bond (e.g., entry no., seizure no., etc.) | Date of Transaction | Transaction district & port code |
| ☐ CONTINUOUS BOND | Effective date | This bond remains in force for one year beginning with the effective date and for each succeeding annual period, or until terminated. This bond constitutes a separate bond for each period in the amounts listed below for liabilities that accrue in each period. The intention to reminate this bond must be conveyed within the time period and manner prescribed in the Customs Regulations. | |

SECTION II — This bond includes the following agreements₂ (Check one box only, except that, 1a may be checked independently or with 1, and 3a may be checked independently or with 3. Line out all other parts of this section that are not used.)

Activity Code	Activity Name and Customs Regulations in which conditions cofified	Limit of Liability	Activity Code	Activity Name and Customs Regulations in which conditions cofified	Limit of Liability
☐ 1	Importer or broker...................113.62		☐ 5	Public Gauger.........................113.67	
☐ 1a	Drawback Payment Refunds............113.65		☐ 6	Wool & Fur Products labeling Acts Importation (Single Entry Only)............113.68	
☐ 2	Custodian of bonded merchandise ....113.63 (Includes bonded carriers, freight forwarders, cartmen and lightermen, all classes of warehouses, container station operators)		☐ 7	Bill of Lading........................113.69	
			☐ 8	Destination of Copyrighted Material (Single Entry Only)...................113.70	
☐ 3	International Carrier.....................113.64		☐ 9	Neutrality (Single Entry Only)..............113.69	
☐ 3a	Instruments of International Traffic.........113.66		☐ 7	Bill of Lading........................113.69	
☐ 4	Foreign Trade Zone Operator.............113.73				

SECTION III — List below all tradenames or unincorporated divisions that will be permitted to obligate this bond in the principal's name including their Customs Identification Number(s). ₃ (If more space is needed, use Section III(Continuation) on back of form.)

Importer Number.	Importer Name	Importer Number.	Importer Number.
		Total Number of importer names listed in Section III:	

Principal and surety agree that any charge against the bond under any of the listed names is as though it was made by the principal(s). Principal and surety agree that they are bound to the same extent as if they executed a separate bond covering each set of conditions incorporated by reference to the Customs Regulations into this bond.	If the surety fails to appoint an agent under Title 6, United States Code, Section 7, surety consents to service on the Clerk of any United States District Court or the U.S. Court of International Trade, where suit is brought on this bond. That clerk is to send notice of the service to the surety at:	Mailing Address Requested by the Surety

PRINCIPAL₄	Name and Address	Importer No. ₃		
		SIGNATURE₅		**SEAL**
PRINCIPAL₄	Name and Address	Importer No. ₃		
		SIGNATURE₅		**SEAL**
SURETY ₄,₃	Name and Address₆	Surety No. ₇		
		SIGNATURE₅		**SEAL**
SURETY ₄,₃	Name and Address₆	Surety No. ₇		
		SIGNATURE₅		**SEAL**
SURETY AGENTS	Name₈	Identification No. ₉	Name₈	Identification No. ₉

PART 1—U.S. CUSTOMS

Customs Form 301 (092189)

Appraisal and Valuation

To appraise your shipment, the Customs Service will inspect the shipment and then declare its value. A sample of the products may be taken to a customs office known as an Appraiser Store. The sample will be returned after it is appraised.

Classification

The Customs Service classifies goods according to tariff schedules. Different types of goods are assigned different percentages of taxation. The amount of duty will vary dramatically, depending on exactly what the items are and how they are made. For example, cotton knit apparel may be taxed at 21%, and nonknit cotton apparel may be taxed as low as 8%. During the classification step, the Customs Service will determine exactly which tax category is correct for your goods.

Liquidation

After the shipment has been appraised and classified, the final step involves figuring out exactly how much duty is owed. If you disagree with the assessed amount, you can file a protest in the U.S. Customs Court within 90 days. Otherwise, you pay the duty and collect your goods.

Again, all of these details can be taken care of by a customs broker. Fees for this type of service generally range from $20 to $50 per $1,000 worth of merchandise. Customs brokers can be found in the Yellow Pages under "Freight Forwarder" or "Customs Broker." Also, your local Trade Administration office, Department of Commerce office, and the U.S. Customs Service are all structured to be as helpful as possible to importers and exporters. It is their job not only to monitor trade laws, but also to encourage foreign trade. An informative booklet, *Importing into the United States,* can be purchased from federal bookstores or directly from: U.S. Customs Service, Attn: Cashier, 300 S. Ferry Street, Terminal Island, CA 90731. The current price is $6.50. The booklet includes extensive information on importing, including requirements for the following:

- Andean Trade Preference Act (ATPA)
- Canada Free Trade Agreement
- Caribbean Basin Initiative (CBI)

- Compact of Free Association (CFA)
- Generalized System of Preferences (GSP)
- Israel Free Trade Agreement (USIFTA)

Freight Forwarders

International freight forwarders act as agents for exporters moving cargo to overseas destinations. These agents are familiar with the import rules and regulations of foreign countries, methods of shipping, U.S. government export regulations, and documents required for foreign trade.

Freight forwarders can assist with an order from the start, by advising the exporter of the freight costs, port charges, consular fees, cost of special documentation, and insurance costs, as well as their handling fees. Freight forwarders may also recommend the type of packing that will best protect the merchandise during transit. They can arrange to have the merchandise packed at the port or containerized.

TRADE ZONES AND TRADE BARRIERS

Foreign Trade Zones (FTZs) are specified areas set up by the U.S. Customs Service in major port cities within the United States. There are currently 180 foreign trade zones. For customs purposes, they are considered to be outside the United States. This allows importers to ship goods to the United States and store them within these areas without passing through customs or paying customs duties. There are two major advantages of shipping to an FTZ. First, if the importer plans to immediately export the goods and is holding them in the United States for only a short time, no customs duties are charged. Second, some goods that will be entering the United States can be altered or modified while in storage in the FTZ, to qualify for a lower customs duty. In addition, if there is an import quota on a certain good, the importer may hold the shipment at the FTZ until the next quota period, or until a buyer is found, if one has not already been arranged.

Trade barriers can take the form of tariffs, or nontariff barriers. They are put in place by governments in order to protect certain domestic industries from difficult foreign competition. For example, if country A makes straw hats for $2 each, but country B can make the same hats for $1, then the government in country A may put a tariff of $1 on any hats from country B, to keep its own hats competitive. Many economists think that barriers hurt the global economy in the long run, and there has been a trend toward free market places, such as the market within Europe (the European Union or EU) and within North America (NAFTA).

Most trade barriers are in the form of tariffs, but nontariff barriers can ultimately be just as costly. They can include, for example, maximum quotas on foreign goods, excessive marking and labeling requirements, excessive pollution control regulations, and unfair classification of imports for customs duties. Before you can ascertain whether you can trade profitably with a country, you must find out what tariffs and other barriers may be in your way. For imports, check with the Customs Service. For exports, ask for assistance at your local Department of Commerce office, or at the commerce department in the country with which you plan to trade. You can also find out this information through your freight forwarder.

There are more than 300 free trade zones in 75 foreign countries. Exporters use free trade zones to receive goods that are reshipped in smaller lots to customers in the region.

General Agreement on Tariffs and Trade (GATT)

First instituted in 1947, GATT is an international agreement designed to reduce trade barriers between countries. It is now the chief international trade agreement. GATT rules limit the use of trade quotas and restrict tariffs. They also prohibit countries from offering trade advantages to specific trading partners.

The World Trade Organization (WTO), the successor organization to GATT, monitors global trade agreements and resolves disputes. The 1994 WTO conference, composed of delegates from 117 nations belonging to the former GATT as well as 8 others, finalized the Uruguay Round of trade agreements, which had been under negotiation since 1986. In addition to establishing a code of conduct for international commerce, these agreements state that trade should be conducted without discrimination, that tariffs should be reduced through multilateral negotiations, and that member countries should consult together to overcome trade problems. The trade pact officially came into effect on January 1, 1995.

Since the inception of GATT, trade negotiations held under its auspices have brought about reductions in tariffs and other trade barriers (although areas of disagreement still persist). Participants agreed to hold talks over a period of years and to expand the negotiations to include discussion of the service industries, investment, government procurement policies, research subsidies, patents and other intellectual properties, and telecommunications.

GATT and the WTO will have tremendous impact on world trade and the import/export business. They will increase the flow of products and services across borders with fewer restrictions. They will also give smaller businesses opportunities to join the world's marketplace.

North American Free Trade Agreement (NAFTA)

The North American Free Trade Agreement (NAFTA) is a 15-year plan for phasing out all barriers to trading goods and services among Canada, Mexico, and the United States. It took effect January 1, 1994. A similar agreement between Canada and the United States has been in effect since January 1, 1989.

The objectives of NAFTA are to eliminate barriers to trade, promote conditions of fair competition, increase investment opportunities, and provide adequate protection for intellectual property rights. NAFTA specifically establishes trade rules for textiles and apparel, automotive goods, energy and petrochemicals, and agricultural products. It also defines standards for technical information exchange and transportation among the nations involved.

NAFTA is opening the doors of trade, especially with Mexico. The management consulting firm of Runzheimer International, in a survey conducted six months after NAFTA went into effect, found that 51% of the 111 multinational companies surveyed plan to expand their business in Mexico as a result of NAFTA. Despite some fears that NAFTA would result in a giant loss of manufacturing jobs, most respondents indicated that they would not close down operations in the United States in favor of less costly Mexican labor. In fact, 23% said they were planning to set up administrative and sales facilities—an indication that goods and services manufactured in the United States are being sold in Mexico. Not only are large multinational companies profiting from NAFTA, but small businesses are as well. One U.S. exporter of automotive care products reports that, since the passage of NAFTA, sales in Mexico have almost doubled.

A Coopers & Lybrand survey reports that 20% of U.S. companies have increased exports to Canada and Mexico since NAFTA was approved, and only 5% of the same companies have set up manufacturing facilities in the neighboring countries.

If current trends continue, NAFTA promises to expand markets for U.S. importers and exporters considerably, in a region already bustling with international trade.

Fair Trade Regulations

Federal and state laws designed to encourage competition prohibit: practices such as contracts, combinations, and conspiracies in restraint of trade; discrimination in price between different purchasers of commodities similar in grade and quality; and unfair methods of competition and unfair or deceptive practices.

The term *deceptive practices* refers to false advertising, misrepresentation, simulation of competitive products, and slandering of competitors. Even on violations by a manufacturer or distributor, a retailer who knowingly accepts an illegal concession offered by the vendor may be considered equally guilty.

Any firm conducting business across state lines is subject to federal regulations—usually those of the Federal Trade Commission (FTC). Any business that advertises in more than one state is subject to FTC regulations. Even the smallest mail order business comes under FTC jurisdiction.

A fairly common statute forbids the sale of any article at less than the seller's cost, if the intent is to injure competitors. Other laws deal with bait-and-switch selling, withholding appropriate refunds on deposits made by customers, misrepresenting warranties and guarantees, and quality requirements for certain products.

Additional federal regulations apply to home-based businesses. Under the Fair Labor Standards Act, home-based operators cannot hire employees for home work in the production of women's apparel or of jewelry that requires a production process defined as too hazardous for home work. To legally employ home workers in other restricted industries (jewelry manufacturing, gloves and mittens, button and buckle manufacturing, handkerchief manufacturing, embroideries, and knitted outerwear), employers must obtain a certificate of authorization and home-work handbooks from the U.S. Department of Labor.

Remember that the Fair Labor Standards Act is federal legislation; individual states may have differing or additional legislation regarding home work. Because of the complexities of these regulations and the penalties imposed for violations, it is essential that you consult a lawyer if your business may be subject to them.

IDEA PROTECTION

As an import/export management company, you will be responsible for advising or executing the appropriate applications either in the United States (for foreign clients) or in foreign countries (for domestic clients). Idea protection laws cover just about every form of original invention or creation, provided that the idea can be presented in some tangible, physical form. It can be a design, a model, or a write-up.

The U.S. government offers six methods of idea protection:

1. Copyright.
2. Disclosure document form.
3. Trademark registration.
4. Design patent.
5. Plant patent.
6. Utility patent.

When importing an item, make arrangements with the foreign manufacturer to apply for a patent, trademark, or copyright on the product and on any materials used to promote, explain, or train customers.

Your foreign clients may already have obtained patents, trademarks, or copyright on the designs of the products they are producing in their country, and they will most likely have appropriate trademark and copyright protection. Still, it is good practice to apply for similar protection in the United States as well. Although the United States is a member of the Universal Copyright Convention and participates in the World Intellectual Property Organization, the protection afforded under these international conventions may not provide the maximum amount of protection needed within the United States.

The same goes for products being exported from the United States into a foreign country. Always apply for the most appropriate and effective protection for intellectual property that is available within that country. This is simply good business practice. Even though the United States participates in every major convention relating to the protection of intellectual property, each has different requirements that may limit or void the protection your client has obtained in the United States.

Copyright

If your client's idea is an original work of authorship in written form, you may be able to obtain protection from a U.S. copyright. You can copyright cartoon characters, sculptures, paintings, plays, maps, songs, scripts, photos, books, and poems. Until recently, you had to publish a work before it could be copyrighted. But now, as long as the material exists in some kind of tangible form, even if it's just a handwritten or typed manuscript, this kind of protection is available.

You only need to have your client include a copyright notice on the material. Three elements make up the copyright notice:

1. The word "copyright," the copyright symbol ©, or the abbreviation "copr."
2. The name of the owner of the copyright.
3. The year of first publication.

Here is an example of a typical copyright:

Copyright © by John Doe, 1995

There are five classes of copyrights:

1. Class TX: Nondramatic literary works—all types of published and unpublished works written in words or other verbal or numeric symbols: fiction, nonfiction, poetry, advertising copy, periodicals, textbooks, and reference works.
2. Class PA: Works of the performing arts—published and unpublished works created for the purpose of being performed before an audience, whether this performance is live or by means of any device or process: dramatic works, musical works, choreographic works, motion pictures, and audiovisual works.
3. Class SR: Sound recordings—claimants may seek to copyright (a) a sound recording alone or (b) a sound recording in addition to the musical, dramatic, or literary work embodied in the sound recording. This class does not apply to the audio portion of a motion picture or other audiovisual work.
4. Class VA: Works of the visual arts—pictorial, graphic, and sculptural works; two-dimensional and three-dimensional works such as models, globes, and works of fine art; photography, technical drawings, maps, and advertisements.
5. Class RE: Renewal registration—a renewal of registration for works originally copyrighted before January 1, 1978, extending the copyright protection for an additional 47 years. All classes of copyrights are eligible for renewal under this class.

The typical procedure for filing for a copyright is to send a copy of the work, with a completed official form, to the Copyright Office, Library of Congress, Washington, DC 20559; (202) 479-0700. To request forms, call (202) 707-9100. There is a $20 fee for each application.

It is advisable to register your client's copyright even though it may be covered under the Universal Copyright Convention. In cases of infringement, it is always good to have a public record of your copyright in the United States, showing the date it went into effect. As protection against prosecution for infringement, it is wise to have your copyright registered with the Copyright Office.

On products you are exporting, have your client affix a copyright notice to the product, and file properly with the U.S. Copyright Office, to afford you protection in countries that participate in the Universal Copyright Convention. In addition, apply for copyright protection in the country or countries to which the product will be exported. For information on copyright laws within specific countries, refer to Copyright Office circulars 38c, *International Copyright Conventions,* and 38a, *International Copyright Relations of the United States.*

Remember, the copyright protects only the uniqueness of the form in which your idea is expressed, not the idea itself.

Disclosure Document Program

You can protect an idea during the development stage through the Disclosure Document Program. This protection is valid for only a two-year period, after which, if you haven't filed for a patent, your file is destroyed. However, if you file for a patent within two years, the Patent Office will maintain your Disclosure Document in its files for the duration of the patent. This can be helpful in the event of a dispute or infringement suit.

To file, you must send the Patent Office the following items:

1. A transmittal letter requesting that the enclosed disclosure be accepted under the Disclosure Document Program.
2. One photocopy of your transmittal letter.
3. A check to cover the filing fee.
4. A copy of your invention disclosure.
5. A self-addressed, stamped envelope.

Your invention disclosure should be a signed document describing your invention's use, function, and structure, and how it differs from similar ideas. Your document must be either a written explanation or a drawing of your invention. Photographs submitted in duplicate and signed and dated by the inventor may be used to complete your file.

Here are some important details:

1. Number your pages and use paper that folds to less than 8 × 13 inches.
2. Sign and date two copies of the document, and have each copy witnessed by two people.
3. Send both copies to the Commissioner of Patents and Trademarks, Washington, DC 20231. One copy will be returned to you.

Trademark Registration

A trademark is any name, word, or symbol with which a business identifies its products, services, or organization. In the United States, legal protection for trademarks depends on how distinctive the law considers the trademark in question. Marks that describe a product's function or characteristics usually aren't granted protection because these names resemble everyday words and the government guarantees everybody's right to use them. Generally, names that are not in common usage—arbitrary, fanciful, or coined terms—receive protection.

Before you register your foreign client's trademark in the United States, make sure that it is not descriptive or already in use. Before you register your mark, be sure to use the trademark symbol properly on your product. For the trademark to be valid, you must insert the superscript ™ or (T). (This applies to your own business as well.)

Once you have used the trademark, you should register it with the Patent and Trademark Office (PTO). Afterward, you must indicate this protection by placing the symbol ® or "Reg. U.S. Patent & TM Off" on your trademark.

Four elements make up the trademark application:

1. A written application, including your name, citizenship, address, whether the trademark is for yourself or you are acting as an agent for a foreign firm, proof of prior use of the mark, description of the product the mark is used on, and the class of merchandising. If you don't know what class your product falls into, you can contact the PTO.
2. A drawing of the mark. If you are seeking protection for a word, a number, or a combination thereof, a drawing is not necessary. You can simply type the word in capital letters on a piece of paper.
3. Five facsimiles or specimens of your trademark. These must be duplicates of the actual trademark, but should not exceed 8 × 13 inches. Specimens must be flat, not bulky or three-dimensional.

If your trademark isn't flat, you can submit five photographs in place of the specimens.

4. The filing fee.

To obtain information regarding trademarks for companies and products in foreign countries, contact either the Patent and Trademark Office, or the World Organization for Intellectual Property. When contacting the Patent and Trademark Office, ask for the following booklets: *General Information Concerning Trademarks; Trademarks; Trademark Laws;* Trademark Section, *U.S. Patent Gazette* (a weekly publication).

Patents

A patent is granted by the U.S. government to a person or to a legal entity and gives the holder exclusive rights to exclude others from making, using, or selling the invention for the duration of the patent.

When filing a patent for your clients, either in the United States or in a foreign country, keep in mind that a patent is valid only in the country in which it is received. If you wish to obtain protection in a country other than the one in which you already are protected through a patent, you'll have to file an application for a patent in that country. This process has been somewhat simplified by the Patent Cooperation Treaty (PCT), which has been signed by more than 30 countries or groups of countries. The PCT provides for a search and a standard application form that replaces the application forms of individual countries participating in the treaty.

The United States offers three types of patents that are available through the Patent and Trademark Office: design, plant, and utility.

Design Patents

A design patent covers the surface aspects of an invention, not its mechanical design or function. Any invention that is unique because of the way it looks rather than the way it works can be covered by this kind of patent. Design patents grant the owner exclusive rights to make, sell, and use the invention for terms of 3, 7, or 14 years. After this period, the invention becomes part of the public domain and can be made, sold, or used by anyone without your permission.

To file a design patent, you will need to submit three forms, drawings of the design, a check for the filing fee, and a receipt postcard for your client. Be careful when having your client prepare drawings to file for a U.S. patent. If you decide the drawings need only show the exterior appearance of the product, not the interior, every detail of the exterior surface of the design should be shown in the drawings. This includes front, rear, and side views of the design, in addition to views from the top and bottom. By omitting a certain angle or view, the application may be rendered invalid or, at least, approval may be delayed. Send the completed application to the Patent and Trademark Office and be sure to make and keep copies of the entire application for yourself and your client.

Plant Patents

Plant patents cover asexually reproducing plants. For a new strain or variety of plant to receive protection by means of a patent, it must be useful, novel, and not obvious from the standpoint of someone who is knowledgeable about the specific technology involved in the invention.

Unlike design patents, plant patents are granted for a period of 17 years and are renewable only by an act of Congress, which is extremely rare. After 17 years, the new strain or variety of plant can be made, used, or sold by anyone without your client's permission.

The application for a plant patent will include a specification, drawings, an oath or declaration and signature, plus a filing fee. No maintenance fees are required for plant patents.

Utility Patents

A utility plant, the main type of patent, covers products that function in a unique manner and produce a utilitarian result. In the United States, a utility patent grants you the right to exclude others from making, using, or selling your invention without the consent of your client. These rights are granted for a period of 17 years. Once the 17-year period is completed, the invention becomes part of the public domain, and your client will have no control over its use.

The application for your client's utility patent will include a self-addressed receipt postcard, a transmittal letter, a check for the filing fee, and a drawing or drawings of the invention. Because this type of invention is patentable for its function, the drawings must show not only the exterior but also the interior of your invention. All the new working parts of the interior and exterior should be shown in detail.

For computer, chemical, or mechanical processes, the application should include a flowchart showing the separate steps involved, with each step described clearly and concisely. For chemical compositions, drawings aren't usually necessary.

To receive a utility patent, you will also need to include a specification. Because of the nature of the product, the specification should deal mainly with its function, not its exterior design. However, a brief description of the exterior should be given.

The specification should be arranged in this order: title of invention; cross-reference to related applications; a brief summary of the invention, indicating its nature and substance and perhaps including a statement of the object of the invention; a brief description of the several views of the drawings (if included); a detailed description; claim or claims; and an abstract of the disclosure.

To complete this application accurately, you will need to solicit the help of a patent agent or attorney because of the complexity of the law concerning utility patents.

WORKING WITH TRADE ATTORNEYS

Finding the right lawyer early is a critical task for you. Lawyers who can meet your needs should possess several key qualities. Among the most important are honesty, experience in international trade law, and availability. Keep looking until you find a lawyer you can trust and with whom you are comfortable. You will want someone who knows the ins and outs of foreign trade and the laws that pertain to import/export businesses.

A good, honest lawyer will tell you if you are out of his or her principal line of practice and may refer you to another attorney who can do a better job for you. Choose a lawyer who has the time and willingness to sit down and talk with you or to discuss a legal problem over the telephone when needed. If you keep calling your lawyer only to be told that he or she will get back to you (and the call comes days or weeks later), find another who appreciates your business and has the time to do justice to your needs. A great lawyer whom you can't reach is worthless.

Closely related to availability is dependability. Make sure your lawyer can follow through on your problems. Lawyers are selling a service, just as you and other business owners are. If the service can't be provided on time and in good order, at a price consistent with its value, find another lawyer.

Make certain you understand your attorney's fee schedule; this is the biggest area of misunderstanding between clients and lawyers. It is best to have your agreement in writing. Generally, lawyers who are experts in business cannot be retained inexpensively. If you want excellent legal advice, you must be prepared to pay for it.

Once you have established a firm relationship with a good lawyer, you will have found an invaluable resource.

How do you find an international attorney? Contact the Export Legal Assistance Network (ELAN) through your regional SBA office. Sponsored by the Small Business Administration and the Federal Bar Association, ELAN helps small and midsize companies find international trade specialist attorneys. The attorney you select should have sufficient experience in the type of transactions you make as well as in international trade law. If you cannot find an international attorney who fits your needs, ask for a recommendation from an international banker with whom you work.

WORKING WITH SHIPPERS

Transporting goods from point A to point B is the job of shippers.

Air freight is quicker and more expensive than ocean freight. By air, a shipment may reach its destination in 3 to 6 days. By ocean, the same shipment may require 3 to 6 weeks. However, air freight is typically about 300% more expensive than ocean freight.

In your import/export business, you will work with freight forwarders and customs brokers. A freight forwarder's services include estimation of freight and insurance costs, packaging, arrangement of container loading, and documentation. A customs broker specializes in handling the customs documentation and red tape, though a customs broker may also be a freight forwarder.

4

SETTING UP YOUR IMPORT/EXPORT OFFICE

Though it is often subject to more regulations than domestic trade, starting an import/export company is actually easier and less expensive than starting almost any type of retail business. One reason is that you will not need to rent an office because none of your customers will actually come to see you. It is far less expensive to simply work from your home, if your local zoning regulations allow it. With professional looking stationery, a separate business phone line, a post office box, and a fax or telex, you will be ready to go. You won't need any storage or warehouse space if you have your orders shipped directly from your client to a buyer.

SELECTING YOUR BUSINESS LOCATION

To many businesses, restaurants, banks, and baseball franchises, business location is a vital component of success. To an import/export service, location is not as important as knowledge of the business. You can set up your import or export business in your home, your own office, or space within a related business's office. Depending on the type of import/export business you establish, you may want an office near a port of entry or foreign trade zone. Let's consider the options.

THE HOME-BASED OFFICE

One obvious advantage of starting an import/export business from home is the small initial outlay of required capital. Starting from home will free up money that would otherwise be spent on leasing an office. Ideally, converting a spare bedroom or den into an office provides the best home-based operation. However, if you don't have one available, a corner of the garage, basement, or even the kitchen will suffice.

You should be aware, however, that to take full advantage of the available tax breaks, you must choose a room—not just a corner of a room—and it must be used solely as an office. If it also contains a TV and stereo and is used as a den, your home office deduction won't likely hold up under the scrutiny of an audit. By law, you can deduct from your income taxes a percentage of expenses equivalent to the percentage of space your home office occupies. If one room in an eight-room house is used solely as your office, you can deduct as business expenses one-eighth of your rent (or deed/mortgage payment) plus one-eighth of your utility bills, and so on. According to recent federal tax legislation, however, no part of the base rate of the first telephone line into your residence can be deducted, even if you use the telephone for business.

Before you begin your business in a home office, take the time to review your local zoning codes. Zoning ordinances that prohibit or restrict business operations in residential areas may directly affect your home-based business. (Taxes and zoning codes are discussed later in greater detail.)

In addition, you should contact an insurance broker to find out whether your home is adequately insured to protect you against the added liability risks of operating a business from your home.

Naturally, you'll want to keep overhead as low as possible when starting out. Don't invest too much in fancy office fixtures and decor that your customers will never see. Once the business is up and running, you can always upgrade.

Rent a post office box to serve as your mailing address. You can rent one monthly from either the local post office or a private mailbox rental facility. Renting from a private facility will allow you to affix a suite number to your post office box, as though you are operating from a commercial office location. This will enhance your image and aid you in opening a merchant's account with a bank. Most banks will not allow you to open a business account if it is known you work from your home.

In some states, it is illegal to refer to your mailbox number as a suite number. In such cases, you could refer to your mailbox as "#," "No.," or "Box" (not "P.O. Box"). Check the laws in your area.

THE COMMERCIAL OFFICE

Unless your local zoning laws do not allow you to start your business out of your home, there is no need to lease an office when you start your business. Most of your business dealings will be over the phone or through the mail, and you will not have any clients coming to see you at your office. If you do have to meet with manufacturers, they will prefer to meet at their offices to save them time. As your business grows, however, you may eventually need to hire additional help, and you may need the extra room a rented office affords.

Depending on the type of business you establish, you may want to have an office adjacent to a customs house, a warehouse, or other related facility. Or you may decide that you'd prefer not to work out of your home. Here are some of your options when considering commercial office space:

- *Office buildings.* These are single-structure buildings with several levels or stories. They are usually located in metropolitan areas, and hold a variety of businesses. Office buildings are normally managed by the developer or a professional management company hired by the developer. Office space is commonly leased out on a triple-net basis, with the tenants sharing in the maintenance costs of the building. Many times, this maintenance cost will include service to your own office as well as security. When your company reaches a point where image becomes a paramount concern, renting office space in an office building may be a consideration, but not until then.

- *Business parks.* Business parks are usually one or more office buildings located on the same lot and, like office buildings, managed by the developer or a professional management company hired by the developer. You'll find business parks in metro as well as densely populated suburban areas. In terms of leasing conditions, they are very similar to office buildings, and, like office buildings shouldn't be considered for office space until you reach a point where image is a prime consideration in the marketing of your business.

- *Freestanding buildings.* Locating your import/export business in a freestanding building in a light-industry area will work nicely. You'll pay a lower fixed rent and, when negotiating your lease, you may have more freedom when dealing with a lessor eager to have a tenant. In addition, you won't be subject to advertising charges, common area fees, or regulation of your business hours. What the freestanding location lacks, however, are the shared (and thus lower) expenses for utilities, pest control, security, trash removal, maintenance, and so on.

LEASING PROPERTY

Among the factors to consider when pinpointing an exact location for your import/export business are:

1. *The rent-paying capacity of your business.* If you have done a sales-and-profit projection for your first year of operation, you will know how much sales you can expect your business to generate. To judge your rental expenses (leased space plus any add-on costs), you can express the total amount you expect to pay, on a monthly or annual basis, as a percentage of projected net sales (gross sales minus returns and discounts) and compare that percentage with those of similar businesses.

2. *Restrictive ordinances.* In almost every city and town are areas as small as a few blocks or as large as many acres zoned for only commercial, industrial, or residential development. Within these broad classifications are further zoning restrictions. A commercial zone may permit one type of business to operate but not another. It's important to check the zoning codes of areas under consideration before spending a lot of time and money on a market survey or pursuing a specific site.

3. *Parking.* Does the particular site provide easy and adequate parking for clients and employees? Is it well lit? Is there sufficient security? What is the condition of the parking area? (Will it need expansion, resurfacing, or striping—possibly at additional cost?)

4. *Terms of the lease.* Leasing considerations can sometimes be the major determining factor in your choice of a site. Occasionally, a site that is otherwise ideal may have to be ruled out because the leasing terms are not right for your business. Remember that terms are negotiable, and the time to negotiate is *before* you sign the lease. (More on this topic later in this chapter.)

Leases are usually strong contracts. If you sign a lease for $1,000 per month for a period of one year, you are agreeing, in essence, to pay $12,000, regardless of what happens to your business. Therefore, some business tenants recommend starting out with the shortest lease term possible until you can see where you are going.

With office-oriented or unproven business, it is safer to arrange for a month-to-month rental at the beginning. Then, if your import/export company outgrows its original location after six months of operation, you won't be faced with the problem of subletting the first space when you move to larger quarters.

It may not always be possible to rent premises on a month-to-month basis, but you should never feel pressured to accept what's offered to you. There will always be another site opening up elsewhere, perhaps one even better suited for your business.

A good lease from your point of view is one that can easily be assigned to another tenant in the event your business fails or you need another facility. Therefore, make certain it contains a provision for assignment or subletting. Such a clause will allow you to close or move your business while permitting you to get another tenant to pay your rental obligation for the balance of the lease term. It will also allow you to sell your business to a new owner who can assume your lease under the same good terms you have.

Flat Leases

The flat lease, the oldest and simplest form of lease, sets a single price for a definite period of time. This lease is becoming hard to find but is naturally the best deal for the lessee. Do not be tempted to go along with a flat lease if the term is too short. A series of short-term leases could cost you more in the long run. Even if your business is successful in your present location, if your landlord increases the rent every time your short-term lease expires, a prime location can quickly become unprofitable.

The short-term lease is a built-in "escape clause" that enables you to leave that facility before your business goes bankrupt altogether, but it's better to find a good location that won't price you out in two or three years. Always do your homework. Sit down and calculate potential costs over the long and short term. Insulate your business as much as possible from threats to your financial well-being.

Step Leases

The step lease recognizes inevitable increases in the landlord's expenses over time. Taxes will go up, insurance premiums will increase, and the cost of repairs certainly will pace wage inflation. The step lease attempts to second-guess what these expenses will be in the future.

The step lease compensates the landlord by annually increasing the monthly rental rate over the term of the agreement.

	Monthly Cost with Step Lease
First year	$600
Second year	$640
Third year	$680
Fourth year	$720
Fifth year	$760

In this example, the rent has been stepped up almost 30% over a five-year period. Is this too high? Too low? If you feel this is too much, you won't like this kind of lease. On the other hand, if you believe this kind of arrangement will be to your advantage, this might be the lease for you.

Net Leases

A net lease takes the guesswork out of the step lease problem. Net leases are based primarily on the premise that the landlord knows the taxes will go up, but doesn't know exactly how much. Therefore, you'll pay the base rent of, for example, $600 per month. If and when the taxes go up, you pay the dollar increase—or your share, if more than one tenant is housed within the same facility.

Where proportionate sharing occurs, your rent is based on the square footage you occupy versus the total size of the facility. If office A has 1,450 square feet, office B has 2,400 square feet, and office C has 850 square feet, then the building has a total of 4,700 square feet. Let's say taxes on the building property go up $880, or 18.7¢ per square foot. Office A's increase is 1,450 × 18.7¢ or $271.15 per year. Office B's increase is 2,400 × 18.7¢ or $448.80 per year. Office C's increase is 850 × 18.7¢ or $158.95 per year. This method ensures that everyone pays a fair share.

There are net-net (or double net) versions of this lease that pick up added insurance premiums as well as tax increases, singularly or on a proportionate basis. Keep in mind that if you do something within your particular business that raises insurance premiums, you alone will pick up the tab.

Triple-net is the version most often encountered, especially in business parks. It includes similar sharing of repair costs by tenants as well as taxes and insurance. Remember, however, this is not your building you are consenting to maintain. If you agree to pay taxes, insurance, and maintenance costs, the landlord might have little concern that these costs are kept to a minimum, when most of the payments are coming out of the tenants' pockets.

Cost-of-Living Leases

These leases ignore specific expense items, tie everything together, and are attached to the cost of living index. In short, they take into account general inflation. At the end of the year, the government's cost-of-living figures are evaluated. If the inflation rate has been, for example, 6.8%, your rent is increased by a like amount.

One common lessee complaint regarding this approach is that cost-of-living indicators depend on consumables' costs, while tax or insurance premium increases tend to lag a year or so behind. Taxes are highly susceptible to given revenue requirements and market conditions in different parts of the country. Evaluate the cost-of-living circumstances in your area to determine whether this approach would be detrimental to your situation.

In any event, there are sufficient economic projections around to get a general idea of what this kind of lease will cost you overall. When you consider that your product costs and your profit will also rise with inflation, and then compare other leases you might be saddled with, the cost-of-living lease may not be so bad after all.

Other Terms

A lease usually covers other important matters, such as who is to pay for any remodeling to be done, liabilities and duties assumed by each party, and permission for the tenant to erect external signs, engage in additional lines of business, or make alterations if needed. A lease is an important legal document; as a small business owner, you should always seek competent legal counsel before signing one.

Negotiate before You Sign

You can negotiate the lease prepared by the lessor. It is not engraved in stone but is extended to you for your consideration. If you accept it without discussion, you have met the conditions entirely. By simply asking, though, you may be able to negotiate something much better, particularly in terms of the length of the lease. If the answer is no, you have lost nothing. You can look elsewhere and usually come back to the first location if you don't find a better offer.

Analyze your own particular requirements thoroughly. When negotiating, ask the landlord to make the additions or renovations to the property that you need *before* you rent. If the landlord won't bear the expense, ask to have the rent deferred or abolished for a beginning period.

After you have chosen a particular site, check the following points before you sign the lease:

- Is there sufficient electrical power? Are there enough outlets?
- Is there enough parking space?
- Is there sufficient lighting? Heating? Air conditioning?
- How large a sign and what type can you erect at your facility?
- Will your city's building and zoning departments allow your business to operate in the facility?
- Does your city or county health department require two restrooms if you have both male and female employees?
- Will the landlord allow the alterations that you deem necessary for your business?
- If you have plate glass windows, who will pay for insurance? (This can be expensive.)
- Will the delivery and shipping of materials and goods to and from the building be easily accomplished?
- Is there any indication of roof leaks? (A heavy rain could cause damage.)
- Is the cost of burglary insurance high in the area? (This varies tremendously.) Can you secure the building against the threat of burglary at a low cost?

THE OFFICE LAYOUT

Whether you start in your home or go immediately into a commercial office, aim for efficient use of space. Typically, an import/export business can be divided into two major realms of activities: marketing and administrative.

If you are starting a one-person operation, you'll bundle these two activities into a single work area. It is important, though, that you arrange this space efficiently. In terms of marketing, plan to have sufficient space to store account records and leads (both client and buyer), as well as reference materials for easy access. You can set up separate alphabetical file cards for contacts with suppliers, customers, sales representatives, and so on, or you can use a system of folders in which you keep copies of all correspondence and replies. Whatever system you initiate, remember that yours is a business of matching buyers and sellers, and producers and distributors.

In addition to adequate space for marketing, you should set aside adequate space for recordkeeping purposes. Accurate recordkeeping is crucial in a business such as this because of all the documentation you'll be dealing with. In fact, a great majority of your space will be dedicated to maintaining business records. You will be amazed at how quickly you accumulate reams of material. The systematic filing and retrieval of these names, products, sources, and representatives are crucial elements in establishing a productive import/export business.

When setting up your office, one of the things you'll have to deal with is the location of a computer. Although you can begin an import/export business without a computer, we recommend that you purchase one right away. The savings in time will help increase your productivity immensely and will enable you to have instant access to many of the U.S. Department of Commerce databases on international trade.

If you are starting in a commercial office space, you should plan your space so you have a reception area where your administrative assistant can sit and greet clients if they stop by, and, of course, an office for yourself. If you plan on hiring more account supervisors, make sure you lease enough space to accommodate them within their own office areas.

OUTFITTING THE OFFICE

For an import/export business, your initial equipment and supplies needs will be minimal. In your office setup, you can trim costs by going with the minimum. A small desk, a chair, and one or two 47-inch-high locking file cabinets will start you off. You will also need bookshelves for the reference materials you'll consult when arranging deals. You can probably get by for under $500 if you buy used furniture and shop around for it.

You'll also need stationery. Whether you work in a small, home-based office, or run a gigantic office with hundreds of employees, most of your business will be done either over the phone or through the mail. Even the smallest company can look impressive if it doesn't cut corners on stationery and other printed material. Your stationery and business cards should present a professional image. Try to avoid low-quality paper and printing.

Although some stationers and office supply stores handle printing, you may be wiser to go to an offset print shop to have your business materials imprinted with your company's logo. Be sure to add USA to your address; much of your correspondence will be with foreign countries.

Local stationers and office supply stores will have most or all of your miscellaneous operations materials. A few hundred dollars should buy you all the letterhead and blank stationery, envelopes, business cards, and recordkeeping equipment (files, ledgers, and index cards) you need.

Ask for referrals from other businesspeople, or let the Yellow Pages guide you to local shops. Check under the categories of "Paper Products—Wholesale," "Office Supplies," and "Stationers—Retail."

Other items you'll need to round out your office needs include:

- Phone lines and utilities.
- Answering machine.
- Telex.
- Fax machine.
- Typewriter (and supplies).
- Copier.
- Computer (and supplies).
- Inexpensive calculator.
- Two prospect index files.
- Calendar.
- Appointment log.
- Stapler.

Phone Lines and Utilities

Most small businesses will find a single-line phone system adequate. However, if your company reaches a point where it outgrows the single line, you will want to invest the extra money and install a multiline (push-button) phone system that allows you to switch back and forth between lines while on one phone. As your business grows, you may then need a computerized, electronic switchboard and a receptionist to operate it.

Some telephone and utility companies require deposits. A deposit may not be required if you own real estate or if you have established a payment record with the company in the past.

For utilities, be sure the wiring in your facility can accommodate any special equipment, tools, or fixtures you have in your business, and expect to pay more than ordinary monthly charges for complex wiring or plumbing needs. Deposits for gas and electricity (when required) will vary according to your projected usage. It is possible to lower them by not overestimating your initial consumption.

Telephone deposits are determined by the number of phones and the type of service required. Unless you need a large number of phones and lines, the deposit will probably range between $50 and $350.

Whether you choose a single-line or multiline system, these are some features you may want to consider when deciding on a phone:

- *Automatic redial.* The phone redials the last number called, or it may dial and redial a number at regular intervals until it gets through. This is now an automatic feature on some telephones, or it can be added to a phone through an attachment.

- *Programmable memory.* Phone numbers are stored and called up automatically by entering a code or pushing a single button. If you call long-distance numbers frequently, this feature is especially helpful.

- *Call forwarding.* All incoming calls to your usual number are forwarded to a number where you can be reached temporarily.

- *Call waiting.* This feature signals you if someone is trying to reach you while you're on the phone. You can take the incoming call while holding the original call.

- *Speaker phone.* An amplifier allows you to hear the other person's voice without using the receiver. It's useful if you're put on hold and want to move around.

- *Cordless phone.* The obvious convenience of freedom of movement may be offset by a cordless phone's poor quality. Research the latest models in *Consumer Reports* before buying.

Your local phone company's business sales rep should have the answers to your specific needs.

If any intended equipment or fixtures will put an unusual demand on the wiring or plumbing, always check with a contractor to be sure there will be no problem.

Answering Machine

This purchase lets you receive calls while you're away from the office. Answering machines come with a variety of features. Basically, all you'll need is a simple machine that will record incoming messages that you can play back later. Make sure your welcoming message is professional and clearly states your name as well as the name of your company. Ask callers to leave their name, number, and a brief message. In this way, if a client or prospective client has a specific question in mind, you can research it and have the answer ready when you return the call. For a suitable answering machine, you should expect to pay between $80 and $200.

Telex

Though the fax machine is taking over, many businesses around the world still rely on the Telex machine to transmit documents through telephone lines. The Telex is similar to an electric typewriter that is hooked up to the phone line. When a person on one end types in a message, the Telex machine at the other end prints the message out. If your foreign business partners rely on a Telex machine for communication, you will have to purchase one yourself. Prices for Telex terminals start at about $1,000. Many companies now rely exclusively on the facsimile machine for transmitting printed material.

Facsimile Machines (Fax)

Fax machines have become standard for the transmission, over telephone lines, of handwritten or graphic information such as maps, drawings, or signatures, as well as typed or printed pages. Fax machines provide an efficient way to communicate information rapidly between you and your clients, prospective clients, or business associates anywhere in the world.

Fax machines now range from small portable units that can plug into any outlet and send documents over phone wires to any other fax, to the larger floor-standing models that many offices use. "Personal" fax machines usually offer a built-in telephone and photocopier that comes with automatic feed capabilities. Some models even serve as answering machines and flatbed copiers. Priced as low as $400, personal fax machines are well worth the cost, especially for home-based entrepreneurs. Check your local Sharp, Xerox, or Canon dealer for more information on the features of specific personal fax machines.

On the high end of the scale are the larger floor-standing models that transmit information via both public and private digital networks, at the incredible speed of three seconds per page. Standard models of these machines usually come with automatic document feeders, one-touch or coded speed dialing, and sequential broadcasting and polling (see pages 96–97) to and from multiple locations. Some employ state-of-the-art laser beam printer technology that allows transmission of documents with a resolution of 400 × 400 dots per inch. This is especially useful if you plan to send graphics-oriented documents. These machines, however, cost about $8,500.

New facsimile boards or "cards" added to an open slot within your computer and coupled with the right software can turn your microcomputer into a fax machine that will be able to transmit and receive documents from other fax-outfitted computers. These add-on cards allow the user to send either a computer file or a scanned image, and to view and edit incoming documents on the computer monitor. Many of these cards come with an integral modem that provides high-speed transmission up to 9600 baud. As an add-on to your personal computer, these facsimile boards are very reasonable (about $250).

Yet, if you receive faxes via a fax board, you live with a major limitation of the technology: the faxes cannot be used with a word processor. The incoming fax is a graphics file that can only be viewed or printed. To enter text into your word processor, you have to type it in by hand. Look into Calera Recognition Systems FaxGrabber, a Windows-based utility that neatly and efficiently converts incoming faxes into text. FaxGrabber can automatically poll your fax board for incoming faxes and convert them into text files. For more information, call Calera Recognition Systems at (800) 544-7051.

Because all fax communication takes place through the phone wire, you need to consider whether to install a second phone line. The fax machine can be hooked up to any phone jack, so you could, in practice, get away with using one phone line for your phone and fax. However, a shared line means you can't use the phone while sending or receiving a document—which is annoying to clients trying to call you. They get either a busy signal or the shriek of a fax machine in their ear. A business fax machine should ideally be hooked up to a second phone line.

One alternative is to invest in an automatic voice/data switch. Plugged into a fax machine, this device can instantly tell the difference between a data call and a voice call, and adjusts the machine accordingly. Some fax machines include an automatic switch, as well as a telephone and answering machine.

Another big decision is what kind of paper you want. Thermal-paper fax machines are less expensive, as is the paper supply. The drawbacks are that thermal paper is flimsy, has an irritating tendency to curl, and fades after a while. Plain paper machines, especially laser models, cost more, but the output quality is much better. Think about who will see your faxes, how often you'll end up copying them onto plain paper for long term filing, and the kind of data you'll be receiving.

Consider these additional features:

- *Memory*—makes it possible to save transmissions if the machine runs out of paper, to send batch transmissions at a later time, and to save and access confidential faxes. Low-end models usually carry enough memory to store up to 30 pages.

- *Transmission speed*—how long it takes to transmit one page. Average transmission speeds range from 10 to 20 seconds per page—longer if there are photographs or illustrations.
- *Document feeder*—allows transmission of multiple-page documents without having to feed the paper through the machine page by page.
- *Delayed transmission*—a special programming that allows a document to be sent at another time, such as during off-peak hours when long-distance rates are lower.
- *Polling/Broadcasting*—automatically calls a group of selected fax machines and either receives documents from them or sends a document stored in memory.
- *Automatic redial/Alternate number redial*—calls back a number after receiving a busy signal, or dials a different assigned number.

Before buying a fax, give this purchase some thought. Fax machines vary in features, price, speed, and image quality. Do a little investigating and a lot of comparison shopping. You'll not only make a better choice, but you'll also learn how to get the most from your fax machine.

Typewriter

You can find a good electric typewriter for $100 to $200, or lease one for about $50 per month. Don't go overboard—as long as the machine produces crisp letters that look attractive and professional, it's fulfilling its purpose. If, however, you'll be using your typewriter for more complex word-processing tasks than just typing letters, but aren't ready to switch to full-scale computerization, companies like Brother, Smith-Corona, Xerox, Panasonic, and others have full lines of sophisticated machines that combine the memory and word-processing features of a computer with the simplicity of a typewriter. Look for such features as: memory (internal or diskette), liquid crystal display, high-speed printout, correction capabilities, a spell-check function, and automatic style features. These high-end typewriters range from $200 to $800.

Copier

A copier is a fixture of the modern office. A few years ago, copier ownership was possible only for companies with sizable equipment budgets. The average personal copier cost $10,000 or more, and was housed in a huge console. Today's copiers are far more compact—and far more affordable. They're small enough to be placed on a desktop and are designed for easier maintenance.

Not every business needs a copier, but office-oriented businesses such as import/export often require one because of the volume of documents that need to be reproduced.

A copier will improve your efficiency and increase your staff's productivity, particularly if there isn't a copying service nearby.

Some copiers offer features like automatic document feeders, collating for multipage documents that can sort by both group and mode, color reproduction, paper cassette choices that range from the standard 8 × 11-inch format to ledger-size options, and reduction and enlargement. Often, all of these features are within a compact unit that can be placed on its own stand or on a desktop.

Some important features to look for when purchasing a copier are the copies produced per minute, reduction and enlargement capabilities, collating and sorting capabilities, paper tray size and capacity, and two-sided copying. Add in the expense of toner cartridges and regular servicing when purchasing a copier.

You may need only a basic copier with multiple paper trays for different sizes of documents, or you may need one with most of the features listed above. A basic copier is suitable for simple reproduction of one-page documents such as invoices and correspondence. The high-end machines will be most appropriate for lengthy documents and the presentation of materials that require color reproduction.

Basic copiers with a minimum of features are often priced around $1,500; high-end office copiers can cost close to $8,000. Copiers can also be leased on a monthly basis for $300 to $500 with a $150 installation/removal charge. Call your local Xerox, Canon, Sharp, or 3-M dealer for more information.

Personal copiers, defined as compact (or mini) copiers for home and private use, handle anything from single sheets (where the user must manually feed in one blank page at a time) to 10 copies per minute (cpm). Major players in the personal copier industry are Canon, Sharp, and Xerox as well as Mita, Panasonic, and Sanyo. You can get a low-end, no-frills personal copier with replaceable toner cartridges for less than $400.

A bit higher on the scale are desktop copiers. Even the plainest desktop copiers have a speed of 10 cpm, which is considered the minimum for a business copier. Many go as high as 20 to 25 cpm. They range from 800 to 20,000 in recommended copy volume per month. For about $2,000 to $3,000 you can get a desktop copier with considerable speed (20 or more cpm) and useful extras like front-loading paper trays, the ability to enlarge originals up to 11 × 17 inches, and zoom reduction/enlargement.

Most desktop copiers are purchased through dealers who throw in service and support as part of the deal. Buying from a dealer costs more—anywhere from 10 to 20% over a discounter, computer super store, or mail order company. The advantages are: an on-site service center and a contract guaranteeing a certain number of service visits throughout the year. You pay a little extra for the service contract, but, at most alternative vendors, this contract isn't even an option. Most copier vendors offer their own warranty, which generally lasts anywhere from 90 days to 3 years.

Ninety-eight percent of all businesses with fewer than 100 employees own at least one copier or plan to buy one in the near future, according to BIS Strategic Decisions.

Voice Mail

Any business owner—or customer, for that matter—knows the one essential ingredient in running a successful business: customer service. You can be hardworking and dedicated, draft a flawless business plan, and enjoy a bottomless source of financing, but if you don't keep customers satisfied and coming back, your business will never succeed. Customers' primary complaints regarding the service they've received often center around phone service: they've called repeatedly, only to hear a busy signal or an endlessly ringing phone, or they are placed on hold indefinitely.

A voice mail system answers and directs incoming calls, takes messages, and costs less than hiring more employees. Formerly available only to large corporations, voice mail is now possible for small and even home-based businesses. For less than the cost of a cup of coffee a day, you can receive your customers professionally without any equipment to buy, operate, or repair.

You can put your voice mail number on your letterhead, business cards, and advertisements. You can also forward your phone to your voice mail box, creating an answering service on your live line or lines when you are either swamped or out of the office. In that way, you can conduct sensitive calls on the same phone line without interruption or fear of losing messages. Many articles and studies have shown the dramatic dollar and time savings when voice mail is implemented in both large and small businesses.

Several telecommunications firms provide voice mail service tailored especially for small businesses. One such company is Lifescript. For a nominal monthly fee, Lifescript will set you up with anything from the simplest single-voice mail box to a complex interactive system involving multiple-choice menus, networking, and paging. When customers dial your voice mail number, they have a chance to listen to or modify their own message before they hang up. Mail boxes will take many messages simultaneously, answer every call on the first ring, and avoid busy signals and holds. Voice mail is an excellent way to give your business a professional image by supplying your customers with the fastest and most efficient phone service possible. For more information, contact Lifescript at 1-800-888-4493, extension 613.

Long-Distance Carriers

Since deregulation of the telecommunications industry, the competition has grown fierce among the primary contenders: AT&T, MCI, and U.S. Sprint. Buying long-distance services from one of the Big Three means buying years of research and development, millions of miles of telephone lines, and the assurance of a well-established company that stands behind its product. Brand-awareness is a big factor in purchasing long-distance services, and many business owners prefer to stick with what they know.

Your next option is regional carriers, which have their own facilities and switching equipment, but usually cover only a limited region: a tri-state area, or the Southwest, for example. They are sometimes called switch-based resellers because they augment their own lines with time purchased from the big carriers.

Regional carriers such as ITT, Metromedia Long Distance, Cable and Wireless Communications, and Allnet Communications Services are gaining popularity with small businesses that place the bulk of their calls to very specific areas. For example, if 80% of your customers are within a 100-mile radius, you could negotiate a good deal with a regional carrier covering that area. On the other hand, if your customers are all over the map, it might not be worth the inconvenience of using several different regional carriers.

Some business owners find it advantageous to sign with the smaller long-distance companies, which, they say, often respond more quickly to customers' problems. But not all regional carriers are created equal; some of them may not offer all the amenities you want, like calling cards or dedicated data lines.

Most cities are served by numerous regional carriers. Look in the telephone directory under "Telecommunications" or "Telephone" for representatives, and ask for a consultation.

Another option is to go through one of the switchless resellers, a small but growing group of competitors out to get a piece of the long-distance pie. Their edge? The same service—for less money. Switchless resellers buy long-distance time in bulk, then resell it to individuals or small businesses. Because they buy in bulk, resellers receive a substantial discount, part of which they pass on to their customers. One reseller in Illinois says that about 95% of his customers are small and medium-size businesses.

Before making this choice, however, research the reseller. Some fraudulent companies are promising big discounts and then reneging. Call the Telecommunications Resellers Association to get a list of qualified resellers in the area, or to verify the reliability of a company that may be soliciting you. When you call the resellers, ask to be put in touch with one or two of their customers, whom you can ask about service, billing, and any problems they may have had.

When choosing a long-distance carrier, keep in mind that there are major network providers like AT&T offering direct line service, and a host of national and regional carriers that lease lines from the major providers and offer long-distance service; or they, in turn, act as "fiber carriers" and sublease those lines to yet another carrier.

Your choice of carrier obviously depends on a number of factors. Analyze the calling patterns of your business and answer these questions before you decide:

- Which area(s) (regional, national, worldwide) do you call most frequently?
- At what time of day will you be making most of your long-distance calls?
- How much do you anticipate spending on long-distance calls each month?
- Do you foresee a seasonal trend in your calling patterns?
- Can the company customize its services to fit your business needs?
- Can the company provide all the service you need: calling cards, conference calling, data services, 800 numbers?
- How responsive is the company, that is, how willing and/or able is the company to solve your problems quickly?
- What billing increments does the company use? Does it offer "first dollar" discounts, or is there a minimum threshold you must cross before a discount kicks in?
- Is billing customized? Can it reflect specific reporting information such as length of call, time of day, and area codes called?

- How many carriers does the company contract with? If it uses more than one, does it consolidate everything for you on one bill?
- Will the company act as a consultant if you need specialized help, such as installing dedicated data lines or linking two office buildings?

Most carriers offer specialized services structured for both small and large businesses. If your business deals only with customers or clients within your state, a regional dedicated Wide Area Telecommunication Service (WATS) line could be the most cost-efficient option.

Be sure to read the fine print in telephone company brochures. Some carriers charge installation and/or start-up fees for their services. Others charge minimum monthly usage or flat monthly fees. Can you meet any minimum usage requirements? Does the discount or service you receive warrant the flat monthly charge? If you require computer telecommunication services, find out whether this option is available.

When choosing a long-distance carrier, you should be familiar with accounting codes, billing units, calling card availability, dedicated access/dedicated line, hotline connection, Local Access and Transportation Area (LATA), least-cost billing, magnetic tape, mileage sensitive/distance sensitive/time-of-day sensitive retail billing, speed dialing, volume discounts, WATS, and any other services that are available.

COMPUTERS AND SOFTWARE FOR IMPORT/EXPORT SERVICES

Although many import/export entrepreneurs begin operations without a computer, they are working at a disadvantage against competitors who are using this technology. Computers have the capability to access important international trade data and reports produced by several government and private organizations. Moreover, computers provide a multitude of functions that will help organize your time and improve your productivity. You can get typing done more quickly and professionally, speed your billing process, or do any one of a hundred other tasks.

For computerization to be cost-justified, it should do at least one, and preferably several, of the following:

1. Help you provide your customers with a product or service not otherwise possible.

2. Provide a measurable decrease in labor costs.
3. Give you a clear competitive edge that your customers or clients understand and benefit from.
4. Give you better profit control and more useful management information.
5. Help you prospect new clients or customers and keep existing ones satisfied.

Despite popular myth, a computer system is no longer that expensive. Minimum cost is usually about $4,420 for the first workstation, with a cost of approximately $2,300 per workstation thereafter. That amount may seem excessive, but the cost includes both the hardware and the software needed to run the system. Although newspapers advertise PCs for less than $1,000, most of these computers are extremely limited and cannot run many of the programs you will want to use.

To get the most out of your computer and its compatible software, purchase a PC based on 486/DX technology, with 4 megabytes RAM, a 120-megabyte hard drive, and high-density 5¼-inch and 3½-inch floppy drives. Couple those features with an SVGA (Super Video Graphics Array) monitor, an SVGA graphics board, a 9600-baud modem, a laser printer, and a mouse controller. Your system will then run all the latest, most powerful software, and will give you enough room for more software and technology in the future. For a complete breakdown of computer-related costs, see Figure 4–1.

Service contracts (if you decide to purchase one) usually run 10 to 20% of the hardware cost per year. If you use a reputable consultant for help with the selection, installation, testing, and training process, his or her fee could cost an additional 5 to 20% of the total system price.

Training, one of the most time-consuming aspects of computerizing, is often necessary. The duration of your training will depend on your previous exposure to computer systems. There are user-friendly systems on the market that are easy to learn. Apple Computers makes the Macintosh, a computer that uses a standard graphics interface for all of its programs, so you don't have to spend countless hours memorizing the proper commands and learning the quirks of each program.

To make the PC more user-friendly, Microsoft introduced Windows in the late 1980s. All software written for Windows uses the Windows interface; each one looks and feels the same as the others, which reduces training time considerably when compared to DOS-based programs.

Whether you choose a Macintosh or a PC, you will need to purchase stand-alone software (programs dedicated to doing a single

Figure 4–1   Computer Equipment Cost Estimates

Hardware

486/33 computer	$	1,295
SVGA monitor		460
SVGA Graphics board		120
Modem-9600 baud/software		350
Laser Printer		810
Mouse		70
Surge protector		15
Printer stand		45
Total Hardware	**$**	**3,165**

Software

Windows	$	90
Word Processing		495
Spreadsheet		495
EX-TRA (Single User)		15,000
Database Management		495
Total Software	**$**	**16,575**

Miscellaneous

Miscellaneous Supplies	$	200
Magazine Subscriptions		45
Total Miscellaneous	**$**	**245**
Total Costs	**$**	**19,985**

task). For DOS, Windows, and Macintosh systems, examples of powerful stand-alone software are:

Purpose	DOS	Windows	Macintosh
Word processing	Microsoft Word 6.0	Same as for DOS	Microsoft Word 5.1
Spreadsheet functions	—	Microsoft Excel 5.0	—
Database files and records	Microsoft FoxPro 2.5	Same as for DOS	Microsoft FoxBASE+ 2.01
Accounting and bookkeeping	Intuit Quicken 7.0	Intuit Quicken 3.0	Intuit Quicken 4.0 or Microsoft Money 3.0

In addition to these programs, you may need telecommunication software for sending and receiving electronic information. The software you select may come packaged with a modem; if it doesn't, Data Storm produces an excellent package called PROCOMM Plus, available in DOS and Windows versions.

An important computer solution that is now just impacting the import/export trade is the Electronic Data Interchange for Administration, Commerce, and Transportation (EDIFACT), which is geared toward implementing a standard format for the electronic interchange of trade and shipment data. More information on EDIFACT can be obtained from the National Council of International Trade Documentation, 818 Connecticut Ave., N.W. Washington, DC 20006, or call (202) 331-4328.

Syntra Ltd. has developed and markets a software program for international trade called EX-TRA Export Processing System. EX-TRA automates the extensive paperwork required in international trade. Modules include export order data entry, order acceptance, shipment processing, invoice processing, and duty drawback. For more information, contact Syntra Ltd., 505 Eighth Avenue, New York, NY 10018, or call (212) 714-0440.

Integrated Software and "Office Suites"

New businesses often run into the same problem: they purchase a computer and want basic office software, but don't know what to buy. Or, they rely on one major application like a word processing or spreadsheet program and then decide they want a complete range of computer capabilities.

One option is to buy an integrated software package such as ClarisWorks or Microsoft Works. A second option is the new "office suites" or software products from Microsoft, Borland, and Lotus. In Borland Office 2.0, you'll get Borland Quattro Pro 5.0 for Windows, Workgroup Edition; Borland Paradox 4.5 for Windows, Workgroup Edition; and WordPerfect 6.0 for Windows. Borland Office gives you an easy avenue for sharing data, and all three applications in the suite support DDE, OLE 1.0, and Borland's Workgroup Desktop. In Microsoft's Office, you'll get Microsoft Excel 5.0 for Windows; Microsoft Word 6.0 for Windows; Microsoft PowerPoint 4.0 for Windows; and Microsoft Mail 3.2. All of these applications support DDE and OLE 2.0. In Lotus Smart Suite, you'll get Lotus 1-2-3 4.0; Lotus AmiPro 3.01; Freelance Graphics 2.01; Approach 2.1; and Lotus Organizer 1.1.

Both integrated packages and software suites offer a full complement of office automation software: word processing, spreadsheet, database, graphics, and communications. The difference is that integrated software contains all these applications in one program, which means that each component has fewer features than its individual counterparts. Software suites, on the other hand, are bundles of full-featured software programs.

For many small business owners, an integrated software package is sufficient, and it comes with a lower price tag—$200 to $400, compared to $600 to $800 for an office suite.

Although integrated packages can handle the basics and are fine for many businesses, other users want the power of full-featured applications. Early software suites from Borland, Lotus, and Microsoft simply gave users a price break for buying three to four applications. The latest versions of mainstream applications offer more consistent user interfaces and better networking capabilities than those in the recent past.

Upgrading Your PC

When people consider adding power to their computers, the first thing they think of is upgrading the central processing unit (CPU).

There are three ways to add a more powerful processor to your computer:

1. Replacing the motherboard.
2. Going through the manufacturer's proprietary upgrades.
3. Getting the new industry standard Intel OverDrive Chip.

You may also need to analyze other options.

Adding RAM can improve your system's performance more than any other upgrade. However, this booster helps only up to a point—after that, adding more RAM will not boost performance any further. Windows stores applications and data it is using in RAM; if there is not enough RAM, the applications and data will be stored in "virtual RAM," and this slows down your computer. By adding enough RAM to store your entire application and data—optimally, 8MB—you can greatly speed up your performance. However, having more RAM than your system needs will not produce any additional benefits.

If you decide you need to buy a faster hard disk, you need to look at *access time* and *transfer rate*. The access time is the time it takes for the hard disk head to physically find the data on the disk; the transfer rate is the length of time it takes to transfer the data from the disk to the processor. If your computer runs at 20MHz or faster, look for a hard disk with an access speed of under 20 milliseconds (ms) and a transfer rate of at least 700KB per second—preferably 800KB per second or faster. Also, be sure your new hard disk has the same kind of hard disk controller you already have.

Graphical applications, such as those that run in the Windows or Macintosh environment, can be quite taxing on any computer system. Graphics display and manipulation require a great deal of processor power, which in turn can greatly slow the operation of your system. Graphics accelerators, which cost anywhere from $99 to $995, are add-in cards you install into the NuBus slots in your Mac or the expansion slots in your PC. These add-ins take on the burden of graphics processing, leaving the computer's CPU to do processing. Companies such as Radius, RasterOps, and Mirror Technologies offer graphics accelerators for the Mac; ATI Technologies and Actix are two companies that offer graphics accelerators for the PC.

On-Line Information Services

One of the most significant technological breakthroughs in personal computing has been the birth of on-line communications. Their ability to link together millions (and potentially billions) of computers allows individuals and businesses to communicate in ways never before possible, and to gain access to more information than they could use in ten lifetimes.

The advent of the fax machine and personal computer brought a whole new dimension to the age of information. Not only is it possible to send published material to someone overseas faster than ten years ago, but it is also possible to send electronic mail (messages sent electronically through a telephone line) to someone in another country in less than ten minutes.

If you're a newcomer to the information-highway generation, you may ask, "What are on-line services and how are they useful to entrepreneurs?" On-line services are electronic networks that connect an infinite number of local computer terminals to each other. This allows the rapid transit of large amounts of information at the wink of an eye and a touch of the keyboard.

By logging onto an on-line service using a local access telephone number and a modem hooked up to a personal computer, a person can perform a variety of functions that will enable him or her to access many different types of information, such as local, national, and global news; reference materials such as those provided in a well-stocked collegiate library; professional and financial data; entertainment; and personal interests and hobbies.

You may already be familiar with a bulletin board service (BBS), which is simply a message board in electronic format, where people can write and post to other BBS members and receive responses. Bulletin board services also contain library file databases, from which members can download any kind of PC file, be it a text file, graphic image, or executable application.

On-line services are simply large BBSs. The most popular commercial on-line services are Prodigy, CompuServe, and America Online (AOL). Each of these services has its own assortment of news information, message boards, file databases, and conference or "chat" capabilities, in which you can hold live (referred to as "real-time") conversations with other people located anywhere in the world.

Many commercial on-line services offer means to connect, known as "gateways," to the Internet, a giant international network made up of smaller networks, each with bulletin boards, file databases, and other information resources. Gateways serve to transfer data between separate networks or applications not normally connected to each other. For example, the on-line service America Online is a separate network outside of the Internet. However, AOL offers gateways through which you can send and receive e-mail (electronic mail) from the Internet, as well as access certain parts of the Internet.

For more information about what the Internet is and how to access and use it, see *The Whole Internet User's Guide and Catalog* by Ed Kroll (O'Reilly & Associates, Inc., 1992).

You can use on-line services for research for your own business or for a client, and you can network with other entrepreneurs in your field or in other industries. On-line services are also good for making contact with consultants and other individuals who can offer valuable advice. You can even go so far as to conduct business on-line with clients in other parts of the world, if necessary. This is certainly one part of the information highway that can be very beneficial for home-based entrepreneurs.

If for no other reason than to have the *possibility* of reaching valuable information sources, no matter how frequently they are used, entrepreneurs who subscribe to one or more on-line services have a distinct advantage over those who do not.

Modems

To access on-line services, you'll need a modem to link you with the service. When purchasing a modem, consider the need for an internal or external modem, fax capability, and, most importantly, the modem's speed.

Internal modems are generally less expensive than external modems. External modems have status lights to let you know whether the modem is in use and connecting with the service. External modems also have plug-in capability with a portable notebook computer.

If you need to fax on a regular basis, it can be very convenient to have the ability to press a button and fax directly from your computer via modem. Look for Class 1 or Class 2 compatibility.

The modem's speed is measured in bits per second (bps). The speed will determine how fast your modem will transmit and receive data. Experts recommend not buying a modem with less than 14,400 bps; many recommend that you buy a faster one (14,400 bps or more). The rate at which your modem will process data will depend on the phone line you use and the software you have, as well as the type of information it is processing. Graphic images with photographs, drawings, and even video and audio files will take more time to process than text.

LEASING VS. BUYING EQUIPMENT

If your equipment investment will be large, compare the potential tax savings available through leasing to the tax advantages of buying. See your accountant for current rulings and to determine whether your potential leases are suitable for write-offs.

If your start-up capital is limited, explore leasing as an alternative. The advantage of leasing is that your initial cash outlay can be significantly less than when you buy on an installment contract. The disadvantage, if you have a legitimate tax-deductible lease, is that you do not acquire equity in your equipment and therefore do not build up your balance sheet.

A financial statement showing a strong net worth is important to any business. In addition, the total cost of leasing over a period of years is higher than if the same item were purchased. Consult your accountant as to the wiser choice for you.

The tax laws generally make the purchase of equipment, whether new or used, more attractive than leasing. Some financing sources offer no-money-down options for equipment purchases or leases. No-money-down leases enable you to own the equipment when the term of the lease is completed.

Asset Remarketing

To save money on equipment costs, you can purchase used equipment through asset remarketers or equipment leasing companies. Sometimes these companies work through wholesalers and dealers, and sometimes they deal directly with business owners. Leasing companies may run classified ads in your local newspaper, and may keep their equipment in warehouses that you can visit.

When purchasing equipment from these companies, most businesspeople say you should look for name brands, and always inspect the equipment before you consider purchasing it. Many owners are thoroughly satisfied after buying this repossessed equipment.

Contracts for Equipment Purchase

Two types of credit contracts are commonly used to finance equipment purchases: (1) the conditional sales contract, in which the purchaser does not receive title to the equipment until it is fully paid for, and (2) the chattel-mortgage contract, in which the equipment becomes the property of the purchaser on delivery, but the seller holds a mortgage claim against it until the amount specified in the contract is paid.

5

MANAGING YOUR FINANCES

For your import/export business to succeed, you must learn to manage your capital skillfully. Being able to control your finances is absolutely crucial: how you succeed in managing your money and accounts will determine whether you can successfully establish your business and position it for future growth. Ultimately, you must ask yourself this question: Can you turn a profit in this venture? At the very least, your capital investment should yield a higher rate of return than could be obtained from an investment in government or other securities earning a guaranteed rate of interest. Skillfully managing your capital, however, will pave the way to establishing your business start-up as a full-fledged profitable import/export business. Please refer to *The Entrepreneur Magazine Small Business Advisor,* also published by John Wiley & Sons, for a discussion of tools that can help you gain financial control of your business. This chapter discusses financial management as it applies specifically to import/export businesses.

INVENTORIES

Some import/export management companies act as distributors for clients: they purchase a product at a new wholesale price less a discount equal to the client's sales overhead. If you act as a distributor for your client, most of the money you use will be spent purchasing products. If you haven't lined up a buyer beforehand, you will have to store your inventory in a warehouse and keep comprehensive records of what you have purchased, what you have on hand at any given time, and what you have sold.

DEBT MANAGEMENT

To get your import/export business off the ground, you will most likely have to raise sufficient capital to finance your venture. To determine the most appropriate type of financing, you will have to evaluate your financial situation and your business capacity to manage debt. You must know when debts will fall payable and judge whether there will be funds to meet those expenses on their due date. If you borrow to pay for exports *after* you have a letter of credit guaranteeing payment upon shipment of goods, you should have no problem paying back your loan as soon as the goods are shipped.

EXTENDING CREDIT

Virtually any business beyond the level of street vending relies heavily on credit for its success. Any time you extend credit to a client, or any time your services are not paid for in cash, you are allowing your customer to use your money interest-free.

There are two types of trade credit: (1) promises and (2) orders. As an import/export management company, you will extend credit to your clients in the form of promises. Promises, also known as promises to pay, can be either invoices or promissory notes. When your clients utilize your services as an importer or exporter and don't pay for those services at the time they are performed, you bill your clients through an invoice. Promissory notes are usually used where the agreed-on cost or service is very high. The client would then sign a promissory note, guaranteeing payment. Later in the chapter, we will discuss promissory notes and how they can be used to protect you against clients that have a poor credit history.

When a customer applies for credit with your company, you will have to make some hard decisions. In weighing a customer's creditworthiness, you should analyze its working capital, receivables, inventories, and, most of all, debt structure. The reports you obtain from services such as Dun & Bradstreet (D&B) will give you a good picture of the customer's business and payment records. With over 9 million businesses and 15 million names on file, D&B can help you acquire and maintain customers, obtain marketing information, assess a customer's credit, or perform your market research.

A customer's working capital should be enough to support his or her volume of business without extending the company to such a degree that it can't keep up with its bills. If the information you receive doesn't satisfy you, ask your business banker to run a quick check. Bankers talk freely with each other within the confidential guidelines, and you should get a good picture.

When extending credit to your customers, spell out the credit terms exactly so there's no chance for confusion. A common term some companies will ask for is "ROG as of the 25th." These companies want the billing date to start upon the receipt of goods (ROG). They ask for the 25th because many American businesses consider the 24th day of each month to be the end of the billing and shipping month, a custom that has solidified over the years.

You might wish to issue all the credit you are granting as EOM, or as of the end of the month. This agreement is generally written up as "net 15 EOM," meaning you expect the customer receiving your goods to pay you by the 15th day of the following month. You also can grant terms that are simply net the number of days you specify from shipment or pickup of goods. For example, if you're trying to increase your cash flow, you might grant only terms of net 15 days. If you've fulfilled your customer's purchase order by shipping out your merchandise on the 3rd of the month, he or she must pay you by the 18th.

Customers will often ask about cash discounts for fast payment. This is a standard practice, but you should decide for yourself whether to allow it. If not managed carefully, cash discounts can become an expensive proposition. If you give a customer terms of 2% 10, net 30, that customer can deduct 2% from the cost of goods if you receive payment within 10 days. This discount can become especially expensive if you operate within slim profit margins. For example, if your margins for a particular product are only 9% after all your costs are figured, then a 2% discount can quickly bite into your profits. On the other hand, quick-paying customers will boost your cash flow and cut down on your bookkeeping chores. If you're trying to pay down any loans or letters of credit, for example, having a quicker cash flow may enable you to pay off your obligations earlier, thereby saving interest charges that are accruing. In some cases, this advantage may more than offset any cash discounts that you extend to your customers. When considering cash discounts, be careful to analyze your financial position and offer the terms with which you're most comfortable.

Avoid the pitfall of extending credit for longer terms than your cash flow can cover. For example, a company may ask for terms of more than 30 days—say, 45 days or even 60 days. In this situation, it is crucial to analyze the operating expenses and debt obligations your business must cover before you extend credit for terms longer than 30 days. Suppose you've agreed to sell $10,000 of widgets to Alpha Company. Alpha likes your product and finds your price attractive. To go through with the deal, however, they request that you grant them terms of net 60 days. Before you rush ahead and try to close a big sale, make sure that you can afford to extend terms out to the requested date. Will it cause you to be caught short of cash in the coming weeks? Keep in mind that a positive cash flow is essential to the financial health of your business. Extending credit should not create any undue risk for your business.

Suppose that, despite the high risk involved with extending the longer terms to Alpha, you really are eager to close the sale. Your first option is to negotiate. Will Alpha accept the terms you can afford to extend? If you have a good relationship with your bank, you might try asking for an extension on your loan or line of credit (or other form of debt) repayment terms, to cover the terms proposed by Alpha. Some banks might be reluctant to extend the terms on debt, especially to new businesses, but having a purchase order (P.O.) or accounts receivable entry in hand as proof of Alpha's pending order will definitely help your appeal to the bank officer.

Another option is available. You might be able to take out a short-term loan to cover your costs of doing business. Remember that whenever you extend a loan or apply for a new one, you must factor these additional expenses into the costs for the deal, because the added interest expenses will affect your profit margins. As mentioned earlier, agreeing to 60-day terms is like agreeing to lend a customer your money interest-free for 60 days.

Extending credit assumes that your customer is creditworthy in the first place. If, in researching a company, you find that its credit history is poor but the business picture looks bright, you might move from invoices with terms into the realm of promissory notes. You get the customer to sign a promissory note stating that a specified amount of cash is due on a certain date. Businesses will sign these documents because they know you have a good recourse with this kind of paper. Should a client not honor a promissory note—or refuse to sign one— you can have your bank draft an order to pay. Orders to pay are transferred to the other business's bank. Businesses don't like this to happen because it tips off the bank that they are not paying their bills.

DOMESTIC BANKING

You need a business bank account. Don't make the mistake of merely seeking the most convenient bank in relation to your office location. If you are serious about developing a successful import/export business, you will need to work with an international bank, a commercial bank that offers at least one full-time international banker, or a bank with international partners.

If you know in advance what countries you will be dealing with, and/or if you are fluent in the language(s) of those countries, consider a bank that specializes in business with that country or region. For example, if you know that you will be importing merchandise from China and Japan, don't be afraid to consider foreign banks like the Bank of Hong Kong or one of the large Japanese banks that operate many branches in the United States, such as Sumitomo Bank or Tokai Bank. Or, if you're exporting goods to Germany, explore the opportunities available at a large German bank such as Deutsche Bank. Because they retain close ties with their countries of origin, these banks may be able to speed the process of opening letters of credit, and they sometimes offer better terms or more advantageous lending guidelines. If you are a minority entrepreneur, don't forget to seek out the minority or disadvantaged business programs sponsored by most U.S. banks.

Regardless of what kind of international bank you choose, your bank will be crucial to the success of your small import/export management company. Banks are used to working with irrecoverable letters of credit, and they can work with other banks in the countries in which you plan to do business. If you use letters of credit as an importer, your bank will be able to draw them up for you. If you are an exporter, your bank must be able to accept a letter of credit from a foreign bank and send off a letter of confirmation to you. The bank must then be able to accept and verify all trade documents, pay the exporter, and forward all documents to the foreign bank or bank branch.

The various services performed by international banks include:

- Advice on export regulations.
- Exchange of currencies.
- Assistance in financing exports.
- Collection of foreign invoices, drafts, letters of credit, and other foreign receivables.
- Transfer of funds to other countries.
- Letters of introduction and letters of credit for travelers.
- Credit information on potential buyers overseas.
- Credit assistance to the exporter's foreign buyers.

Different import/export management companies will have different needs. Determine what your needs will be, then interview the bank managers in your area, by phone or in person, to find the best bank for your business.

Interviewing banks to find the right one will give you a psychological advantage with the bank manager and will provide an opportunity to establish a relationship with him or her. Ordinarily, when you just walk in to open an account, you are handled by a new accounts clerk and never come in contact with the bank executives. The closer the relationship you develop with someone at the bank manager level, the better your chances of obtaining loans and special favors in marginal situations.

Don't pretend to know everything, in an effort to impress your banker. You may be an expert in your field; the bank manager is definitely an expert in banking. Learn to talk to your banker using his or her vocabulary. (The Glossary at the end of this book will give you some basic terms and their meaning.) Good rapport will help your present situation and improve your position the next time you have a request.

In a branch-banking state, you will probably be doing business with a large bank that has many branches. Managers change frequently. Watch for changes and maintain that all-important relationship by introducing yourself to each new manager.

The fact that your account will be small at the start is not a major drawback. Remember, you are offering the prospect of big future transactions, and there is inherent glamour and adventure associated with international commerce. Bankers are people, too. You'll find that some of them get more fired-up at the thought of working with a promising entrepreneur than others do. Give the bank manager your account and develop reciprocal interest, so that the manager has a sense of participating in your success. He or she will be a big help in establishing credit references for you, checking references of your contacts, and handling letters of credit, which will be your major form of financial exchange.

Independent banks without any branches, or small chains capable of meeting your needs, will provide the most personalized service. In a small bank, your account may be important; in a large bank, you may never be noticed.

Take time to find the most suitable bank, then avoid moving your account if at all possible. If you move your account constantly, it will be hard to establish a good bank reference to obtain credit from your suppliers.

One long-lived myth is that collecting your money from overseas transactions is very difficult and default is common. This is not true. Your banker (in a large bank that has an international department) has all the expertise necessary to handle foreign transactions, almost all of which will involve letters of credit. In addition, your international banker will often assist you by locating new overseas markets, developing data on the business climate in the country to which you are planning to export, introducing you by mail to overseas banking and trade contacts, and investigating foreign firms' credit references, among other services.

When opening your business account, the bank will need your social security number or your federal employer identification number, your driver's license, and (for partnerships and sole proprietorships) a fictitious name certificate. If you have formed a corporation, bring your corporate seal as evidence of your status. You will need a financial statement when requesting a VISA or MasterCard franchise.

Practically every growing business experiences some rough financial periods and a few growing pains, and requires financing of some type sooner or later. Watch for signs of upcoming problems so you and your banker can deal with them in advance, not after the problem has grown serious.

Plan your growth program and presell your banker. Foresight demonstrates that you are an astute professional manager who is on top of every situation. Your chances for obtaining a loan under marginal conditions will be improved 50% by anticipating your needs.

INTERNATIONAL BANKING

More than 300 U.S. banks have international banking departments with specialists familiar with specific foreign countries and various types of commodities and transactions. These large banks, located in major U.S. cities, maintain correspondent relationships with smaller banks throughout the country. Larger banks also maintain correspondent relationships with banks in most foreign countries or operate their own overseas branches, providing a direct channel to foreign customers.

Some banks specialize in certain types of businesses or have departments to handle different types of trade. Some banks only go after big money. Those interested in attracting borrowers from small businesses are likely to be more attentive to the needs of new and growing firms. You can usually judge them by their eagerness to obtain your business account. To assist you in making a judgment, here are a few questions to ask your prospective banker:

1. Is it necessary to maintain certain balances before the bank will consider a loan?

2. Will the bank give you a line of credit, and if so, what are the requirements?
3. Does the bank have limitations on the number of small loans it will grant or the types of businesses to which it will grant loans?
4. What is the bank's policy on the size or description of checks deposited to be held for collection?
5. Will checks under that size be credited immediately to your checking account balance? (This question is very important, and you must press for a definite answer.)

If you do not have a previous business account to serve as a reference, a few banks may hold all checks for collection until they develop experience with you. The bank's decision to exercise this precaution may depend on your personal credit rating.

OVERSEAS PRIVATE INVESTMENT CORPORATION

The Overseas Private Investment Corporation (OPIC) is a U.S. government agency that provides project financing, investment insurance, and a variety of investor services in more than 135 developing nations and emerging economies throughout the world. OPIC encourages American overseas private investment in sound business projects to improve competitiveness, create American jobs, and increase U.S. exports. Its direct loan program is available, for amounts of $500,000 to $6 million, to finance projects sponsored by or significantly involving U.S. small businesses or cooperatives. Its loan guarantee program covers projects requiring $2 million to $25 million, but can be as large as $50 million. In most cases, OPIC's finance commitments don't exceed 50% of the total project costs.

OPIC can insure U.S. investments (both assets and business income) against the risks of war and civil strife overseas. It offers specialized insurance coverages for U.S. investors involved in contracting, exporting, licensing, or leasing transactions in developing countries. In addition, OPIC offers competitively priced advisory services to small and medium-size U.S. businesses contemplating investment in overseas markets.

OPIC currently has a development program for central and eastern Europe and the newly independent states of the former Soviet Union. This program can provide eligible U.S. investors with up to 75% of the total costs of conducting market-entry strategy assessments, business plan development, and other analyses in more than 20 countries.

The Overseas Private Investment Corporation can be contacted at 11100 New York Avenue, N.W., Washington, DC 20527, (202) 336-8400.

Working with Banks around the World

Once you have put together a deal with a buyer and a seller and have agreed on a price, you can handle the transfer of money from the buyer to the seller in one of these ways:

1. Cash in advance from the buyer.
2. An "open account."
3. Goods shipped "on consignment."
4. Collection basis.
5. Letter of credit.

All of these methods of payment were designed to ensure that the seller will be paid for any goods shipped. Each method has its own benefits, though the best by far is the letter of credit, especially early on, when you are relatively unsure of the companies with which you will be dealing.

Currency Exchange

The U.S. dollar is the most widely accepted form of currency in the world and stands as the world's economic benchmark. Even so, a dollar isn't worth a dollar everywhere in the world. It is worth a fluctuating number of yen, marks, dracmas, rubles, or other currency units. The difference between the value of two currencies is called the rate of currency exchange. Whenever you are setting your prices, you will have to pay close attention to the rate of exchange for the currencies you are dealing with. These rates will go up and down with the U.S. economy, and you may have to alter your prices accordingly. When the U.S. dollar goes down in relation to other currencies, most people in America view this with dismay because the dollar is not worth as much against foreign currencies.

This decline also makes things difficult because, as an importer, you will have to pay more in dollars to purchase your products. As an exporter, though, when the dollar drops, U.S. goods will cost less on the global market, and you can either lower your prices or keep them the same and take a higher profit. To make the currency swings favorable to you, it may make good sense to import goods from countries whose currencies are weak in relation to the U.S. dollar—such as emerging economies—and export to countries whose currencies are generally stronger, such as European countries.

As an exporter or importer, you sometimes will be responsible for exchanging into U.S. dollars the foreign currencies you deal in. Generally, you will be involved in two types of transactions:

1. A *spot transaction* involves the sale of U.S. dollars and the purchase of foreign currency (or the reverse) for immediate delivery. For example, if you sell shoes to a company in France, you must quote a price in either U.S. dollars or French francs. The exchange rate may change before the deal is completed, but the price is already set. If you quote the price in dollars, the French company assumes the risk of a change in rates because it will have to pay the dollar value no matter what. A change in rates may be to the French purchaser's benefit, or it may not. If you quote your price in French francs, you are assuming this risk. On the date of payment, you will have to have a bank exchange the francs to dollars (or buy dollars with the francs). If the franc is weaker, you will have lost a percentage of profit, but if the franc is stronger and the dollar weaker, you will have gained in profit.

2. A *forward transaction* lets you avoid fretting over whether the exchange rate will go up or down. You simply purchase the foreign currency at the time you make the deal. For example, if you quote a price in French francs, you then immediately purchase the francs from the bank at the rate that coincides with your price quote. In this way, both parties are free of risk. However, if the foreign currency increases in value, you will have lost an extra percentage of potential profit.

Generally, it will be easier to find a buyer if you agree to accept payment in the buyer's currency. If you operate in this manner, watch the foreign currency prior to pricing your goods. You should be able to spot any trends in the currency and set your price quote according to what you think the exchange rate will be when the deal is completed.

Cash in Advance

Under this arrangement, the buyer pays cash for the products before they are even shipped. Because the buyer must then completely trust the seller to follow through with the deal, this method is used only occasionally, in a strong seller's market, when demand for a product is particularly high. It may also be used for small deals, when the parties do not feel that using another method payment, such as a letter of credit, is worth the cost in time and money.

When a manufacturer needs a good deal of money up front to produce goods for sale, it may demand partial cash in advance, such as 25%, to offset its costs.

Open Account

In an open account, the buyer has an account with the seller. When the buyer receives the goods, payment is sent to the seller. In essence, the seller is offering credit to the buyer, and this practice can be risky. Typically, exporters use an open account only when they are dealing with someone with whom they are extremely comfortable. Cash in advance puts all the risk with the buyer; an open account puts all the risk with the seller, and for this reason, is not common.

On Consignment

Under this system, the seller ships goods without being paid, and is not paid until the buyer sells the goods. This system is by far the riskiest and is not advisable for any deal. If the buyer cannot sell the goods, they are simply returned without payment, causing the seller both headaches and unwelcome shipping costs.

Collection Drafts

The collection draft method and the letter of credit are similar (and both are different from the three methods described above). A bank acts as an intermediary between the buyer and seller, in an effort to minimize the risks of the buyer and seller. If buyers and sellers could completely trust one another, the collection drafts and letters of credit would not be necessary, but such cases are extremely rare.

With collection drafts, the seller ships the goods and the seller's bank sends a bill of lading (which is necessary to pick the goods up) and other specified shipping documents to a bank in the buyer's country. The buyer's bank will not release the bill of lading to the buyer until the goods are paid for. Once the buyer pays for them, it can pick up the goods. The buyer's bank sends the payment back to the seller.

To complete this type of deal, the seller must draw up, through its bank, a *draft*, or an order for the buyer's payment. There are three types of drafts:

1. *Sight draft.* Payment is required before the goods can be received by the buyer. The seller retains the title to the goods until they have reached their destination and are paid for. It is called a sight draft because, as soon as the goods have arrived, or are theoretically "in sight" on the dock, the draft is payable. The risk in this type of deal is that the buyer may change his or her mind when the goods are en route, and decide not to buy them. It is then the full responsibility of the seller to pay for return shipment of the goods.

2. *Time draft.* The seller is extending credit to the buyer. The buyer has a specific amount of time (i.e., 30, 60, or 90 days) to pay for the goods, from the date he or she picks up the goods and accepts the draft. With some time drafts, payment is due within a specific number of days after sight (or arrival) of the goods. If a specific date for payment is stated, the document is known as a date draft.

3. *Clean draft.* The shipping documents are sent to the buyer at the same time as the goods. This is, in effect, like sending the goods on an open account: the buyer must follow through with payment after receiving the goods. This rare type of draft is only used when the seller has extreme confidence in the buyer.

Letter of Credit

In the most simplified explanation of a letter of credit (L/C), the buyer arranges with an international bank to pay the seller as soon as the goods have been shipped. All the seller needs to do is bring proof of shipment and any other agreed on documents to the local branch of the named international (or any other designated bank) to be paid. The buyer is then safe because no payment will be given unless the goods are coming, and the seller is assured of payment if the goods are sent. With a collection draft, the buyer must pay a bank before he or she can pick up the goods. With an L/C, the seller must ship the goods before the bank will pay. The L/C is the preferred method of payment because the seller does not have to worry that the buyer will cancel an order after the goods have been shipped.

Most letters of credit involve two different banks. The buyer goes to his or her bank and has the L/C issued to be paid through the seller's bank. These two banks then cooperate to fulfill the terms of the L/C. When the letter is issued, the buyer may ask for any number of documents to be presented before the letter is payable. These terms are crucial for the beginning import/export entrepreneur: they serve to establish what shipping arrangements will be acceptable. The buyer thus controls how the goods are shipped, the price, and so on.

As a new importer, the easiest and safest way to negotiate the price of your goods will be to ask for pricing on the goods that is:

- C.I.F. (cost + insurance + freight) to the port of destination or
- D.P.D. (delivery paid + duty) your warehouse door.

Under both denotations, the seller (the exporter) arranges all shipping, insurance and freight; in the case of D.P.D., customs duties and delivery right to your warehouse door are included. There is a caveat, however: many exporters will only quote up to C.I.F.

The most common documents that will accompany a letter of credit before it is payable are:

- *Bill of lading* is a document signed by the captain, agents, or owners of the vessel transporting the goods, as evidence that the goods have been shipped. It represents a receipt for the merchandise and a contract to deliver it. (See Chapter 6 for information on the various forms of bills of lading.)
- *Packing list*, similar to a commercial invoice, provides information on how the goods were packed, the number of goods in the shipment, how they are numbered, and the weight and dimensions of each item. This is important for verification of the payment as stated in the letter of credit, and for customs purposes and pick-up.
- *Invoice* is a required commercial document that contains a full log of information: name and address of the shipper, seller, and consignee (the buyer); reference numbers (such as P.O. number or L/C confirmation number); date of the order and shipping date; mode of shipment and delivery and payment terms; description of goods, prices, and quantities. The invoice essentially represents the agreement as well as the terms under which it is to be executed.
- *Marine insurance papers* prove that the seller has provided marine insurance and indicates the type and coverage. If you are an importer, have the seller arrange and pay for this coverage, especially when working through L/Cs. The seller will receive payment as soon as the goods are shipped, and having insurance will cover your investment (the goods) should anything happen during shipping. Unless you are comfortable with another arrangement, it would be wise to request "All Risk" insurance, payable in U.S. dollars, for up to 110% of the value of

the goods. You're then insured against not only mishandling of the goods during shipment, but against declarations of war, weather, riots, and strikes.

- *Certificate of inspection* certifies the quantity and quality of the goods and their conformity to the order. If the inspection is "standard export inspection," the shipper or shipping company will nominate a standard inspector, or, if you prefer, you can hire a private weights and measures inspection company to conduct an accurate inspection of your goods.

Most letters of credit are issued as *irrevocable,* which means that the terms can be amended only with the consent of all parties involved. *Revocable credit* L/Cs also are issued, but these can be amended or canceled at any time without notification of the seller, and so are inadvisable because of their high risk factor. A *confirmed* L/C means that the seller's bank guarantees payment by the buyer's bank.

Costs for a Letter of Credit or Collection Draft

Typically, if you have no import credit record and you have to open an L/C—as the importer, or buyer of goods—you will be required to put up 100% of the L/C amount in cash or other marketable securities up front. As you build your credit record, however, your bank will grant you credit terms for your L/Cs, provided you sign a promissory note backed by sufficient collateral (cash, marketable securities, real estate, or other convertible assets). Payment terms will vary from bank to bank, and according to your creditworthiness and the amount of money you request. Credit terms for an L/C typically run from 30 days to 90 days, depending on your needs and your standing with the bank.

In the United States, the interest rate for the L/C amount is usually tied to the prime rate, plus some margin, say, 1.5% to 2.75%. For example, let's say you would like to purchase $20,000 worth of bicycle parts from China through a letter of credit. The prime rate is currently 11.0%, and your bank's margin is 2.0%, with terms out to 60 days. This means that you would have 60 days to repay the $20,000, while interest accrues at 13.0%. In addition to the interest charges, you will have to pay a small commission and other miscellaneous charges such as opening fees and cable or telex charges. As the buyer, you may be asked to pay both the issuing and confirming banks' charges for a letter of credit or draft. In most cases, however, the buyer and seller take care of their own respective L/C opening charges. These fees usually run between .25% and 1.0% of the transaction. In some rare cases, if the buyer refuses to pay for a letter of credit and asks for an open account arrangement, it may be in the seller's best interest to go ahead and pay for the L/C in order to make the sale without incurring undue risk.

Let's take a step-by-step look at what happens in an L/C transaction. In this example, let's say that a Japanese retailer has agreed to buy 2,000 snowboards from you at a certain price and under certain import conditions, such as paid delivery to the port in Kobe, Japan. Once this agreement has been reached, the following steps are taken:

Step 1. The Japanese buyer is issued an L/C by his bank. If the buyer's bank does not grant him terms for the L/C, he will have to put up 100% collateral for the value of the L/C.

Step 2. The Japanese bank prepares the L/C, including instructions on which documents are necessary from you, the seller.

Step 3. The Japanese bank sends this L/C to your bank here in the United States and requests confirmation. (A foreign bank will sometimes choose a correspondent bank with whom it usually works in the United States, but you can request a specific international bank that handles your business.) For our purposes here, let's say that the Japanese buyer agrees to work with your bank.

Step 4. Your bank prepares and sends a letter of confirmation, along with the L/C, back to you, the exporter.

Step 5. You read over the conditions, which may include, for example, that you provide insurance for the shipment, and you make sure that you can meet all conditions listed, including the date of shipment.

Step 6. If you can meet the conditions of the L/C, you then arrange for your freight forwarder to send the goods to the port or airport.

Step 7. Once the goods are loaded for shipment, the freight forwarder completes the necessary documents and returns them to you.

Step 8. You take these documents, which indicate compliance with the conditions of the L/C, to your bank.

Step 9. When your bank verifies that the conditions have been met, the bank pays you the agreed-on amount and sends the documents to your buyer's bank in Japan. (This is why careful recordkeeping and documentation are so important. These signed papers function just like a check. When they are presented to a bank, the bank will issue full payment for the goods "at sight.")

Step 10. When the Japanese bank receives the documents, it sends the money due to your bank.

Step 11. If the buyer doesn't already have terms with his bank, he pays his bank any money he may owe on the L/C, after which the bank hands over the documents to him so that he may collect the shipment from the shipping company.

CREDIT AND COLLECTIONS

As an exporter, you will need cash as soon as your first orders come in. You may have an L/C from the buyer, but you still have to come up with money to pay for the goods you are shipping, and be paid yourself. There are a few ways you can go about this. If you have sufficient collateral, you should have no problem getting a short-term loan from a bank. If not, you may be able to use the L/C as collateral, as long as you do not have a poor credit rating. The bank can see that, because you already have an order for the goods, you are a pretty low risk. All you have to do to be paid is ship the goods, and you will then be able to pay back your loan.

A third way to handle this situation is to obtain credit from the manufacturer, but such an arrangement will take some convincing. If you are just getting started, you will not be able to supply trade references, and your bank probably will not give you a credit rating if your account is new.

Honesty and a personal financial statement may open the coffers. If your supplier is small, the manner in which you present yourself will be an important factor in obtaining initial credit. If you are dealing with a large supplier and the credit manager is protecting the supplier's position, you may find the going tough. Again, a personal visit may accelerate your acceptance. If you already have an L/C, obtaining credit will be easier. Many suppliers will send a bill 30 days after the products have been shipped. This should give you ample time to get the documents to the bank and be paid yourself.

Credit Records

Create a permanent credit record and maintain it separately from your invoices. Show the date, the invoice number, the amount of any new charges, a running balance of the total amount owed, the date and amount of each payment received, and a record of any invoices, collection letters, and collection phone calls made to each customer. Using these records to review your receivables is an important aspect of your entrepreneurial responsibility.

Good receivables can become overdue collection problems, and losses can result if they are not monitored frequently and carefully. Your review should pinpoint potential problems at an early stage, to lower the probability that the account will become a loss. Credit experts advise that the difficulty of collecting an account increases in direct proportion to its age.

International Collection Methods

To avoid letting an overdue account age so that it becomes uncollectible, deal with it early. First, send another copy of the most recent bill, with the notation "Past due" or "Overdue notice" stamped on the front. If this does not bring a response in the form of payment or an arrangement for payment, the common second step is to send a letter. Draft a form letter that has a friendly, courteous tone. You want to maintain good relations with the customer; he or she may have overlooked the billings or be temporarily hard-pressed.

Reminders should be sent routinely when payment of bills is late. Your customers should know you are aware of their tardiness. You can lessen the impersonal aspect of a form letter by having appropriate spaces for filling in by hand, the amount owed, writing the customer's name at the top, and personally signing the letter. Keep reminders friendly and sympathetic, but also firm and short.

Sending a letter or series of letters, each less friendly and more threatening than the last, may not always evoke the desired response. If the debtor does not respond, you must proceed to stronger collection methods.

Confrontation by telephone or in person is the next step because it forces a response. The initial contact should be in private, appealing to the debtor's sympathies, pride, and sense of justice. Make his or her embarrassment work in your favor. Try to get a firm commitment on the amount you can expect and when you can expect it. If your pleas don't have the desired effect, inform the debtor of the collection actions you will take if payment is not received by a certain date.

A small fraction of your credit customers may be totally immune to polite and gentle approaches. If they don't respond to your warnings and have not begun to correct the situation in spite of your consideration, it is time to give up on them as customers and take the drastic measures required to collect your money. Choose from the following alternatives the method most appropriate for each account:

1. *Notify other creditors.* In the process, you will learn how much your debtor owes them, and how quickly you must act to collect your share. This tactic will prevent the debtor from receiving additional credit extensions elsewhere.

2. *Send a sight draft to the debtor's bank, directing the bank to pay the amount owed.* Payment of this draft requires the debtor's consent, but the draft may be approved to avoid further embarrassment with the bank.

3. *Use a collection agency, but only as a final resort.* An agency will take 25 to 33% of the amount(s) it collects—even 50% on amounts under $50. Still, this is better than taking a total loss. Collection agencies are listed in the Yellow Pages. If an agency proves ineffective, take your account to another agency as soon as the first contract expires. Different agencies use different methods. One agency may produce better results with your customers than another. Keep in mind that any amount collected while an account is signed over to the agency is subject to its fee, whether the payment resulted from its efforts or yours. For this reason, make sure you have exhausted your own methods before turning to a collection agency.

4. *Garnish the debtor's wages, savings, or checking accounts, or any other assets you can find.* The legal expense you will incur makes this approach impractical unless you are seeking collection of several hundred dollars or more.

5. *Hire a lawyer.* Some lawyers have a good deal of experience in collection proceedings. A lawyer's time, however, will be expensive regardless of whether you receive payment on the account.

6. *Take your case to small claims court.* This is an inexpensive and informal method of bringing suit, but even a judgment in your favor does not guarantee payment. Also, the presence of legal technicalities can mean that even though you are in the right, the judge or referee may decide against you, out of sympathy toward the story the debtor tells.

Factoring Houses

A factoring house, or factor, is a company that buys another company's receivables. If you have receivables that you are having a hard time collecting, or if you need payment immediately for receivables that pay slowly, the factor will pay you the amount due, minus a percentage as commission, and then collect the bill independently. This strategy will free up your cash more quickly and release you from the burden of collection, but you will lose a percentage of your sale to the factoring house.

If you make an agreement with a factoring house "with recourse," you are still ultimately responsible for repaying the factor if your buyer defaults. If the agreement is "without recourse," the factor is solely liable for collecting from the buyer. Factors purchasing receivables without recourse will charge a much larger percentage because of the added risk on their part.

Foreign Credit Insurance

One way to alleviate worry about foreign creditors' defaulting is to purchase insurance that covers such a situation. The Foreign Credit Insurance Association (FCIA), an insurance agency associated with the Export-Import Bank of the United States (refer to Chapter 2), provides coverage for companies extending credit overseas.

The sidebar, "Foreign Exchange," gives an overview of payment methods for international trading.

In America, getting paid for your work is relatively straight-forward. You sign a contract, complete the job, present the invoice or purchase order, and wait for payment.

Getting paid for products or services when exporting, however, is not so simple. In fact, before you sell a single item, it would behoove you to take a crash course in "Export Payment Methods 101" (check with your local small business development office or export council).

But don't let all the new terms and definitions scare you, advises Susan Corrales-Diaz, whose Orange, California, company, Systems Integrated, manufactures automated controls for electric power and water management equipment. She knew almost nothing about exporting when she started six years ago, but today exhibits an impressive knowledge of what it takes to collect overseas.

"I didn't know very much at all when we started," remembers Corrales-Diaz with a rueful laugh. "One of my more seasoned salesmen had experience in China, so we decided to go into that market, where we knew there was a good infrastructure."

To educate herself, Corrales-Diaz began attending seminars and reading books. She learned about a "whole rainbow assortment of ways to get paid," but quickly discovered that until you are actually using them, their applications can be difficult to understand.

Payment of Choice

Looking for a head start in understanding all the payment methods available to exporters? Here's a rundown:

- An *open account* is "the easiest and most dangerous way [to obtain payment for exports]," says Bob Lee of the U.S. Commerce Department's Trade and Project Finance Division. "You may do a [credit check] to make sure the customer has enough money and to see what their payment record is, but basically you don't go beyond that. Then you hope in 30, 60, or 90 days that you'll receive payment." This method, says Lee, robs you of legal recourse should your foreign buyer decide not to pay. "Open accounts should be reserved for your very best customers or countries you feel are very stable," advises Lee.
- *Documentary collection* involves sending an overseas bank the title documents for the goods to be exported

and a blank check (called a draft) along with instructions not to surrender title until the buyer signs the draft. "The draft has the amount of money [due you] filled in and a space for the buyer to sign," explains Lee, adding that the draft can be a sight draft paid immediately or a time draft paid so many days after it's signed. The draft is drawn up by you after negotiating conditions with the customer, such as what bank to send it to, what documents to include (for example, bill of lading, invoice, insurance, pro forma invoice), when and how payment will be made, and where to ship the goods. The drawback to this method, says Lee, is that the buyer may refuse to sign the draft, and because a bank is not a collection agency, your goods may just sit on the dock. "The advantages are that it's a convenient, well-understood mechanism that is cheaper to use than obtaining a letter of credit," he says, adding that this method works best with small and medium-sized orders.

- *A letter of credit* is the second most secure way to recover payment for your exports, Lee believes. "There are two kinds of letters of credit, and they can by used for many different things," says Laura MacLellan, president of the Export Managers Association of California. "The standby letter of credit is used to collect in the event someone doesn't do something [such as ship the goods or pay the invoice] on time. It can be used as a form of insurance, a performance bond, or even as a collateral with a bank." The commercial letter of credit, says MacLellan, is usually what the exporter receives from the buyer's bank as payment once proof the order has been completed is assembled. Letters of credit are usually tailored to each transaction and can include information such as how much the order cost; when, how and where it will be shipped; what inspection certifications should be included; and who pays for what. All this should be agreed on beforehand in a pre-letter-of-credit contract or agreement, MacLellan says, because any deviation requires amending the letter of credit, which can be extremely time-consuming and expensive. "The letter of credit is safe because it's issued by a commercial bank and can be created to follow the regulations of the International Chamber of Commerce (ICC)," says MacLellan. "The ICC 500 is a standard set of rules banks worldwide play with. No lawyers are needed [to enforce the letter of credit]."

- *Credit cards* can also be a viable way to accept payment. Exporters don't necessarily need to have a customer's card in hand, says Brad Hennig of VISA. Once they have merchant status, all they need is the customer's card number and selected other information to call in for point-of-purchase verification. Steve L. Abrams of MasterCard says the company's Purchasing Card can be a good option for export payments. "We created this card to facilitate small purchases, which we define as those under $25,000." The American Express card offers several benefits for use in export payment as well, says spokesperson Marcos Rada. Lack of a preset spending limit is one plus; also, if you process electronically, you could receive payment within three business days.

- *Cash*, of course, is always an option. "The safest payment method, although it's not commonly used," says Lee, "is cash in advance." He adds that exporters should use cash only for small-ticket items. Have the buyer send a check in U.S. dollars, and then ship the goods express mail. While getting cash upfront may be the ideal way to receive payment for exporting, it does not give customers the payment flexibility you may need to attract them, nor does it give you a competitive edge.

According to Corrales-Diaz, there are myriad ways to combine the various payment methods. "Our letter of credit is [combined] with a sight draft," she says, "but you can also have a letter of credit with a time draft or an open account backed by a standby letter of credit." She stresses that personal understanding of the drafts and letters of credit can't replace working with a knowledgeable, experienced international banker who can explain the subtle nuances of each method.

"All these different [payment methods] have degrees of risk associated with them," says Corrales-Diaz. "As a seller, you should understand what your competitors are doing in a country and then choose payment methods [that allow you to compete] yet protect you as much as possible."

Cynthia E. Griffin, "Foreign Exchange," *Entrepreneur*, October 1994, p. 58.

6

MAINTAINING RECORDS

Among the many good reasons to maintain accurate records of your business operation, perhaps the two that make it absolutely necessary are: (1) accurate financial records are required by law, and (2) you need accurate records to assess the financial health of your business. With accurate and trustworthy records, you can steer your business toward maximum profits.

As with any business, accurate records must be kept to determine the tax liabilities of your import/export business. Regardless of the type of bookkeeping system you employ, your records must be permanent, accurate, current, and complete, and they must clearly establish income, deductions, credits, employee information, and anything else specified by federal, state, and local regulations. The law does not require any particular kind of records, only that they be complete and separate for each business.

From a managerial standpoint, maintaining accurate records is vital to the day-to-day operation of your import/export business. As you become more successful in your business, you will be handling a multitude of various documents and records for each client, especially those related to your letters of credit and shipping and receiving. Careful records will help document the distribution and sales of your clients' exports or imports. Carefully documented information about your business's financial condition will help you identify and correct any income or expense problems before they become major problems.

ACCOUNTING METHODS AND SYSTEMS

Two systems of accounting are used for recordkeeping purposes—
(1) cash basis and (2) accrual basis. When you start in business, establish the type and arrangement of books and records most suitable for
your particular operation, keeping in mind the taxes for which the
business is liable and when they fall due. Which system will be best for
your import/export business depends greatly on your sales volume,
how you legally choose to form your business, and whether you extend
credit. If you are not proficient in this area, seek the aid of a professional accountant. Setting up a system for good recordkeeping need be
done only once; doing the setup efficiently makes maintaining the system much easier.

Cash Basis

With cash basis accounting, you do business and pay taxes according to
your real-time cash flow. Cash income begins as soon as you receive income from a sale. Expenses are paid as they occur. Both income and expenses are put on the books and charged to the period in which they
are paid or received.

   If you're on a cash basis system, you can defer income to the following year as long as it isn't actually or constructively received by you
in the present year. A check received by you in the present year but not
cashed until the following year is still income to you for the present
year. Therefore, if you want to shift income to the following year, you
will either have to delay billing until the following year or bill so late in
the present year that a payment before year-end is unlikely.

   If you want to accelerate expenses to the present year, you should
pay those bills received and log them as the present year's expenses.
An expense charged to your credit card will count as an expense in
the year it was charged, not when you pay the card company. Be careful about paying next year's expenses in advance. Generally, expenses
prepaid in excess of one month have to be prorated over the specified
payment period. However, dues and subscriptions can be currently
deducted if prepaid for the forthcoming year.

Accrual Basis

With accrual basis accounting, income and expenses are charged to the
period to which they apply, regardless of whether money has been received. For instance, if you complete a deal but have yet to be paid for

goods shipped, you recognize all expenses incurred in connection with that contract during the period in which it was supposed to have been completely paid and expensed, regardless of whether you have been paid yet. If an employee works for you this month but you haven't paid him, you still take the deduction for that expense because that person has earned the money.

The accrual method is mandatory for purchases and sales when and where inventories are used in the business, for example, if you purchase imports and hold them in a store or warehouse. Under the Tax Reform Act of 1986, if your gross sales receipts exceed $5 million per year and your business is a corporation, partnership, or trust, the Internal Revenue Service (IRS) will not permit you to use the cash method of accounting. You must use the accrual accounting method. There are several exceptions that permit some businesses to use the cash method of accounting no matter how large their gross receipts. Those exceptions are made for the farming business, partnerships without corporate partners, sole proprietorships, and qualified personal service corporations—those performing services in the fields of health care, law, accounting, actuarial science, performing, or consulting. In addition, 95% of the stock of the corporation must be owned by shareholders who are performing services for the corporation.

With accrual basis accounting, it doesn't matter when you receive or make actual payment. Income is reported when you bill. Expenses are deductible when you are billed, not when you pay. This accounting method has more tax benefits for a company with few receivables and large amounts of current liabilities. Advance payments to an accrual-basis taxpayer are held to be taxable income in the year received.

Unlike payments for services rendered, advance payments for merchandise are reported by an accrual-basis taxpayer when properly accruable under this method of accounting. But if you choose this accounting procedure, you must use it for all reports and credit purposes. If you run two or more businesses at the same time, you may use different accounting methods. You can choose to run one business on the cash basis and the other on the accrual basis.

PRIMARY AND SECONDARY RECORDS

When developing a recordkeeping system, your goal is to keep it as simple as possible. Your time is valuable, and if your records are too complex, you will spend too much time maintaining them. Additionally, complicated records may require hiring an accountant or bookkeeper part-time or full-time. Develop a comprehensive but easily understandable recordkeeping system.

Regardless of whether you use computers, manual entry, or some combination of both, keep in mind that as you enter data into your records, the information should have a direct bearing on the financial condition of your import/export business. Don't maintain records that are irrelevant and time-consuming. Maintain up-to-date records of current and pertinent information in a manner that can be uniform throughout the entire system.

BOOKKEEPING SYSTEMS

Double-entry bookkeeping, which makes use of journals and ledgers, is usually the preferred method of keeping business records. Transactions are entered first in a journal (Figure 6–1). Monthly totals of the transactions are then posted to the appropriate ledger accounts. Five categories of ledger accounts are: (1) income; (2) expenses; (3) assets; (4) liability; and (5) net worth. Income and expense accounts are closed each year; asset, liability, and net-worth accounts are maintained on a permanent and continuing basis.

Single-entry bookkeeping, although not as complete as the double-entry method, may be used effectively in a small business, especially during its early years. The single-entry system can be relatively simple. The flow of income and expense is recorded through a daily summary of cash receipts, a monthly summary of receipts, and a monthly disbursements journal (such as a checkbook). This system is entirely adequate for the tax purposes of many small businesses.

Generally, your import/export business will generate four basic records for which you are accountable through your recordkeeping system:

1. Sales records.
2. Cash receipts.
3. Cash disbursements.
4. Accounts receivable.

Sales records include all income to be derived from the performance of your service. Sales can be grouped into one large category called *gross sales* or into several subcategories depicting different client accounts so that you know which ones are performing well in the markets you've targeted. These records will provide you with an indication of changes that need to be made in the marketing plan for particular accounts.

Figure 6-1   Sample General Journal Form

GENERAL JOURNAL

MONTH OF _____

DATE	ACCOUNT DEBITED	ACCOUNT NUMBER	AMOUNT	ACCOUNT CREDITED	ACCOUNT NUMBER	AMOUNT

Cash receipts account for all moneys generated through the collection of accounts receivable. This is *actual income* collected during a given accounting period, which is different from earnings entered in your sales records. Remember, your sales records account for all sales made, not moneys collected.

Cash disbursements are sometimes referred to as operating expense records or accounts payable (Figure 6–2). All disbursements should be made by check if possible, so that business expenses can be well documented for tax purposes. If a cash payment is necessary, a receipt for the payment, or at least an explanation of it, should be included in the business records. All canceled checks, paid bills, and other documents that substantiate the entries in the business records should be filed in an orderly manner and stored in a safe place. Breaking the cash disbursement headings into different categories such as rent, maintenance, and advertising may be easier to deal with than one large category.

A petty cash fund should be established for expenses that must be paid immediately and are small enough to warrant payment by cash (Figure 6–3). The Small Business Administration suggests that you account for petty cash by cashing a check for the purpose of petty cash and placing the money in a safe or lockbox. Record items purchased through the petty cash fund on a form that lists date of purchase, amount, and purpose. When the petty cash fund is almost exhausted, total the cost of all the items and write a check for the specified amount in order to replenish the account.

Accounts receivable (Figure 6–4) are sales stemming from the extension of credit. Most import/export management companies invoice their clients for services rendered; therefore, they are extending credit to their clients based on prearranged terms. You need to maintain these records on a monthly basis so you can age your receivables and determine how long your credit customers are taking to pay their bills. If an account ages beyond a 60-day period, start investigating the reasons why the customer is taking so long to pay. (We have covered the extension and collection of credit in Chapter 5.)

RECORDING INCOME AND EXPENSES

A manual or a one-write system of recording financial transactions is a system whereby each check that you write is recorded automatically in the cash disbursements journal. This is popular with many small businesses because it saves time. If you are writing a low number of checks per month, it makes sense to use a manual or one-write system. Maintaining your general ledger on a normal basis should

Figure 6–2   Sample Accounts Payable Aging Report Form

AGING OF
ACCOUNTS PAYABLE

REPORTING PERIOD

FROM: ——————————————— **TO:** ———————————————

DATE	INVOICE NUMBER	ACCOUNT	ACCOUNT NUMBER	DESCRIPTION	AMOUNT			
					30 DAYS	60 DAYS	90+ DAYS	TOTAL

Figure 6–3   Sample Petty Cash Form

PETTY CASH JOURNAL

REPORTING PERIOD

FROM: _____ **TO:** _____ **BALANCE ON HAND** ☐

DATE	VOUCHER NUMBER	ACCOUNT	ACCOUNT NUMBER	PAYEE	APPROVED BY	TOTAL	BALANCE

TOTAL VOUCHER AMOUNT	$
TOTAL RECEIPTS	$
CASH ON HAND	$
OVERAGE/SHORTAGE	$
PETTY CASH REIMBURSEMENT	$
BALANCE FORWARD	$

AUDITED BY:

_____

APPROVED BY:

_____

Figure 6-4 Sample Accounts Receivable Aging Report Form

AGING OF
ACCOUNTS RECEIVABLE

REPORTING PERIOD

FROM: _____ **TO:** _____

DATE	INVOICE NUMBER	ACCOUNT	ACCOUNT NUMBER	DESCRIPTION	AMOUNT			TOTAL
					30 DAYS	60 DAYS	90+ DAYS	

give you all the financial information you need to make good business decisions.

If you write a large number of checks per month, consider changing to batch processing of your general ledger postings (Figure 6–5). Data processing services will handle this for you. Hiring a data processing service will save you the time of doing it yourself and the expense of hiring a full-time data processor. Develop expense codes for the types of checks you write. Then make an adding machine tape of the totals and send the tape to the data processing center. Within about five working days, you will receive a computer printout of your general ledger, with all of your checks listed according to their expense codes.

If you are spending a lot of money in cash rather than via checks, you should list these expenditures on an expense report form. Printed forms, readily available at stationery stores, designate separate categories: travel, entertainment, office supplies, and so on. Attach your receipts to the form on which you report the expenditures. Now add the expense codes and write yourself a check for reimbursement of expenses (or give your bookkeeper the form and receipts, and ask for a reimbursement check). Ultimately, all cash disbursements, even out-of-pocket expenses, are handled by check. For example, if you spend $200 out of pocket, fill out an expense report, pay yourself back for what you spent, and file the report and receipts. With this system, you know these expenses are entered into your bookkeeping system, and you have documentation available for the IRS.

Pay as much as you can by check, to have a record of all debits to your company. Most bookkeeping veterans agree that it is best to work out of one checkbook for a business, if at all possible. Nothing drives an accountant crazier than interaccount transfers. They are the source of many businesses' financial problems.

In some lines of business, legal restrictions prevent running a business out of one checkbook. Lawyers and collection agents are usually required by law to maintain trust accounts on behalf of their clients. These accounts represent funds held in trust on the client's behalf (for example, court-awarded damages or collection monies) until they are disbursed in response to presentation of client receipts or, ultimately, to pay service fees.

DEPRECIATION

There are two kinds of depreciation: (1) cash-value and (2) tax-related. Cash-value depreciation is based on the difference between the cost of the equipment and the fair market value of it at any point in time. If a

Figure 6–5 Sample Form for General Ledger Postings

GENERAL LEDGER

ACCOUNT _____ **MONTH OF**_____

ACCOUNT NUMBER _____

DATE	ITEM	EXPENSE CODE	TRANSACTION		BALANCE	
			DEBIT	CREDIT	DEBIT	CREDIT

piece of equipment that cost $15,000 in January had a market value of $11,000 in December of the same year, the cash-value depreciation would be $4,000. In other words, your actual expense of owning the equipment would have been $4,000 for one year, or $333 per month.

Tax-related depreciation is purely an accounting device to take advantage of the maximum allowable deduction permitted by law when figuring your annual net taxable income. Tax-related depreciation is determined by a formula laid down in the Internal Revenue Code. It has nothing to do with the actual condition of your equipment or its loss in value at the end of each year's use.

Cash-Value Depreciation

If you buy a piece of equipment, depreciation of its cash value should be included as an expense on your monthly operating statement. If you lease a piece of equipment, the monthly lease payment will be a part of your monthly operating expenses. (Cash-value depreciation is frequently figured into the cost of an equipment lease and need not necessarily be figured separately by you.)

Many equipment-leasing agreements have a clause providing for what is known as a depreciation reserve—money set aside in an amount that corresponds with the declining value of the equipment. When the lease is up, the equipment is going to be sold either to the lessee or to a third party. If it goes for a price over and above its depreciated value, the difference can be refunded to the lessee. If, however, the equipment is sold for a price that is less than its depreciated value, the lessee must pay the difference to the lessor. This is where the depreciation reserve comes in. It is usually a part of the lease and should be considered a monthly expense of running the business.

Straight-line or uniform depreciation is the most frequently used method of depreciating new equipment. In straight-line depreciation, the equipment loses an equal part of total value in every year of its life.

Suppose you buy a $15,000 printing press with a 10-year useful life, according to your accountant's schedule. The straight-line depreciation rate would be calculated by dividing its price by its useful life into the $15,000 for a rate of $1,500 a year. If you are in the 28% tax bracket, $1,500 in depreciation will save you $420. Suppose you need only 20% down ($3,000) to buy a $15,000 machine, and you finance your machine on the installment plan. The interest you pay on any amount owed is going to be another tax deduction for you. That means your total cash savings of $4,536 ($420 × 10 + $336) will more than offset your down payment of $3,000.

Depreciation for Taxes

The depreciation method used on financial statements is often different from the method used on your tax return. For your tax return, your accountant will most often use a tax-approved depreciation schedule that will give you the largest possible deduction on your tax return (and, therefore, reduce your taxes).

The Tax Reform Act of 1986 revised the depreciation rates that may be used for federal income tax purposes on all equipment, real estate, and similar assets purchased after December 31, 1986. This new method is often referred to as MACRS (modified accelerated cost recovery system). (The method used for earlier acquired assets is referred to as ACRS.)

Assets purchased before that date and used in your trade or business are depreciated using a different schedule that generally gives you a larger depreciation deduction than the current rates do. Keep in mind that, in many states, rules that are entirely different from those used on your federal income tax return are in effect for allowable depreciation methods on state tax returns.

You can learn the rules for depreciation of assets used in your trade and business by ordering Publication 17 from the Internal Revenue Service and ordering IRS Form 4562 with the accompanying instructions.

Depreciation Schedules

If you are depreciating real estate used in your business or held for investment, the time period over which it is depreciated depends on whether it is residential property (such as apartments) or commercial property (such as stores, offices, and so on). Residential real property is depreciated over 27.5 years using the straight-line method. Commercial real property is depreciated over 31.5 years using the straight-line method.

Several different depreciable lives are possible for depreciable personal property used in your trade or business: 3, 5, 7, 10, 15, and 20 years. Almost all equipment—automobiles, trucks, typewriters, desks, and machines—will be depreciated using either a 5-year or a 7-year life. You should consult IRS publications to determine what types of assets use other lives.

Equipment that fits into the 5-year or 7-year-lives class can be depreciated using the 200% declining balance rate: the equipment is depreciated using twice the straight-line rate. However, in the years of acquisition and disposition of the equipment, you can take only half of a full year's depreciation, no matter in which month of the year the equipment was purchased.

Some of the items included in the 5-year depreciation class under MACRS are:

1. Automobiles and light trucks.
2. Computer-based telephone central office switching equipment.
3. Research and experimentation property.

The 7-year MACRS depreciable life applies to most forms of equipment used in business: typewriters, computers, desks, chairs, and fixtures. For example, if you purchase a $1,400 computer that has a 7-year MACRS depreciable life, the depreciation in the first year would be $1,400 ÷ 7 = $200. You can take twice the straight-line rate depreciation of $400, but, in the first year, you are limited to a half-year's worth of depreciation, which would mean $200 depreciation.

After the initial year's depreciation, you would calculate your depreciation for each subsequent year using the following formula:

$$\text{Initial cost} - \text{Prior year's depreciation} \times [1 \div 7] \times 2$$

Certain properties, such as luxury automobiles used less than 50% of the time for business, are limited to straight-line depreciation.

Automobiles that are used for business and cost more than $12,800 are limited to $2,560 depreciation in the first year, $4,100 in the second year, $2,450 in the third year, and $1,475 for all subsequent years.

Except for automobiles, under Internal Revenue Code Section 179, you can immediately deduct up to the first $10,000 of equipment purchased for your business each year and avoid depreciating it over a period of time. However, if you place in service personal property in excess of $200,000 in any one year, the $10,000 is reduced, dollar for dollar, for all property purchased in excess of the $200,000. In addition, the $10,000 deduction is limited to the taxable income of your trade or business before taking this deduction. If the equipment is sold, this deduction must be recaptured.

These points are current at the time of publication but may change from year to year. Make sure your financial adviser(s), particularly your tax adviser(s), are made aware of any changes that may occur in tax-related depreciation guidelines.

OTHER RECORDS YOU SHOULD RETAIN

Records supporting entries on a federal tax return should be kept until the statute of limitations (ordinarily, three years after the return is due) expires. Copies of federal income tax returns should be kept forever; they may even be helpful someday to the executor of your estate.

In addition to the four basic records discussed earlier and your tax documents, you should maintain records for three other important items: capital equipment, insurance, and payroll.

Capital Equipment

Equipment records should be kept for major purchases such as your computer system, so that you can determine what your depreciation expenses will be for tax purposes. Don't keep records on small items like staplers, tape recorders, and answering machines. Don't list leased equipment in this section. Leased equipment should be entered under cash disbursements because you do not own it. Leased equipment is a liability that is payable each month.

Maintain records only on capital equipment you have purchased, whether outright, on a contract basis, or through a chattel mortgage. Major equipment you have purchased is considered an asset even though you may have financed it. As you pay off your loan obligation, you build equity in the equipment, and the amount of that equity can be entered onto your balance sheet as an asset.

Information you should record for each piece of equipment includes: date purchased, vendor's name, a brief description of the item, how it was paid for, the check number (if appropriate), and the full amount of the purchase.

Insurance

Keep all records pertaining to your company's auto, life, health, and fire insurance policies, and any special coverage you may obtain to decrease the risk of liability in a specific area, such as cargo insurance. List the carrier for each policy and the underwriting agent who issued the coverages. Maintain records on any claims made against your policies. You may need them to resolve any misunderstandings that may arise.

When updating your records, enter all information about the payment of premiums: the date the check was written, the amount, and the number of the policy it was written for. This detail will help you in payment disputes and for tax purposes.

If you are an importer servicing any national or chain accounts, you sometimes will be asked to provide product liability insurance, often in excess of $1 million. Keep these records in a file that is easily accessible. You will have to provide proof of insurance periodically.

Payroll

Any employer, regardless of the number of employees, must maintain all records pertaining to payroll taxes (income tax withholding, Social Security, and federal unemployment tax) for at least four years after the tax becomes due or is paid, whichever is later.

SHIPPING RECORDS

You will need to maintain files containing the shipping records for each account you service. Most of the shipping records you'll be dealing with are known as *collection documents.* If you are the exporter, you may choose to use a freight forwarder who will take care of filling out and processing all of the appropriate forms. Once you've met all the shipping conditions on the importer's letter of credit, you will then take these documents to your bank, where they will be checked to see that all the stipulations of the importer's letter of credit have been satisfied. Your bank, through an arrangement with the importer's bank, will then issue payment for the goods "at sight." You receive payment right there at your bank. In a sense, then, these documents represent cash, in much the same way that a business check represents cash— both will provide the presenter with payment on sight.

If you're the importer, you or your customs broker will use these collection documents to claim your cargo after the shipment arrives in port. You must take care of any import duties and customs fees, as well as any necessary inspections. Once your goods have been cleared, they will be released over to you.

Although collection documents will vary from country to country and from importer to importer, in general, they will include some combination of the following forms:

1. *Bill of lading* (Figure 6–6). This document is signed by the captain, agents, or owners of the vessel transporting the goods, as binding evidence that the goods have been shipped. It

Figure 6-6   Sample Bill of Lading

BILL OF LADING

TRAILER/CAR NUMBER: _____

BILL DATE: _____

TO			**FROM**		
Consignee			Shipper		
Street			Street		
Destination			Origin		
City	State	Zip	City	State	Zip
Route:			Special Instructions:		

FOR PAYMENT, SEND BILL TO			**SHIPPER'S INSTRUCTIONS**
Name			
Company			
Street			
City	State	Zip	

NO. SHIPPING UNITS	TIME	DESCRIPTION OF ARTICLES, SPECIAL MARKS & EXCEPTIONS	WEIGHT	RATE	CHARGES

REMIT C.O.D.	C.O.D. AMOUNT: $	C.O.D. FEE
TO:	If this shipment is to be delivered to the consignee without recourse on the consignor, the consignor shall sign the following statement:	PREPAID ☐ COLLECT ☐
ADDRESS:		TOTAL CHARGES $
NOTE: Where the rate is dependent on value, shippers are required to state specifically in writing the agreed or declared value of the property. The agreed or declared value of the property is hereby specifically stated by the shipper to be not exceeding	The carrier shall not make delivery of this shipment without payment of freight and all other lawful charges.	Freight Charges are collect unless market prepaid
$ _____ per	_____ Signature of Consignor	CHECK BOX IF PREPAID ☐

RECEIVED subject to the classifications and tariffs in effect on the date of the issue of this Bill of Lading, the property described above in apparent good order, except as noted (contents and condition of packages unknown), marked consigned and destined as indicated above which said carrier (the word carrier being understood through this contract as meaning any person or corporation in possession of the property under the contract) agrees to carry to its usual place of delivery as said destination. If on its route, otherwise to deliver to another carrier on the route to said destination. It is mutually agreed as to each carrier of all or any of said property, over all or any portion of said route to destination and as to each party at any time interested in all or any said property, that every service to be performed hereunder shall be subject to all the Bill of Lading terms and conditions in the governing classification on the date of shipment.
Shipper hereby certifies that he is familiar with all the Bill of Lading terms and conditions in the governing classification and the said terms and conditions are hereby

Shipper	Carrier	
Per	Per	Date:

Mark with "X" or "RQ" if appropriate to designate Hazardous Materials Substances as defined in the Department of Transportation Regulations governing the transportation of hazardous materials. The use of this column is an optional method for identifying hazardous materials on Bills of Lading 172.201(a)(1)(iii) of Title 49. Code of Federal Regulations.

represents a receipt for the merchandise and a contract to deliver it. Bills of lading can come in several forms, including:

- *Clean.* The bill of lading is clean if the shipping company has not noted any irregularities in the packing or the condition of the goods. This is generally the standard bill of lading.
- *Straight.* The bill is nonnegotiable with a stipulation as to the party to whom the goods are consigned. This is usually the preferred type of bill for beginning importers because it offers the buyer the most protection by prohibiting the release of the goods to anyone but the party specified on the documents.
- *On board.* The bill is issued once the goods are on board the vessel. This is an older shipping term that is used less frequently now. It confirms only that the goods have been placed on board, and does not carry any other guidelines or stipulations.
- *On deck.* The goods are being transported on the vessel's deck. This is relevant only if the goods are required to be placed on deck—livestock, for example.
- *Order.* The bill must be endorsed by the shipper.
- *Order notify.* The bill must be endorsed by the shipper and the consignee must be notified when the ship reaches its port of destination. If you are the importer and the L/C is "Marked Notify," the shipper will notify you in advance when the ship or plane will arrive in the United States. This remark is particularly helpful to the beginning importer. Many companies will stipulate that both the customs broker and the consignee (the buyer) must be notified.
- *Through bill of lading.* Several carriers are involved; perhaps one carrier is responsible for overland and another for ocean shipment. If you're an importer located in the interior of the country, you will need to become familiar with through bills of lading because you will ultimately receive your goods via truck or rail.

2. *Commercial invoice.* This type of invoice accompanies a shipment and should include the names and addresses of the shipper, seller, and consignee, as well as reference numbers (such as the original P.O. number or the L/C confirmation number), date of the order, shipping date, mode of shipment, delivery and payment terms (including L/C opening date), description of goods, prices, and quantities. This essentially represents the agreement and terms of the deal.

3. *Consular invoice.* Some countries require an additional invoice prepared in the language of their country, and on official forms, primarily for export customs purposes.

4. *Certificate of origin* (Figure 6–7). Some countries require a separate certificate of origin, even though this information is included on the commercial invoice. This is especially important when importing goods that must pass through regulatory approval, such as medical gowns and gloves or food preparation disposables. The Food and Drug Administration, for example, requires certificates of origin for all products under its authority. Sometimes, especially in countries with emerging economies, this document might be simply a statement by the manufacturer on its own letterhead, that the goods were manufactured at that factory. The statement will probably be stamped by the appropriate authority from that country.

5. *Inspection certificate.* The quantity, quality, and conformity of the goods to the order are certified after an inspection. The inspection can be a "standard export inspection," in which the shipper or shipping company nominates a standard inspector, or, if the buyer prefers, he or she can hire a private weights and measures inspection company to conduct an accurate inspection of the goods.

6. *Dock receipt* (Figure 6–8). This receipt is especially relevant to your customs broker. It merely confirms that the goods have arrived at the designated U.S. harbor. This form is used only if the importer is responsible for shipment from the U.S. port. Your customs broker will take care of this document.

7. *Certificate of manufacture.* When the buyer intends to pay for goods before shipment, this certificate proves that the goods have indeed been manufactured and do fulfill the general product requirement terms. When first starting out, you will be better served by avoiding any agreement where you must pay for your goods before shipment. You can protect yourself if you use letters of credit: the seller will not be paid until the goods are shipped. If you cannot use an L/C, use this certificate as proof that the goods are on hand and ready to be shipped.

8. *Packing list.* Similar to the commercial invoice, the packing list (Figure 6–9) or packing slip (Figure 6–10) provides information on how the goods were packed, the number of goods in the shipment, how they are numbered, and the weight and dimensions of each item. This is important for verification in the payment of the L/C and shows to whom the goods are consigned.

Figure 6–7   Sample Certificate of Origin Form

DEPARTMENT OF THE TREASURY
UNITED STATES CUSTOMS SERVICE

Approved through 12/31/96
OMB No. 1515-0204
See back of form for Paper-
work Reduction Act Notice

NORTH AMERICAN FREE TRADE AGREEMENT
CERTIFICATE OF ORIGIN

Please print or type

19 CFR 181.11, 181.22

1. EXPORTER NAME AND ADDRESS

2. BLANKET PERIOD *DD/MM/YY*

FROM

TAX IDENTIFICATION NUMBER:

TO

3. PRODUCER NAME AND ADDRESS

4. IMPORTER NAME AND ADDRESS

TAX IDENTIFICATION NUMBER:

TAX IDENTIFICATION NUMBER:

5. DESCRIPTION OF GOOD(S)	6. HS TARIFF CLASSIFICATION NUMBER	7. PREFERENCE CRITERION	8. PRODUCER	9. NET COST	10. COUNTRY OF ORIGIN

I CERTIFY THAT:

• THE INFORMATION ON THIS DOCUMENT IS TRUE AND ACCURATE AND I ASSUME THE RESPONSIBILITY FOR PROVING SUCH REPRESENTATIONS. I UNDERSTAND THAT I AM LIABLE FOR ANY FALSE STATEMENTS OR MATERIAL OMISSIONS MADE ON OR IN CONNECTION WITH THIS DOCUMENT;

• I AGREE TO MAINTAIN, AND PRESENT UPON REQUEST, DOCUMENTATION NECESSARY TO SUPPORT THIS CERTIFICATE, AND TO INFORM, IN WRITING, ALL PERSONS TO WHOM THE CERTIFICATE WAS GIVEN OF ANY CHANGES THAT COULD AFFECT THE ACCURACY OR VALIDITY OF THIS CERTIFICATE;

• THE GOODS ORIGINATED IN THE TERRITORY OF ONE OR MORE OF THE PARTIES, AND COMPLY WITH THE ORIGIN REQUIREMENTS SPECIFIED FOR THOSE GOODS IN THE NORTH AMERICAN FREE TRADE AGREEMENT, AND UNLESS SPECIFICALLY EXEMPTED IN ARTICLE 411 OR ANNEX 401, THERE HAS BEEN NO FURTHER PRODUCTION OR ANY OTHER OPERATION OUTSIDE THE TERRITORIES OF THE PARTIES; AND

THIS CERTIFICATE CONSISTS OF   PAGES, INCLUDING ALL ATTACHMENTS

11a. AUTHORIZED SIGNATURE	11b. COMPANY	
11c. NAME *(Print or Type)*	11d. TITLE	
11e. DATE *(DD/MM/YY)*	11f. TELEPHONE NUMBER	*(Voice)*	*(Facsimile)*

11.

WOLCOTTS FORM #952 NAFTA CERTIFICATE OF ORIGIN - NEW 1-94 (price class 6-2P)

Customs Form 434 (121793)

Figure 6–8 Sample Dock Receipt Form

DOCK RECEIPT

2. EXPORTER (Principal or seller-licensee and address including ZIP code)	5. DOCUMENT NUMBER
	5a. B/L OR AWB NUMBER
	6. EXPORT REFERENCES
ZIP CODE	
3. CONSIGNED TO	7. FORWARDING AGENT (Name and address - references)
	8. POINT (STATE) OR ORIGIN OR FTZ NUMBER
4. NOTIFY PARTY/INTERMEDIATE CONSIGNEE (Name and address)	9. DOMESTIC ROUTING/EXPORT INSTRUCTIONS

12. PRE-CARRIAGE BY	13. PLACE OF RECEIPT BY PRE-CARRIER	
14. EXPORTING CARRIER	15. PORT OF LOADING/EXPORT	16. LOADING PIER/TERMINAL
16. FOREIGN PORT OF UNLOADING (Vessel and air only)	17. PLACE OF DELIVERY BY ON-CARRIER	11. TYPE OF MOVE / 11a. CONTAINERIZED (Vessel only) Yes No

MARKS AND NUMBERS (18)	NUMBER OF PACKAGES (19)	DESCRIPTION OF COMMODITIES in Schedule B detail (20)	GROSS WEIGHT (Kilos) (21)	MEASUREMENT (22)

DELIVERED BY:

RECEIVED THE ABOVE DESCRIBED GOODS OR PACKAGES SUBJECT TO ALL THE TERMS OF THE UNDERSIGNED'S REGULAR FORM OF DOCK RECEIPT AND BILL OF LADING WHICH SHALL CONSTITUTE THE CONTRACT UNDER WHICH THE GOODS ARE RECEIVED, COPIES OF WHICH ARE AVAILABLE FROM THE CARRIER ON REQUEST AND MAY BE INSPECTED AT ANY OF ITS OFFICES

LIGHTER _____

TRUCK

ARRIVED— DATE _____ TIME _____

UNLOADED—DATE _____ TIME _____   FOR THE MASTER

CHECKED BY _____   BY _____

PLACED   LOCATION _____   DATE _____

ONLY CLEAN DOCK RECEIPT ACCEPTED.

Figure 6–9   Sample Packing List Form

PACKING LIST

DATE: _____

PURCHASE ORDER NO.: _____

SOLD TO: _____   SHIP TO: _____

_____   _____

_____   _____

_____   _____

ITEM NO.	QUANTITY ORDERED	QUANTITY SHIPPED	DESCRIPTION	UNIT PRICE	TOTAL AMOUNT

PACKED BY: _____   **SUBTOTAL** [ ]

WEIGHT: _____ # OF CARTONS: _____   **SHIPPING & HANDLING** [ ]

DELIVERY: _____ PARTIAL: _____ COMPLETE: _____   **% TAX** [ ]

BACK ORDER #: _____ DELIVERY BY: _____   **TOTAL** [ ]

TERMS:

_____ COD

_____ CASH

_____ CHECK

_____ CHARGE

_____ ACCOUNT

RECEIVED IN GOOD CONDITION BY _____

Figure 6–10   Sample Packing Slip Form

PACKING SLIP

ORDER NO.: _____   SOLD TO: _____   SHIP TO: _____

SHIPPED VIA: _____   _____   _____

CONTACT: _____   _____   _____

PRODUCT NO.	DESCRIPTION	QUANTITY	PRICE	AMOUNT	DISCOUNT	TOTAL

NO. OF PIECES _____   DATE SHIPPED _____   CHECKED BY _____

WEIGHT _____   FILLED BY _____   DELIVERED BY _____

9. *Insurance certificate.* This certificate confirms that marine insurance has been provided for the cargo and indicates the type and coverage. If you are a beginning importer, it is a good idea to have the seller arrange and pay for this coverage, especially when working through L/Cs. Because the seller will receive payment as soon as the goods are shipped, having insurance will cover your investment (the goods), should anything happen during shipping.

BUSINESS PAPERS

Carefully preserve all business papers. All purchase invoices, receiving reports, copies of sales slips, shipping bills, invoices sent to customers, canceled checks, receipts for cash paid out, and cash register tapes must be meticulously retained. They are not only essential to maintaining good records, but may be critical if legal or tax questions are ever raised.

How Long Should I Keep These Records?

Price Waterhouse, one of the Big Six accounting firms, offers the following guidelines:

- Income tax returns, revenue agents' reports, protests, court briefs and appeals: Retain indefinitely.
- Annual financial statements: Retain indefinitely. Monthly statements used for internal purposes: Retain for three years.
- Books of account, such as the general ledger and general journal: Retain indefinitely. Cash books: Retain indefinitely, unless posted regularly to the general ledger. Subsidiary ledgers: Retain for three years. ("Ledgers" refer to the actual books or the magnetic tapes, disks, or other media on which the ledgers and journals are stored.)
- Canceled payroll and dividend checks: Retain for six years.
- Income tax payment checks: Retain indefinitely.
- Bank reconciliations, voided checks, check stubs, and check register tapes: Retain for six years.
- Sales records such as invoices, monthly statements, remittance advisories, shipping papers, bills of lading, and customers' purchase orders: Retain for six years.
- Purchase records, including purchase orders, payment vouchers authorizing payment to vendors, and vendor invoices: Retain for six years.
- Travel and entertainment records, including account books, diaries, and expense statements: Retain for six years.
- Documents substantiating fixed asset additions, such as the amounts and dates of additions or improvements, details related to retirements, depreciation policies, and salvage values assigned to assets: Retain indefinitely.
- Personnel and payroll records, such as payments and reports to taxing authorities, including federal income tax withholding, FICA contributions, unemployment taxes, and workers' compensation insurance: Retain for four years.
- Corporate documents, including certificate of incorporation, corporate charter, constitution and by-laws, deeds and easements, stock, stock transfer and stockholder records, minutes of board of directors' meetings, retirement and pension records, labor contracts, and licenses, patents, trademarks and registration applications: Retain indefinitely.

PAYROLL AND TAXES

Every government entity, bureau, or agency that has any legal jurisdiction whatsoever over your business requires that you submit something in writing, usually accompanied by a payment, on a monthly, quarterly, or annual basis.

Figure 6–11 is a list of typical business taxes. These taxes don't apply in every state or city. Billing for any other taxes you must pay in your area will come automatically to you. In other words, the agencies doing the collecting will find you.

Payroll records present another set of problems. An employer, regardless of the number of employees, must maintain all records pertaining to payroll taxes (income tax withholding, Social Security, and federal unemployment tax) for at least four years after the tax becomes due or is paid, whichever is later.

There are 20 different kinds of employment records that must be maintained just to satisfy federal requirements. These records are summarized as follows:

Income Tax Withholding Records

1. Name, address, and Social Security number of each employee.
2. Amount and date of each payment of compensation.
3. Amount of wages subject to withholding in each payment.
4. Amount of withholding tax collected from each payment.
5. Reason that the taxable amount is less than the total payment.
6. Statements relating to employees' nonresident alien status.
7. Market value and date of noncash compensation.
8. Information about payments made under sick-pay plans.
9. Withholding exemption certificates.
10. Agreements regarding the voluntary withholding of extra cash.
11. Dates and payments to employees for nonbusiness services.
12. Statements of tips received by employees.
13. Requests for different computation of withholding taxes.

Social Security (FICA) Tax Records

1. Amount of each payment subject to FICA tax.
2. Amount and date of FICA tax collected from each payment.
3. Explanation for the difference, if any.

Figure 6–11   Typical Business Taxes

TAX REPORTING SUMMARY

FEDERAL

DESCRIPTION	FREQUENCY
Income tax	Annually
Estimated income-tax deposits	Quarterly
Self-employment tax	Annually
Income-tax withholding	Quarterly
Income-tax withholding deposits	Quarterly or more often
FICA (Social Security) tax	Quarterly
FICA tax deposits	Quarterly or more often
FUTA (unemployment) tax	Quarterly
FUTA tax deposits	Quarterly or more often

STATE

Income tax (state of residence)	Annually
Income tax (state where business is located)	Annually
Estimated income tax (state of residence)	Quarterly
Estimated income tax (state where business is located)	Quarterly
Withholding tax	Quarterly or more often
Withholding tax deposits	Quarterly or more often
Sales tax	Quarterly
Conservation tax	Quarterly
Retail sales license	Quarterly (when business starts)

COUNTY

Personal property business tax	Annually
Merchant's inventory tax	Annually
Merchant's license	Quarterly

LOCAL

Sales tax	Quarterly
Transportation tax	Quarterly
Earnings tax	Annually
Earnings tax withholding	Quarterly
Business earnings and profits tax	Annually

Federal Unemployment Tax (FUTA) Records

1. Total amount paid during calendar year.
2. Amount subject to unemployment tax.
3. Amount of contributions paid into the state unemployment fund.
4. Any other information requested on the unemployment tax return.

Payroll for a small firm is a simple task with a good pegboard or write-it-once system. Any office supply store can show you samples of different one-write systems. A good accounting clerk can be taught how to use one in about 15 minutes. Most accountants recommend these systems because they reduce errors and save time in making payroll entries.

As a business owner and employer, you will be responsible for collecting various state and federal taxes and remitting them to the proper agencies. In addition, you will be required to pay certain taxes yourself.

When reading the following information, remember that at the time this book went to press, all tax information reflected current law. Congress has been passing tax legislation at the rate of one major act every two years. Therefore, it is important that you check for any major tax changes before making a decision that will affect the tax structure of your business.

Employer Tax Identification Number

If you employ one or more persons, you are required to withhold income tax and Social Security tax from each employee's paycheck and remit these amounts to the proper tax-collecting agency.

For tax purposes, you will need to obtain an employer identification number (EIN) from the federal government (ask for IRS Form SS-4) and, if your state has an income tax, from the state as well. Call the local numbers of the federal and state agencies listed in your telephone directory. The federal agency will send you your number as well as charts to determine payroll tax deductions, quarterly and annual forms, W-4 forms, tax deposit forms, and an instruction manual on filling out forms.

Income Tax Withholding

The amount of pay-as-you-go tax you must withhold from each employee's wages depends on the employee's wage level and marital status, the number of exemptions claimed on the withholding exemption certificate (Form W-4), and the length of the payroll period. The percentage withheld is figured on a sliding basis, and IRS percentage tables are available for weekly, biweekly, monthly, semimonthly, and other payroll periods.

Social Security (FICA) Tax

The Federal Insurance Contributions Act (FICA) requires employers to withhold two different taxes: Social Security and Medicare. You need to know the difference between the two types because the tax rates are different.

As of early 1995, the FICA tax (for both employers and employees) is 6.2% for old-age, survivors', and disability insurance (OASDI), commonly known as Social Security, for wages through $60,600; and it is 1.45% each for Medicare on all earnings (there is no limit). For self-employed individuals, the 1995 OASDI tax rate is 12.4% on wages through $61,200 and 2.9% for Medicare on all earnings (no limit).

As an employer, you have two responsibilities in regard to FICA: (1) you must withhold 7.56% from your employees' wages as FICA; and (2) you must pay another 7.65%, matching the amount of Social Security tax the employee pays.

Both the federal withholding and the full 15.3% FICA tax are reported on Form 941, Federal Payroll Tax Return. Form 941 is filed quarterly, and as long as total taxes due per quarter are less than $500, you can pay the entire amount when you file the return. The returns are due the last day of the month following the end of the quarter.

As a new employer, if you don't fall under the less-than-$500 quarterly exemption, you qualify with the IRS as a monthly depositor. You must deposit FICA and federal withholding for every calendar month by the 15th day of the following month. January taxes, for example, must be deposited by February 15. Monthly deposits must be made with Form 8109, Federal Tax Deposit (FTD) Coupon. If you are a new employer, the IRS will send you an FTD coupon book five to six weeks after you receive your EIN.

Charts and instructions for Social Security deductions come with the IRS payroll forms. Be aware that Congress has accelerated the requirements for depositing FICA and withholding taxes. Failure to comply subjects a business to substantial penalties.

You must file four different reports with the IRS district director in connection with the payroll taxes (both FICA and income taxes) withheld from your employees' wages:

1. Quarterly return—taxes withheld on wages (Form 941).
2. Annual statement of taxes withheld on wages (Form W-2).
3. Reconciliation of quarterly returns of taxes withheld, along with annual statement of taxes withheld (Form W-3).
4. Annual Federal Unemployment Tax return (Form 940).

Federal Unemployment Tax

In addition to the FICA taxes, the Federal Unemployment Tax Act (FUTA) requires payment under certain conditions. If, during the calendar year, you paid total wages of $1,500 or more in any quarter or had any employee who worked at least one day during 20 different weeks, you must pay FUTA tax on behalf of your employees.

The FUTA rate is 6.2% of the first $7,000 of wages. Any state unemployment tax rate you pay is subtracted from your federal rate, up to 5.4%. If you qualify for the full 5.4% credit, your FUTA rate could be reduced to 0.8%. You pay your employees' FUTA tax when you file Form 940, Employer's Annual Federal Unemployment Tax Return (or Form 940EZ, with restrictions). Form 940 is due on or before January 31 of the following year.

W-2 and W-3 Forms

Form W-2 provides the employee and the government with a record of the employee's earnings and withholding for federal income tax, state income tax, and FICA taxes. The form must also contain the employee's full name, address, and Social Security number.

Form W-2, Wage and Tax Statement, is a five-part form that must be mailed or delivered to each employee by January 31 of the year following the end of the tax year. The employee gets three copies; the fourth copy is for your records; the fifth copy must be mailed to the Social Security Administration (SSA).

The SSA copies of Form W-2 must be summarized on Form W-3, Transmittal of Income and Tax Statements, and mailed to the SSA by February 28.

State Payroll Taxes

Almost all states have payroll taxes of some kind. You must collect them and remit them to the appropriate agency. Most states have an unemployment tax that is paid entirely by the employer. The tax is figured as a percentage of your total payroll and remitted at the end of each year. The actual percentage varies with the state and the employer.

Some states impose an income tax that must be deducted from each employee's paycheck. As an employer, you are responsible for collecting this tax and remitting it to the state. A few states have a disability insurance tax that must be deducted from employees' pay; in some states, this tax may be split between employee and employer.

Most states have patterned their tax-collecting systems after the federal government's. They issue similar forms, employer numbers, and instruction booklets. As discussed above, you may apply for an employer number and various forms and booklets by calling the local office of the appropriate state agency.

Independent Contractors

Hiring individuals as independent contractors requires filing an annual information return (Form 1099) to report payments totaling $600 or more made to any individual in the course of trade or business during the calendar year. If this form is not filed, you will be subject to penalties. Be sure your records list the name, address, and Social Security number of every independent contractor you hired, along with pertinent dates and the amounts paid to each person. Every payment should be supported by an invoice submitted by the contractor.

Other than licensed real estate agents, very few people who perform services on your premises qualify as independent contractors. The IRS uses 20 criteria for determining whether a worker is an employee of an independent contractor. Such factors as performing services for more than one firm, determining how the work is to be done, use of one's own tools, hiring and paying one's own employees, and working for a fee rather than a salary are indicative of independent contractor status. If the IRS feels an individual should have been treated as an employee, you will be liable for payroll taxes that should have been withheld and paid, plus penalties and interest.

An independent contractor must have:

1. Business license.
2. Cards, stationery, and a real business address.
3. Business bank account.
4. Regular service to various customers.

To support the position that a worker is an independent contractor, businesses should conclude independent contractor agreements with certain information. They should describe the method of payment as based on a job rather than on time, and avoid establishing hours of work; avoid noncompete or exclusivity clauses, and indicate that the person can work for anyone else; allow the independent contractor to determine who will perform the work and how it is to be done; provide for termination of service under specified conditions but avoid employment-at-will language; permit the independent contractor to provide supplies, tools, and equipment; and indicate that the independent contractor is responsible for any damage, errors, or losses in connection with the engagement.

Personal Income Tax

Operating as a sole proprietor or partner, you will not be paid a salary like an employee; therefore, no income tax is withheld from money you take out of your business for personal use. Instead, you must estimate your tax liability each year and pay it in quarterly installments on Form 1040 ES. Your local IRS office will supply the forms and instructions for filing estimated tax returns. When applying for the forms, also request the *Tax Guide for Small Business* (Publication 334).

At the end of the year, you must file an income tax return as an individual and compute your tax liability on the profits earned in your business for that year.

Corporate Income Tax

If your business is organized as a corporation, you will be paid a salary like other employees. Any profit the business makes will accrue to the corporation, not to you personally. At the end of the year, you must file a corporate income tax return.

Corporate tax returns may be prepared on a calendar-year or fiscal-year basis. If the tax liability of the business is calculated on a calendar-year basis, the tax return must be filed with the IRS no later than March 15th each year.

Reporting income on a fiscal-year cycle is more convenient for most businesses because they can end their tax year in any month they choose. Pursuant to the Tax Reform Act of 1986, if a corporation's income is primarily derived from the personal services of its shareholders, the corporation must use December 31 as its year-end for tax purposes. (Most Subchapter S corporations (a legal form under which the owner(s) of the corporation avoid double federal taxation) are required to use December 31 as year-end.)

Retroactive to January 1, 1993, the new corporate tax rates are as follows:

- 15% on the first $50,000 of annual income.
- 25% on the next $25,000 of annual income.
- 34% on all taxable annual income over $75,000 but less than $10 million.

If a corporation has taxable income over $10 million, then it pays a flat 35% tax.

Sales Taxes

Sales taxes are levied by many cities and states at varying rates. If you sell imports on a retail level, you will be required to collect sales tax. Most cities and states provide specific exemptions for certain classes of merchandise or particular groups of customers. Service businesses are often exempt altogether. Contact your state and/or local revenue offices for information on the law for your area so that you can adapt your bookkeeping to the requirements.

Levying taxes on *all* sales would present no major difficulties, but since this is not the case, your business will have to distinguish tax-exempt sales from taxable sales. You can then deduct tax-exempt sales from total sales when filing your sales tax returns each month. Remember, if you fail to collect taxes that should have been collected, you can be held liable for the full amount of uncollected tax.

Advance Deposits

Many states require an advance deposit against future taxes to be collected. In lieu of the deposit, the bureau will accept a surety bond for that amount from your insurance company. If you have a fair credit record, the bond is usually simple to obtain through your insurance agent. The cost varies according to the amount and the risk; 5% is a rule of thumb, but 10% is not unusual for small dollar amounts.

If your state requires a deposit or bond, you can keep the amount down by estimating sales on the low side. This is a wise tactic because most new business owners tend to overestimate early sales.

Seller's Permit

In many states, you will not be able to sell imported goods to retailers unless they can show you a sales tax permit or number, also called a seller's permit. Usually, a business permit is acceptable as a seller's permit.

STANDARD BUSINESS DEDUCTIONS

There are a variety of business expenses you may be able to deduct from your income before you determine how much of it the government gets. They include general and administrative expenses, automobile expenses, entertainment and travel, and some tax adjustments. This section gives an overview of these standard business deductions. For more complete and up-to-date information, talk with your accountant or request pamphlets on these topics from the Internal Revenue Service.

General and Administrative Expenses

There are deductible general and administrative expenses in your business. These include all office expenses such as telephone, utilities, office rent, salaries, legal and accounting expenses, professional services, dues, and subscriptions to business publications.

Many people working out of their homes want to claim a home office expense. That deduction was severely limited by the Tax Reform Act of 1986, which said that one could claim a home office only if it was the sole and primary place of doing business. If you have another office somewhere, you will not be able to deduct the cost of a home office. You might still deduct some business-related telephone charges made from your home, as well as business equipment and supplies, but you will not be able to deduct any part of your rent or depreciate any part of the property as a business expense.

A deduction is allowable to the extent that a portion of your home is used exclusively and regularly as your principal place of business for any business that you operate. Normally, that portion of your residence must be used to meet clients, store inventory, and perform your work. If you perform the majority of your work somewhere else, the home office may not be deductible.

Home office expenses that are eligible for deduction include all normal office expenses plus interest, taxes, insurance, and depreciation on the portion of your home used exclusively as your office. The total amount of deduction is limited by the gross income derived from that business activity, reduced by all of your other business expenses other than those connected with the home office. Therefore, a home office cannot be used to produce tax losses for an otherwise profitable business. Any disallowed losses can be carried over and used in a year when the limitation is not exceeded.

Allocation of home office expenses is generally made on the basis of the ratio of square footage used exclusively for business to total square footage of the residence.

Computers are becoming part and parcel of virtually all business. The Deficit Reduction Act of 1984 severely limits the conditions under which computers in the home can be used as a means of limiting tax liability. Actually, the test is simple: a home computer used for business over 50% of the time can qualify for appropriate business deductions or credits.

Section 179

The biggest tax break for start-up entrepreneurs is the newly revised rule on depreciation for equipment purchased in 1993 and after. The government allows you to take a depreciation deduction based on the usable life of equipment purchased for your business. One such depreciation deduction is called Section 179, which allows you to deduct up to $17,500 for equipment used in the course of doing business. This deduction had previously been $10,000.

Therefore, if you purchased equipment on or after January 1, 1993, you could deduct up to $17,500 for each piece of equipment, provided that (1) you do not exceed $200,000 and (2) the amount is less than or equal to your taxable income. If the amount exceeds your taxable income, the excess would then be carried forward to the next tax year.

Automobile Expenses

Almost everybody doing business in the United States has to drive an automobile to conduct that business. At this writing, business-related automobile mileage is deductible at 28¢ a mile. Once your vehicle is fully depreciated, you can deduct only 11.5¢ for each mile driven. Keep abreast of any changes the IRS may make.

Calculating your straight mileage deductions is very simple. Suppose you drive a car 20,000 miles a year. Of those, 12,000 miles are for business purposes. Your deduction is 28¢ × 12,000 miles, or $3,360.

The distance you drive from your home to your place of business is not deductible, but mileage you drive from your place of business to any other location for business purposes is. Business miles accumulate when you drive for the purpose of either *doing* business or *seeking* business; going to talk to a potential client or doing something related to the promotional aspects of your business entitles you to deduct for business mileage. Keep in mind that you are required to maintain a log of your business miles for tax purposes. Enter your mileage on your appointment calendar at the end of each day.

Entertainment and Travel

If, in your business, you entertain clients for promotion, you have to maintain a log to deduct for entertainment, travel, and related expenses. Use a standard appointment calendar to write in whom you were entertaining, the nature of the business, where you were, and how much you spent. Contrary to popular belief, you do not need receipts for expenditures on entertainment under $25—but you must maintain your log. In certain instances, you can even claim business-related home entertainment; have clients or prospects sign a guest log. If you prepare a meal or serve drinks, your expenses are deductible as part of the expense of doing business.

However, not all entertainment expenses can be deducted. The laws regarding deductibility are changing frequently. Until 1987, you could deduct 100%; after that, it was 80%. It's now down to 50%. Talk with your accountant or contact the IRS for the latest requirements for business entertainment deduction.

For entertainment expenses, all of these elements must be proved:

1. The amount of expenditure.
2. The date of expenditure.
3. The name, address, and type of entertainment.
4. Reason for entertainment and the nature of the business discussion that took place. General goodwill is not accepted by the IRS.
5. The occupation of the person being entertained.

Since 1986, a deduction is no longer permitted for travel, food, and lodging expenses incurred in connection with attending a conference, convention, or seminar related to investment activities such as real estate investments or stock investments. However, the costs of some seminars are deductible.

Business travel deductions include the cost of air, bus, taxi, or auto fares; hotels and meals; and incidentals such as dry cleaning and tips. However, the rule is that you must stay overnight in order to claim travel/incidentals deductions.

The things you do to expand your awareness of and expertise in your field of business are tax-deductible. Accordingly, deductions are allowed for subscriptions to relevant publications and for convention expenses.

Tax Adjustments

If the IRS wants to look at one of your tax returns, the examination must be done within three years of the time you filed it. The exception to this occurs when the IRS alleges fraud for any reason. The IRS may look at tax returns that have been filed at any time, when it believes that deductions were claimed with the intent to defraud the government out of tax revenues or when a taxpayer has unreported income. If you are doing a proper job of tracking your tax credits and liability, the IRS has three years to look at your records.

The statute of limitations from assessment of taxes starts from the date you file your tax return. If you fail to file your tax return, the statute does not start to run. If you omit from gross income an amount in excess of 25% of the gross income reported on your return, the statute of limitations for an audit and assessment is six years.

Conversely, this means you have three years to straighten out tax problems as they arise. If you discover something that results in a change in your taxable income in any of three previous years, you may file a one-page amended return form, known as a Form 1040X, and indicate the necessary changes on the amended return. It may mean you'll be paying more taxes. On the other hand, if you've had business deductions you didn't take, you can file an amended return and claim a refund—plus interest.

Inventory Valuation

You don't automatically get a deduction for purchasing inventory items for your business. You must reduce the amount paid for inventory purchases by the value of the inventory at the end of the year. For example, if you paid $10,000 for merchandise in one year, and your inventory at the end of the year is $7,000, you can deduct only $3,000 for purchases in the year, even though you paid $10,000.

A change in how your inventory is valued can save a substantial amount of taxes. Given the trend toward rising costs, a switch to the last-in, first-out (LIFO) inventory method in a typical year will give your company a one-shot loss deduction for the increase in prices of the items in your inventory. The switch to LIFO is made by filing Form 970 with your tax return. Once you adopt the LIFO method, IRS approval is required to return to FIFO (first-in, first-out).

WORKING WITH ACCOUNTANTS

A good accountant will be your single most important outside adviser. The services of a lawyer and consultant are vital during specific periods in the development of your business or in times of trouble, but your accountant will have the greatest impact on the ultimate success or failure of your business.

Once you are in operation, you will have to decide whether your volume warrants a full-time bookkeeper, an outside accounting service, or merely a year-end accounting and tax preparation service. Even the smallest unincorporated businesses employ an outside public accountant to prepare their financial statements.

When you borrow money, your bank manager will want to see your balance sheet and your operating statement. If these have been prepared by a reputable public accountant, they will have more credibility than if you prepared them yourself. (If you are borrowing less than $500,000, most banks will accept unaudited financial statements prepared by a public accountant.)

Public accountants must meet certain proficiency levels in order to be licensed by the state in which they practice. This does not ensure that an independent business accountant will automatically do a good job for you, but it does narrow your chances of running into an unqualified accountant.

If you are organizing a corporation, your accountant should counsel you in the start-up phase in order to determine the best approaches for your tax situation. If you are starting as a sole proprietor or in a partnership, you'll want the accountant to set up a bookkeeping system you can operate internally.

Experienced independent accountants will usually be familiar with accounting problems peculiar to your business and will be able to advise and direct you wisely. Before the calendar year ends, always ask your accountant to organize your records for the tax year coming to a close.

Ideally, an accountant should help organize the statistical data concerning your business, assist in charting future actions based on past performance, and advise you on your overall financial strategy with regard to purchasing, capital investment, and other matters related to your business goals. Today, however, much of the accountant's time is spent keeping the business owner in substantial compliance with shifting interpretations of laws and regulations.

Accountants specialize in legal requirements that affect you. This is why you need their services if you expect to succeed as a small business operator. If you spend your time finding answers to perplexing questions that accountants can answer more efficiently, you will not have the time to manage your business properly. Spend your time doing what you do best, not trying to do your own accounting.

Where do you find a good accountant? Ask other small business owners, your banker, or your lawyer for recommendations. How much do good accountants charge? Their fees, like those of lawyers, doctors, and other professionals, vary widely. A small-town accountant in business for himself or herself may charge $60 and up per hour. Some of the large, nationally known firms might charge $100 to $250 per hour or more for the services of their personnel.

7

MARKETING YOUR IMPORT/EXPORT SERVICE

The driving force behind any successful import/export management company is sales. You earn revenue by handling the export or import of your clients' products to buyers in the targeted countries; if you have no clients, you have no products. Thus, when planning your sales and marketing campaign for products you already represent, you mustn't forget the importance of recruiting new clients for your own business. To sell both your company and your clients' products, you will need to demonstrate that you can add value to the trade channel in which your products reside, and one of the chief ways of doing so is to engage in successful marketing and promotion.

Numerous avenues are designed to attract the attention of prospective buyers and sellers. Some of the more popular methods of advertising and promotion for import/export management companies are international and domestic trade fairs, industry trade shows, and general merchandise catalogs. (See the sidebar, "Tricks of the Trade," for more sources of assistance.) To effectively sell your clients' products and ideas at these events, you will need product information and brochures in the native languages of your target countries. And though most import/export companies don't utilize heavy advertising in traditional media, they do advertise via trade and industry journals, trade shows, direct mail, person-to-person sales presentations, and a small amount of mass market print media.

This chapter discusses what you should know in order to most effectively advertise and promote both your business and the products offered by your import/export clients. Remember: the marketing of your own business must be inextricably entwined with the marketing of your merchandise. You need to sell your company and any merchandise you represent.

Marketing your import/export management company will involve two steps:

1. Convincing prospective clients that they have products worth exporting.
2. Persuading them to use your import/export management company to begin their exporting project.

Only a small percentage of domestic producers currently export their products. For the most part, your goal through marketing is to convince these companies that their product holds a great deal of promise within specific countries. (Make sure you've done some basic market research on a particular product before you make a sales presentation.) Initially, direct mail and cold calling will usually work the best. Once you've grabbed the attention of your prospective clients, you'll need to arrange appointments to sell them on *your* service, preferably in person.

Before you make initial contact with any manufacturers, you should have completed some basic market research. Find out what items are selling well in the marketplace. Focus initially on products that you know well or use yourself, or that are bestsellers in their market niches. Know the approximate prices at which the products are selling, as well as the prices of any competing products or brands. It's important to keep in mind that when you contact the manufacturer for the first time, you won't know whether you will be able to import the targeted merchandise profitably. First, you will have to find out the product's import price and set up some additional market research to see how much sales potential you can realize in the product. A typical scenario for a beginning importer or exporter would go as follows:

1. Find a product that you know well or that is a bestseller in its market niche.

TRICKS OF THE TRADE

"You might be happy to know that the government actually *works* for us," says Joe DiStanislao, SCORE counselor of Newport Beach, CA. In fact, he says, "The U.S. Department of Commerce is not only ready, willing and able, but actually *anxious* to assist U.S. companies to export, thereby enhancing our balance of trade."

Founder and CEO of a food brokerage company, DiStanislao did quite well for himself representing major imported and domestic food and confections. Now, he sees the attention has turned to exports, especially with the recent passage of NAFTA.

As a retired executive, DiStanislao is Chair of the New Membership Committee for SCORE and counsels businesspeople at the U.S. Export Assistance Center in Long Beach, CA. Following is a sampling of the government services available through the U.S. Department of Commerce International Trade Administration that he recommends to U.S. export companies and export managers:

1. *A Customized Sales Survey.* Given a particular product, this survey provides actual leads to foreign companies (covering over 59 countries) who might have an interest in representing the product or acting as a licensed or joint-venture partner. The survey also shows key competitors, competitors' prices, customary entry and distribution (e.g., product labeling requirements) for each country. Benefit: This saves companies a lot of time and expense traveling to various countries to do market research. Fee: $800–$3,500.

2. *Export Contact Assistance Services.* This assists businesses in the development of an overseas marketing plan. The Department of Commerce can generate a list, using their Commercial Information Management Systems (CIMS) database, of research contacts for a selected industry. "Companies can get a list of customers that fit the pistol for them," says DiStanislao, "for just 25 cents a name." Benefit: This saves time and money on market research by giving instant access to specific industry contacts, with current company names, addresses, and phone numbers. Fee: 25 cents per name; minimum required: $10.

3. *Contact Services for Agents/Distributor Services.* The Department will seek out foreign agents, and sales representatives and/or distributors to handle a company's product in selected countries. Benefit: Instead of flying over and looking in the Yellow Pages, this list shows who already sells that item in that country and how to contact them. Fee: $250 per country (in Canada, $250 per province).

4. *Gold Key Service.* If an export manager or company thinks selling its product or service face-to-face is the best way to go and is planning a trip to a particular country, this service guarantees prescreened appointments for a day at a foreign company with a key decision maker. This service not only locates foreign distributors in 46 countries, but arranges predetermined meetings with key decision makers at an embassy, hotel, office, etc. They just need two to six weeks' notice. Benefit: This gives the export manager more leverage in selling their product or service, makes such a meeting convenient for both parties, and does not require too much up-front time to plan. Fee: $100 to $600 per day that the service is used.

5. *Trade Shows/Missions.* The Department of Commerce can also set up appointments between companies participating in trade events, international trade fairs, trade missions, etc. Benefit: This gives the export manager the added advantage of knowing who will be at the show in advance and having a predetermined time set up for meeting, without interruptions. Fee: Varies by event.

Finally, DiStanislao adds that export companies can subscribe to the *Journal of Commerce* by calling 1-800-221-3777 for a daily listing of trade opportunities as reported by embassies and consulates around the world. And if a company wants to jump onto the information superhighway, computer access of opportunities is also available on the Economic Bulletin Board (EBB) at 202-482-1986.

So, if you are trying to sell furniture in Italy, clothing in Spain, vacuums in Japan . . . or are exporting any product or service, says DiStanislao, "Why not utilize your government for success abroad?"

2. Contact the manufacturer, explaining that you would like to sell the company's products abroad. Indicate that you need to do some market research, and find out as much as you can about the product, including the cost, the various trade channels used for sales, whether the company can provide any advertising assistance, what size orders can be filled, and how long it takes to fill orders.

3. Do a pricing analysis. How much can you sell the product for in a targeted country? What type of commission can you add while keeping the price competitive? What are the shipping costs, tariffs, operating expenses, and so on?

4. Find a distributor, agents, or sales reps. Do they think they can sell the product at the price you've calculated?

5. Once you are satisfied that a viable market exists for the product, formulate an initial marketing plan, take it back to the manufacturer to work out the details, and draw up a preliminary contract.

Keep in mind that companies wishing to export their products will be searching for firms such as yours. To gain them as clients, you must sell them on the fact that their sales will increase—at virtually no additional cost to them—if they contract *you* to represent them in the overseas market. To expose yourself to these companies, you will need to schedule a limited amount of advertising through specific media geared toward that market.

FINDING DOMESTIC EXPORTERS

Before contacting any manufacturers through direct mail or a cold call, you should have begun your market research in countries where you plan to do business. Familiarize yourself with the potential markets in those countries and with the types of products that are in great demand within those markets. By doing this, you'll be more prepared when marketing your company directly to prospective exporters. You'll know what type of products will be more stable in the countries you are targeting, and you can concentrate the major portion of your marketing efforts toward companies producing those types of goods.

Once you have developed an understanding of the products that you think have export potential, you can begin marketing your services. In the opening stage, you will find it easier to start marketing your services to manufacturers in your general area. The first way to do this is through direct mail. Again, your job as a beginning importer/exporter will be easier if you pick companies that manufacture products that you believe in or know well. The more familiar you are with a product or market, the more convincing your sales pitch will be. Even before you compose your letter, however, try calling some targeted companies and asking for the name of the person to whom the letter should be addressed. In that way, you'll know that the letter will go directly to the correct person.

When you know the names of the persons to contact, write a letter introducing yourself and your company. Outline briefly the potential of the overseas market, as well as the potential of the product within that market. State reasons why and how *your company*, above all others, would be able to position the supplier best. If you already have contacts with foreign distributors, let the manufacturer know that you have foreign representatives for overseas sales. Ask the addressee if you can set up a personal meeting. If no call comes within one to two weeks, contact the person by phone and set up an appointment to meet personally at his or her office.

Another way to contact manufacturers is through a cold call. For the most part, cold calling is cheaper than direct mail, but it requires a lot more perseverance to be effective. However, if it is done well, a cold call can be much more effective than direct mail.

Because cold calling requires you to deal directly with the prospect, you should know how to use telephone sales techniques that get the prospect to listen and increase your chances of making a sale. Here are some basic telephone and telemarketing tips:

- *Create a selling mood.* You'll want to come across as knowledgeable, friendly, helpful, and trusting. Speak firmly and clearly, but amplify your voice so you don't lose the person.

- *Be specific.* Tell the person about the advantages of exporting and how you can help the company enter the international market. A vague message will make your listener lose interest, become distrustful, or suspect that you must have something to hide.

- *Control the time.* Don't tell a bunch of chatty stories. And don't try to top a story the person tells. This is not a contest. If a prospect wants to show off, allow that latitude; you'll reap your rewards when you make a sale.

- *Control the pace.* Slow down, for emphasis, when making important comments. You'll then get the listener's attention at just the right moments.

- *Don't use a lot of "ums" or "ahs."* If you can't think of anything to say, say nothing. Moments of silence can be used to your advantage; filling them up with meaningless sounds takes this advantage away and is annoying to listeners.

- *Ask questions.* They can be very effective. Phrase them so that they cannot readily be answered in the negative: "Do you like to see results?"; "Do you want this year to be your best ever?" By getting prospects to keep saying yes, you're making them think positively about you and your export management company. Such questions force the prospect to listen and to continually agree with you. Focus your questions on what, why, and where. The prospect is tied down by questions starting with "Wasn't it . . . ?", "Hasn't it . . . ?", "Don't you agree . . . ?", and "What would you say to . . . ?" These openings accomplish a series of closes that are parallel to the points, in telephone sales, where the prospective client has to make a decision, however small or seemingly insignificant. The closes build to the most important one—arranging for an appointment at which you can finalize the deal through a contract for formal representation.

- *Listen.* Most of us, particularly salespeople, like to talk. One of the worst things you can do in cold calling is to monopolize the conversation. If you don't let the prospect get a word in, he or she will conclude that you're not really listening and will decide not to listen to you. And with a prospect who is not listening, you're unlikely to strike any deal in the near future. You are not the center of attention; your prospect is. Steer the conversation away from yourself.

- *Don't use unnecessary humor.* You can use humor, but be smart about it. Jokes that fall flat or make you sound silly will not project the image you want. The best way of avoiding a bad joke is to not crack jokes in the first place. Just as you like to feel important, so do your prospective clients. Because you are trying to sell something to them, don't build yourself up, particularly at the expense to your listeners. Make each listener the center of your attention.

It is not enough for the prospect merely to listen to you. You've got to listen to your prospect. One of modern America's most conspicuous weaknesses is the inability to listen. Many people don't understand the techniques necessary for effective listening. When conducting cold calls, listening is essential if the marketing is to succeed.

Here are some hints:

1. *Don't interrupt.* It's not only rude, but it says you are not listening. Once the prospect comes to that conclusion, you can forget any chance of landing that account.

2. *Don't rush the person.* If the prospect is a slow speaker, be patient. Speeding the prospect up will likely cause antagonism.

3. *Meet objections.* Listen to what the prospect says, and read between the lines. You want to address the real problems that confront you, not the surface problems. The prospect may come up with several surface problems that have nothing to do with a nagging main objection. By listening carefully, you'll be able to decipher the real problem and confront it.

4. *Decide on a sales pitch.* A prepared script is essential when starting out (but *never* read from it during a prospect contact). Prepare answers to questions you think will be asked, and counterpoints to objections that may be raised. Turn objections and questions into positives. Get the prospect to agree to something. When you become thoroughly familiar with your pitch, throw the script away.

5. *Don't take rejection too hard.* At no time are you more likely to be rejected than when you try to sell something—especially if you make a cold call to a small businessperson. All the listener has to do to get rid of you is hang up—and many contacts will do so. If cold calling is going to be a successful sales tool for you, you will have to resign yourself to being dumped on. It's a numbers game; when turned down by a prospect, shrug it off and dial the next telephone number.

6. *Don't expect to close a deal over the phone.* Cold calls are used for one main purpose—to arrange an appointment to meet with a prospective client and discuss his or her company's export potential.

Once you've been able to set up a meeting, stress the fact that you will handle all the technicalities of the sale, such as shipping, paperwork, and the securing of payment. The manufacturer has little to lose; this will be a low-cost, low-risk chance to enter a lucrative market not previously considered. Remember: You should have done some research up to this point, and you should know the price of comparable products in the foreign market, the size of the market, and the approximate costs that you will have to add to the price, such as shipping, freight forwarding, and insurance. The more you already know when you meet with a manufacturer, the more he or she will trust you and your business skills.

FINDING FOREIGN EXPORTERS SO YOU CAN IMPORT GOODS

We said earlier that the entire world is a market. You can participate in and profit from importing virtually any item that people buy. If you see any item on a shelf that's not produced domestically—whether it's a bottle of wine, a flashlight, or a pair of shoes—someone is importing it. If you don't already know what type of merchandise you would like to import, try to figure out the market strategies you would like to pursue. For example, are you interested in importing products that have brand-name identities, or are you chiefly interested in price and volume? Would you consider becoming an import merchant and taking title of the goods, or do you prefer serving only as a sales agent for the time being? How much capital do you have at your disposal? Enough for a container full of merchandise or just a few boxes? These are the types of questions you must consider. How you answer them will affect what types of goods you import and how you will find their producers.

The most obvious way to find products for import is to visit foreign countries in search for goods. This assumes, however, that you have the capital and time to embark on such an exploratory trip. If you know what type of goods you want to import, you can usually figure out where to go to find them. For example, Switzerland has an international reputation for producing top-quality watches; Japan is well known for exporting affordable, high-quality electronics. These two industries have much higher profiles than you, as a beginning importer, might be able to tackle, but you can still find plenty of markets that are ready for you to cover.

If you're interested in general merchandise, traveling in search of goods may be the best way to find immediate results. Many foreign manufacturers would never seriously consider selling their goods in the United States, even though the market could be highly profitable for them. The most effective way to find these companies is to go out and look for them.

Before you arrange for any buying trips overseas, however; consider this: Don't limit yourself by looking only at *products* you wish to import. Consider also the *strategies* you want to use to make your profits. Are you more interested in importing products with brand-name identities, or in low price and volume? If the latter, you most likely will have to target countries that are low-cost producers of goods, such as China, India, or Mexico. Because these countries are often emerging economies, your importing mission may be a little more complicated and require a little more patience. But don't be daunted by these obstacles. The profit potentials in these types of ventures often are much greater, especially for the beginning importer.

Because traveling and searching for goods to import can be complicated and expensive, many experienced importers simply don't go to all that trouble. Instead, they wait for manufacturers to contact them. This is an easier way to go, for two reasons: (1) you don't have to go anywhere to search for products, and (2) you don't have to convince the manufacturer to export the goods. Companies that contact you already want to export. All they need is a way to drum up sales in the United States.

As the importer, you will act as a distributor or agent. Generally, you will buy either direct from manufacturers, or from foreign export management companies that handle a number of goods. You can utilize the same resources that you employ for finding buyers in foreign markets for your domestic exporting clients. After all, foreign exporters or their agents will be using the same avenues to search for distributors and reps in the United States. You either can buy the goods from your own account and then resell them at a profit, or you can find sales for the manufacturer or exporter and take a commission.

As a beginning importer trying to locate foreign suppliers, some of your best resources will be international and domestic trade shows and conventions, buyers' directories, industry contacts, the Business-to-Business Yellow Pages, and trade group journals. As free markets have grown throughout the world, many countries or regional trade groups have begun to sponsor trade shows in the United States for the benefit of sellers in their home countries or regions. China and Hong Kong, for example, sponsor several large import/export trade shows throughout the United Sates each year.

Another good resource for finding supplier leads is the embassy or consulate of the foreign country whose products you want to import. Many countries or geographic regions maintain trade development offices where you can find specific information on manufacturers of everything from toothpicks to truck tires to fur coats. Often, a single phone call can result in a long list of suppliers eager to do business with importers in the United States. Hong Kong, in addition to sponsoring trade shows, staffs trade development offices in Los Angeles, New York, and several other large cities. These offices exist solely to promote trade between countries; their *job* is to help you find suppliers.

Another good resource for import trade leads is the U.S. Department of Commerce. The International Trade Division can help you locate various trade groups and development agencies that have lists of the suppliers you are looking for. There are other effective ways of finding suppliers:

- Attend international trade shows and fairs, such as the huge Canton Trade show in Canton, China.
- Read focus publications such as industry or trade journals.
- Make sure you are listed in the major international directories, such as:

  —Blytmann's.
  —The International Yellow Pages.
  —The international telex directory.
  —The international facsimile directory.
  —The U.S. Importer and Exporter directory.
  —The World-Wide Chamber of Commerce Directory.

In addition, if you're familiar with the Internet or other on-line systems, you might try reviewing the numerous directories for further information regarding international business opportunities.

After you've located foreign suppliers that manufacture products you think will have potential in the United States, you may have to sell them on the idea of entering the U.S. market and convince them that you're the most appropriate person to help them do so. Send the prospective client a letter, a telex, or a fax. A telex or fax will be more effective, if you can find the contact numbers for the supplier. (Refer to the appropriate international directories.) Standard international mail is notoriously slow and it may take weeks for a letter to be delivered (if ever, in some places).

In your communications to suppliers, outline the various opportunities available in the United States for their products, and emphasize that you will handle all of the logistics of importing their products with little extra cost to them.

If the companies are located in an English-speaking country, or if you can speak the country's language, follow up with a call or fax a few days later, to strengthen your position and show true interest in becoming the importer for their products. Keep in mind, however, that some international calls still aren't the best quality, despite the recent huge investments in telecommunications systems worldwide. The main problem with international calls to some countries is the pause between statements. Be patient when calling internationally. Allow enough time between statements so you don't cut off a statement made by the supplier.

To make a call internationally, dial the international code, 011, followed by the country code, the city code, and the local telephone number. The country and city codes can be found in your local telephone book. If you are dialing from a touch-tone phone, pressing the pound key (#) after entering the local telephone number will speed up the connection process.

If you are acting as a sales agent, it's highly unlikely that you'll be able to close the deal on the first or even the second call. In some cases, you may have to present a marketing plan for the product and provide the supplier with information about your company, including a list of current clients and proof of your creditworthiness. You may even have to arrange a visit to the supplier in order to close the deal. If you feel strongly about the potential of the product in the U.S. market, a personal visit to the supplier may be beneficial in the long run.

If the goods in which you're interested are not branded (brand-name), copyrighted, or otherwise restricted in any way, perhaps the best profit potential lies in being an import merchant. In this scenario, you buy the goods outright and then sell them to distributors yourself. Provided you have the necessary capital and the marketing power, your contact with the foreign supplier will be geared more toward negotiation. Ask that all relevant information, such as price, terms of quote, and financial requirements, be in written form. If you are an import merchant, keep in mind the old adage: "Money talks." If you're serious about purchasing their goods, most foreign suppliers will be eager to talk. Just be sure that the price quoted will allow you enough room to make an acceptable profit. If you're ready to buy, be prepared to negotiate through a letter of credit. Virtually every foreign supplier will require some form of guaranteed payment such as a letter of credit, especially for a first-time customer.

Regardless of whether you're a sales agent or an import merchant, you should perform the necessary market research and analysis for the product's potential, and prepare a marketing plan. You must be able to sell the goods within the price structure begun by the foreign supplier. If you can't make the sales, then you can't succeed as a business. This is why a well-defined marketing plan is so important. If the supplier sees that you are serious enough to put together a comprehensive plan that details your marketing strategy, you may be able to overcome any apprehensions that the supplier may have about working with you.

One note of caution: Don't offer too many specifics when preparing a marketing plan for presentation. Although most of the prospects you'll be dealing with will be earnest concerning your query, you should take measures to protect yourself in all international dealings at all times. Ask that all correspondence be confirmed in writing, which is easily done via fax. Provide prospective suppliers with enough information in the initial marketing plan to whet their appetite, but don't reveal all your cards. Instill the feeling that they will not be able to penetrate the U.S. market as effectively without you.

Finally, try to get exclusive distribution rights to the goods, at least for the area you are selling in. Many importers look for three-year exclusive rights at first, with the stipulation that the rights are renewable each year after that. If you are selling products from a manufacturer that does not already sell in the United States, you will not have to worry about exclusive rights, at least initially. However, if the products sell well and you do not have exclusive rights, another importer may buy from the same manufacturer and undercut your price. If the manufacturer is afraid to give you rights for this length of time, try to negotiate a deal. For example, sign an agreement stipulating that if you sell X amount of product within a specified time period, you will retain the rights. This is the same type of deal you may give to a foreign distributor if you are exporting goods. In effect, it lets the importer try out for the job without undue risk to the exporter.

Person-to-Person Sales

If the prospect is interested, after receiving your call or letter, but is not sold on using your company as its means of exporting, you will have to do more legwork to close the deal. First, ask the supplier for any available information on its product—and some samples, if possible. Explain that the information and samples will be used to further explore the market potential, and develop a presentation that outlines the marketing strategy you plan to pursue.

From the information and samples, figure out every possible expense you will have, and come up with a preliminary price. Then, if you have already contacted distributors, find out whether this price will sell in their market. If so, arrange for further meetings to establish representation. If you have no distributors or agents, find one who will represent you at this price. Get as much information about your agents and distributors as possible so you can evaluate their performance in the market. These data are crucial for your presentation. Your completed presentation should consist of:

1. A marketing plan for the product.
2. A brochure that describes your company and includes a current client list (if you have one).
3. A personal resume.
4. An appropriate folder that shows your company name and logo.

After this portfolio is prepared, it's time to meet with the prospect.

You must arrive at the presentation looking sharp and professional, even if you live in a casual area. Be prompt: being late for this appointment is a sure way to hurt your chances.

Your *pitch* should include an explanation of how cost-effective the exporting of the product can be, the potential return, the fee structure, and the costs involved to export the product. Your angle is that exporting opens additional markets to the manufacturer, at a very minimal cost. You'll handle all the logistics. All the manufacturer has to do is fulfill the orders that come in and prepare them for shipment.

As mentioned earlier, the marketing plan you present at the meeting should only touch on the general methods you will use to distribute the product. Don't detail for the prospect the exact strategy you have planned. Your presentation is a private sales tool. Keep it that way.

How do you close a deal? Once you've convinced the prospect that exporting will be profitable and its cost will be minimal, you'll close the deal by having the prospect sign a *sole agent contract* that protects you in the international market and specifies the terms of the agreement. A sole agent contract should cover the various guidelines of the agreement, including: responsibility for promoting the product, sales territory, method and time of payment, required letters of credit, product modification, annual sales forecast, and so on. You should have a lawyer prepare your standard contract at the start-up stage of your business. Be sure you have printed copies with you when you visit your prospects.

Many export management companies require exclusive distribution rights for three years when they represent a new client, but when you are starting out you probably will not be able to demand such a long-term arrangement. One alternative is a contract that stipulates that if you sell X numbers of products in Y months, then you will retain exclusive rights for an agreed-on time period.

PRODUCT PROMOTION—DOMESTIC AND FOREIGN

The primary method of promoting export sales is through person-to-person contact with potential buyers. There are many different ways to find these buyers, ranging from U.S. Commerce Department lists to international trade shows. The Commerce Department's Export Development Offices (EDOs), located throughout the world, can assist you in finding buyers, performing market research, and fulfilling shipping and customs requirement. They also steer U.S. exporters to local trade fairs and exhibitions.

Perhaps your most effective and most accessible resource will be your own creativity and common sense. For example, if you're importing latex gloves for general-purpose use, you might consider searching out distributors that operate in the foodservice, janitorial, and paper industries, all of which in some way use latex gloves. This might be as easy as calling up a local janitorial supply store and inquiring about the names of some of the larger janitorial supply distributors or about any trade publications that might be helpful to you. Often, the simplest methods garner the greatest results. Just a few questions to the right people can result in far more information than you might have imagined.

Trade Associations and Journals

Perhaps the most focused and far-reaching tool at your disposal is trade associations. Two of their chief aims are: (1) to function as industry advocates and (2) to serve as clearinghouses for information on the industry. Most trade associations also publish a journal or newsletter that not only gives the latest inside information on the industry, but also offers a host of potential contacts and customer opportunities. You may find customer leads just by leafing through the pages and taking note of the various companies that are mentioned in the articles and advertisements. Be careful to check all the different trade associations; many industries have more than one. The plastics industry, for example, has more than five different major trade groups, each with a slightly different industry focus.

As an offshoot, there are companies that provide industrywide directories covering everything from hardware store chains to foodservice distributors. Typically, these directories will list a company name and address, as well as a short profile of the business—annual sales, a breakdown of management names and contacts, and so on. This background information is enormously valuable to the beginning importer. One company that produces many directory titles is Business Guides, Inc., publishers of Chain Store Guides®. To obtain any of its 20 or more different market directories, each packed with important information, call 800/927-9292.

Trade Fairs

Attending trade fairs may be your best channel to valuable person-to-person contacts, regardless of whether you're an exhibitor with a booth or just an attendee. A trade fair, or trade show, is designed for the sole purpose of bringing together buyers and sellers. If you set up a booth with samples and/or literature about your products, people who stop to examine them are already interested in purchasing products;

otherwise, they would not be at the show. You must then convince them that your products and prices are the best. Trade shows can be regional, state-oriented, or national. It's up to you to decide which will be most beneficial for your marketing plan and which will provide the most possible sales for your dollar. Although trade shows work equally well for both importers and exporters, they are more costly for exporters, who have to exhibit far from home. It is not uncommon for import/export management companies to ask their clients to help defray some of the expense of trade shows. You may also consider dividing costs among yourself, your client, and your overseas agent.

The U.S. Commerce Department can help exporters find trade shows that most suit their needs. The Certified Trade Fair Program recruits U.S. businesses for overseas trade fairs. For trade shows in the United States, look in the library or contact: Tradeshow Week, 12233 W. Olympic Boulevard, Suite 236, Los Angeles, CA 90064; (213) 826-5696. You can also contact the local Commerce Department office, the Chamber of Commerce in the area you plan to visit, or the International Chamber of Commerce, located in New York: (212) 254-4480.

Mail Order

Another way to sell your imports or exports is through mail order, a strategy that can be implemented in several ways. One approach is to build a catalog with a range of related products you handle through your company and send the catalog to wholesalers or retail buyers. A drawback to this method is the cost involved. You not only have to produce the catalog, but you also have to obtain the names of the people and companies to whom you'll send the catalogs, and pay substantial postage. (Mailing lists can be derived from your own prospect and customer lists, and from rentals.)

Another possible arrangement is to have a catalog house include your client's product(s) in its catalog. This is perhaps the most cost-effective method because the catalog house will bear all the overhead expense of producing and distributing the catalog. Once orders come in for the product, all you have to do is worry about fulfillment.

Whether you choose to produce your own catalog or distribute through a catalog house, fulfillment can be a concern. You have two options regarding fulfillment:

1. *Warehouse the products.* If importing, you can purchase the products directly and warehouse them in the United States. When orders arrive, the product is readily available for

shipment. If exporting, you can arrange to have the products warehoused through your commission rep. Keep in mind, however, that warehousing a product is a costly proposition. It also places you in a position where you will have to track the inventory to establish lead times and safety margins, and package and ship the product.

2. *Drop-ship.* Once orders are received through the catalog, they are sent to the manufacturer along with payment less commission for fulfillment. This is much easier from your perspective. However, drop-shipping in international trade takes a long time, even with rush orders, and slow delivery could hurt your client.

The advantage of mail-order promotion is that you can distribute the product on a mass basis while keeping your overhead to a minimum. You can also use your mail-order catalog as a handout at a trade fair. Interested buyers can see all of the products you import or export, and they can place orders immediately, or take a copy with them and decide what to order later.

In addition, your product catalog can appear in *catalog exhibitions* sponsored by the US&FCS. These are comprehensive displays of catalogs and other product information at American embassies and consulates or in conjunction with trade shows.

For mail order to be successful, however, you must sell products that have good potential to produce a worthwhile return. Some of the criteria you should use to gauge a product before you decide on its suitability for mail order include:

- *Can it be sold for a high gross profit?* Operating a mail-order business is expensive, and you must be able to sell the product *competitively* with a liberal enough gross profit—the sale price less *your* cost of acquiring or producing the product. Look for a gross profit that's at least three to four times what the product costs you. For example, if the product costs you $2, it should sell for at least $8 or $10 (gross profits of $6 and $8, respectively). This is possible; many products are available that produce this kind of profit margin.

- *Is it easy to target your market for the product?* You have to attack specific markets one at a time, to do your most effective marketing. Can you pick out the men who will use it? Can you pick out the women? Can you pick out the people who are over 30 or in their teens? Can you determine the target market and go after it selectively?

- *Is your product utilitarian?* People usually buy impulse items—little toys, novelties, small food items—at a retail store because they see them on the cash-register counter. They don't shop for them. Along the same line, they don't normally shop for impulse goods via mail order. (Christmas and other gift-giving items are exceptions to the rule.) Stay with something that has longevity.

- *Can your product be described in an ad?* This point is very important. Some products must be demonstrated; people have to see and feel them. These products are not going to sell in mail order. Stick to something that is somewhat tangible and easily describable. Go with something that can give a strong impression in your ad.

Having the right product is not the only element of success with mail-order sales. You also have to be able to selectively target your market. That means obtaining names of people who meet your demographic profile as defined through your market research. If you contract through a catalog house, you won't have to worry about mailing lists. If you develop and distribute your own catalog, you will.

Mailing lists can be rented from list brokers. You can find them in your Yellow Pages under "Advertising—Direct Mail." Mailing lists today are closely targeted, so you can get lists in just about any category you want. The one-time rental fee for these names is usually between $45 and $75 per 1,000 names, with a minimum rental of 5,000 names.

How do you pick a list? Use the RFM formula: R stands for recency, F for frequency, and M for money. Because people and businesses move and their economic profiles change, recency is vital to the success of a list. Frequency refers to how many times the people on the list purchased your type of product. Money refers to how much they spent.

Because good mailing lists are essential for the success of a direct-marketing campaign, check out the list as thoroughly as possible. Buy only from established services. Ask how many times the list has been sold in the previous six months, and get the names and telephone numbers of some of the buyers. Call them and ask what their response rate was with the list, how many pieces were returned because of bad addresses, and whether they thought the list was worth the cost.

Established businesses are often able to trade their lists with other established businesses. As a newcomer, you won't have the name or the credibility that established businesses have earned. But this exchange is something to aspire to, because it is basically a no-cost way of building a list.

Informative Labels

You should impress on your clients that they can build goodwill among both dealers and consumers by providing informative labels on products. When you market a U.S. product in a foreign country where the language is different, you will have to have these labels translated and reprinted in the native language. You may also have to state sizes and measurements in metric units so that the local consumers will understand them.

When creating labels, you must let people know how your product works. Salespeople do not always tell a customer how to use and care for a product, and sometimes the customer forgets. Extensive studies on informative labels show that they increase the sales of better-quality products. Through good labeling, small manufacturers with a superior product can overcome some of the effects of large competitors' extensive advertising.

In addition, specific marking or labeling is used to meet shipping regulations, ensure proper handling, and help receivers identify shipments. Keep in mind that certain products that fall under regulatory guidelines must be clearly marked in the prescribed way. For example, if you're importing latex gloves that have not been approved for medical use, you cannot use the description "Exam gloves." If you do, the Food and Drug Administration (FDA) will not release your gloves until you change each inner box and outer carton to read "Industrial Use" or "General Purpose." Your customs broker will be able to inform you of any regulatory guidelines that you must follow, but it is your responsibility to forward the information to your supplier.

The overseas buyer usually specifies export marks that should appear on the cargo for easy identification by receivers. Exporters need to put the following markings on export (outer) cartons to be shipped:

- Shipper's mark.
- Country of origin.
- Weight marking in pounds/kilograms.
- Number of packages and size of cases in inches/centimeters.
- Handling marks, using international pictorial symbols (if appropriate).

- Cautionary markings in English and the language of the country of destination (if appropriate).
- Special labels for hazardous materials (if appropriate).

ADVERTISING BASICS

Somewhere along the line, almost any product for sale will need to be advertised, but this is usually left to the retailer and/or the manufacturer. If you are merely a sales agent, you are the go-between for the manufacturer and retailer, so you should find out what the manufacturer is willing to offer in terms of advertising assistance. It may have preformatted print ads that a retailer can use as-is or modify to fit the local language and customs. It may also help pay for ads that the retailer puts together.

Though you may not be actively involved in the advertising of the product itself, you can implement a limited advertising program geared toward generating leads for buyers.

The advertising process involves four steps:

1. Budgeting, based on what you can afford and the media where your advertising and promotional dollars may be most effectively spent.
2. Determining the best way to reach your prospective buyers without wasting your money on advertising that reaches nonproductive audiences.
3. Choosing a minimal number of points to be emphasized in your advertising.
4. Gathering facts on the advertising media and the company market, to justify the dollars to be spent.

How much is enough for an ad budget? Many retail businesses peg their ad budgets at 2% to 5% of their projected gross sales. This ratio, generally referred to as the *cost method*, theorizes that an advertiser can't afford to spend more money than it has. For instance, if your projected gross sales for the first year are $300,000 based on the business plan, and you are using the cost method to determine your advertising budget (figuring 5%), you would have $15,000, or about $1,250 a month, to work with.

That may not seem like much, and for companies that base their advertising budgets on the amount of money needed to move the product, it won't be enough. This is called the *task method* of estimating. There are many different ways to determine the amount of money needed to move a product, but perhaps the most common way is simply through experience.

Companies just starting out, however, won't have past records to guide them. Using the task method during start-up to determine an advertising budget, you'll have to refer to your business plan and market survey. You want to find out what media will be appropriate and what the cost will be to effectively advertise using those media.

Depending on the size of shipments and the scale of the manufacturers you are dealing with, advertising media can include:

- Magazines (including trade and industry publications).
- Newsletters.
- Other media (catalogs, samples, the Yellow Pages, and brochures).

In appraising prospective advertising media or comparing them in effectiveness, you should consider the following factors:

- *Cost per contact.* How much will it cost to reach prospective buyers?
- *Frequency.* How frequent should these contacts or message deliveries be? In your business, is a single, powerful advertisement preferable to a series of constant, small reminders, or vice versa?
- *Impact.* Does the medium in question offer full opportunities for appealing to the appropriate senses, such as sight and hearing, in presenting design, color, or sound?
- *Selectivity.* To what degree can the message be restricted to those people who are known to be the most logical prospects?

Selecting Magazines and Newsletters

You can find publications that will be appropriate for a domestic advertising campaign by looking through reference sources like *The Business Publication*, published by Standard Rate and Data Service (SRDS), 3004 Glenview Road, Wilmette, IL 60091; (708) 256-6067. *The Business Publication* lists all the relevant information about domestic trade and business publications, and a list of international publications can be found in the International Section. You'll find a short description of each publication and its editorial content, who the publication goes out to, and a breakdown of circulation figures. Using this information, you can compile a list of suitable publications.

To obtain more in-depth information on the publications you've listed, contact their ad representatives and ask them to send you a media kit. The kit will contain a sample copy and detailed information about the editorial content, a breakdown of readership demographics, the publication's ad rates, and an audited circulation statement from the publisher. Audited circulation statements are issued through the Audit Bureau of Circulation (ABC) or the Business Publications Audit (BPA). Audited circulation statements are sworn statements by the publisher, verified by an outside source, that the publication is distributed to the number of people claimed in the circulation figures.

With this information in hand, you can determine the cost-effectiveness of advertising in a publication by determining an efficiency ratio between the circulation and the ad rates. This ratio is called the CPM, or cost per thousand—the cost of advertising divided by the circulation in thousands. If the circulation is 30,000 and the rate for a full-page ad is $600, divide the $600 by 30 to yield a cost of $20 per thousand. This is the common denominator used to evaluate the cost-effectiveness of advertising in a publication.

To make your print media ads count most, buy space at the best rates. Often, advertising costs less if more space is purchased. For example, if your campaign calls for 45 inches of column space at $4.50 per inch, the cost will be $202.50. The publication's rate card may reveal that 50 inches can be purchased at a rate of $4 per inch, for a total of $200.

If you're selling in a specific industry, focus on publications that cover only that market. Usually, industry associations and trade groups will publish their own magazines, which are often the standard for the industry. For example, one successful importer involved in the specialty packaging and paper trade advertises only in *Management News,* the official publication of the National Paper Trade Association, the largest organization representing the paper products industry. She reports that the focus of the magazine and its target audience fit her needs perfectly. The magazine is read by purchasing agents and sales reps at many of the top distributors, the very group she wants to target.

Newsletters are great print vehicles for reaching specialized markets. Because circulations are typically small, rates for advertising in newsletters are very reasonable, but the CPM may be relatively high. Their circulations are also closely targeted because of their specialized editorial content. In terms of cost-effectiveness, this is one of the best types of print media to purchase. But you have to be careful. Many newsletters aren't audited publications. They operate on a controlled circulation basis, so you have to take the word of the publisher that the newsletter is distributed to the number of people claimed.

Don't scatter your ads. Skipping from one publication to another seldom gets results. It destroys the effectiveness of consecutive advertising and, most importantly, you lose the handling and consideration privileges received by consistent advertisers. Long-term status can make a great deal of difference when you want to secure a favorable position for your ad in the publication. If you can specify position, go for the upper locations that are the most visible to someone flipping through a newspaper or magazine.

You may want to experiment with the buying patterns in your target community. If, for example, you notice that you ads receive the most response when placed just before payday for a large local industry, then by all means save your advertising dollars for these prime times.

Brochures

As a method of explaining the services you offer as an import/export management company, a brochure conveys professionalism. You may want to include a client list in your brochure, as well as significant items that will appeal to your prospects: your experience in specific markets and products, the rate of return for your clients, and a synopsis of the overall performance of your company since its inception.

Your company brochure does not have to be a fancy four-color printing job. If you want to keep expenses down, go for a light-color card stock measuring $7\frac{1}{4} \times 8\frac{1}{2}$ inches. With one center fold lengthwise, the brochure fits easily into a no. 10 envelope. This presentation makes the brochure an ideal companion for your direct mail marketing efforts as well as an adjunct for your sales presentation. We stress the size because an ordinary-size sheet of paper will tend to blend in with other stacks of paper, and a splashy, oversize brochure may convey the impression that there's no substance to your style.

Use the brochure to advertise your services in a soft, yet no-nonsense fashion. You are selling your prospects on using your import/export management company and convincing them that their company has a lot to gain by exporting their products. The brochure should convey the message that your company and its well-trained, qualified employees can save them trouble, time, effort, and money, while expanding their market worldwide. If you know that you write well and persuasively, write the brochure yourself. If you have any doubt about your ability to do a top-notch job, trust the writing and the design to professionals.

Be careful about typeface, which should be easy to read and no smaller than 10 point. It should take no more than a minute for anyone to scan your brochure, but those 60 seconds should be packed with memorable information. Many companies do not use brochures. But why not give yourself the extra advertising edge a brochure can provide?

The Yellow Pages

Most local businesses advertise their goods and services in the Yellow Pages. You should advertise your company in the local Business-to-Business Yellow Pages as well, and you should also contact NYNEX at (800) 544-4988, to have your business listed in the International Yellow Pages. Your advertisement may be illustrated and may vary in size from a simple one-line listing to a quarter-page spread. In the local Business-to-Business Yellow Pages, you may want to include only your listing. In the International Yellow Pages, a space ad along with your listing would be most appropriate.

DESIGNING YOUR AD

To put together an effective advertisement, you first have to analyze the products you want to advertise, the company you represent, and the type of customers you want to contact through the ad. Next, you have to design an appeal—that is, something that will benefit the target audience—and incorporate it into your ad copy. Here are some guidelines that, if followed, will help you create strong, response-getting ads:

- *Create a sense of immediacy.* Because response diminishes over time, advertising relies on getting people to act immediately. Most people like to be led—particularly when in unfamiliar territory. Tell your audience what response you want. At different points throughout the ad, and especially at the conclusion, ask for a physical response: "Act quickly," "Limited time offer," "Call now," and so on.
- *Repetition sells.* Keep weaving and reweaving the same sales pitch throughout the ad, each time throwing in a slightly new slant to the significant features and benefits of your products. Repetition sells because the more times someone hears or reads something, the more believable it becomes. Repetition is particularly important in advertising (as in speeches), because it normally does not pull in the full attention of the audience. Many people find writing repetitiously difficult because they were taught in school to avoid redundancy at all

cost. When writing ad copy, forget this training and repeat, repeat, repeat.

- *Hit the buttons.* Different people will be turned on by different things about your products. One person may admire quality, another may like easy maintenance or the newness or simplicity of an item. Decide what is different and exciting about your products, then tell your audience how and why they need what you have to sell.

- *"Sell the sizzle, not the steak."* This is an old advertising axiom. It means sell the action, not the product. There's nothing wrong with talking about the features of your product, but unless you spell out how the customers will directly benefit, your ad won't have maximum effectiveness. To excite your audience, you must display and/or describe your product in a captivating way. This does not mean fancy words or constructions that might confuse the reader/listener/viewer. Use plain, simple language. Be straightforward. Keep your ad copy at a level understandable by an 11- or 12-year-old; anything higher, and you'll lose much of your audience.

- *Evaluate other ads.* Collect all kinds of ads and study them. This is a habit of all good ad-makers. Use ideas that are worthwhile. Don't be a martyr, trying to create everything new because you want to be different. Put your own imagination to use, but learn to emulate the strengths of others who are successful with their advertising.

The next element you'll need to include is visual art. Your visual element should create human interest, emotion, and realism. If you can afford photography in print ads, use it. Photographs are generally more believable than illustrations, and they're usually better remembered. As with television advertising, you're creating a visual image that conveys a message.

There are other ways to add visual impact to a print ad. One technique is to create an ad with a lot of white space if you're advertising in newspapers, yellow space if you're advertising in the Yellow Pages. These kinds of ads work well because of the dense columns of type used in these publications. Anything that breaks up the pattern stands out.

This variation is true not only for the design of the print ad, but for its size as well. Ads that are different in size from standard formats will stand out in a publication. For instance, a diagonal ad will break up standard media formats, as will running three ads in rapid succession. Placing an ad that runs across two pages is another widely used method.

PUBLICITY

A newspaper editor's major problem is filling the paper with newsworthy items. Local newspapers are most interested in local news, and you are, in fact, a local business owner. When you start your import/export management company, when you do something charitable, when something unusual happens to you, your business, your clients, or your employees—these are newsworthy events that are worth letting the media know about. Why is publicity so important, and what will it do that advertising won't? In general, a news story or magazine article takes more time to read than an ad. The more time a reader spends with your story, the more likely that he or she will remember you.

Reach is another factor. You can place news and feature stories in more periodicals than you could afford to reach through paid advertising. Besides, an article in a respected newspaper or magazine, or an appearance on radio or television, occurs only if it meets the standards of the editor or programming director. It therefore gives your story a third-party credibility that cannot be duplicated with paid advertisements.

It's important, when you begin any publicity campaign, to make the right media contacts. For newspapers, the most likely contact is the city editor; for radio or cable television, contact the programming director. Just call the newspaper or broadcast station, ask for the person, and be sure you have the correct spelling of the name and the correct address. This is common courtesy and is extremely important to some media people. Take the time to find the right people. This approach will pay off for you.

Keep alert to anything that can give you publicity. Not everything may be accepted by the media, but whatever is accepted will be a form of free advertising for you. Be sure to reprint all your publicity stories and news releases. Use them as highly credible advertising handouts and mailers.

COOPERATIVE ADVERTISING

Although your main concern is finding buyers to distribute products either in a foreign country or domestically, you shouldn't drop your responsibility for further promoting the product. Ultimately, your success depends on how well the product sells to end users. To ensure good sales, you should inquire about a cooperative advertising program with the manufacturer.

Advertising is a big expense, and the distributors you deal with (and the ones they deal with) may not have a large advertising budget.

In addition, these distributors will most likely be dealing with several different products and the advertising they plan may be strictly institutional, not product-oriented. As the agent of the manufacturer, you should make sure your distributors know of cooperative advertising programs sponsored by the manufacturer.

Cooperative advertising will not only reduce the distributors' advertising expense, it will also promote your client's product in a cost-efficient and effective way that will help both the manufacturer and retailer or distributor to reach their target markets.

Although cooperative advertising policies differ from manufacturer to manufacturer, most arrangements pay a portion of the advertising costs and supply the retailer with material to include in the ad, whether it is a print, radio, or television spot. Make sure the manufacturer, or its agency, develops ads in the language of the country where the product will be advertised.

Dealer-Assistance Programs

Importers and exporters who deal directly with retail distributors will find they need considerable assistance from their suppliers. Like most merchants, they need help in product management, especially with reference to advertising, display, buying, stock control, and sales promotion. The importers and exporters who have been most successful in withstanding corporate chain competition are those that have inaugurated dealer-assistance programs. As one supplier explained, "We have learned that our job is to help the retailer move the merchandise out the front door. Only then will there be a demand for us to bring more in through the back door."

Exporters generally depend more heavily on personal selling than on advertising, with 10 to 20 times as much budgeted for the former. Catalogs, price lists, sales letters, and dealer-aid material—all usually furnished by the manufacturer—constitute the principal forms of exporter advertising. The objective is to pave the way for personal selling and to minimize the time spent on sales calls.

Hardly any direct merchandise advertising is undertaken by the exporter personally. The main goal of promoting products, for the exporter, is to make connections with large-scale buyers. When selling on a retail level, the advertiser cannot meet with every potential customer and explain the benefits of his or her products. As an exporter, however, you are seeking just a few buyers who will purchase large orders of products, making meetings with buyers much easier. If you work with agents or distributors, they will do this work for you.

8

MANAGING YOUR OWN
IMPORT/EXPORT
SERVICE

As you gain experience in importing and exporting, you will focus a large part of your time on business management. You will buy and sell products, or act as a liaison between buyers and sellers. In previous chapters, we've discussed how to approach customers, where you can find buyers for the products you sell or represent, what's involved in conducting research and putting together a marketing plan, the legal aspects of importing or exporting, and how to track your financials. This chapter will take you through the actual logistics involved—the day-to-day operations.

WORKING WITH IMPORT DISTRIBUTION SYSTEMS

Distributing imports can be a much more hands-on process than exporting. An exporter will work with a sales representative in a foreign country. This sales rep is, in fact, an importer. As an importer in the United States, you will be responsible for selling products directly to wholesalers or retailers. You may get these products directly from manufacturers, or you may work with a foreign export company. You may buy the goods directly from your own account and act as a wholesaler yourself, or you may simply act as an agent, generating sales for a commission. No matter how you decide to organize yourself, you must be a dedicated salesperson.

Before you can sell, you have to determine a price for your goods. As a general guideline, you can figure a price by adding your landed cost (buying price + duties + miscellaneous costs such as drayage) plus your expected profit margin, and comparing the total with what the market will bear. If you've done your market research properly, you should be able to find some price at which you will be able to sell your stock and still make an acceptable margin of profit. After you've determined this price, you will implement the selling and distribution strategies detailed in your marketing plan (developed through your market research). Your major goal, as an importer, is to reach the target market as defined in your marketing plan.

You begin executing your marketing plan by first looking at your position within the trade channel. As mentioned in Chapter 2, you should be aware of which partners add cost to the product you are selling, and determine whether that cost is equal to the value received. You want your distribution channel to be as efficient as possible so that the perception of value held by your customers is strong and convincing.

Once you've located retailers or wholesalers that carry similar goods to your own, call to find out who is in charge of purchasing and set up an appointment to talk about your goods. Bring to the meeting all of the information you can on your merchandise, including samples, brochures, and price lists. You must be able to show the value and quality of your product. Your customer is in business to make a profit, too, and if he or she feels that your goods won't bring in profit, then you have not done your sales job properly. Keep in mind, too, that some retailers buy for their stores the same way their customers buy for themselves—on impulse. It will be your job to convince them to place an order. Show the buyer your market research and outline the great sales potential for your goods in your customer's market niche.

New buyers may want to start out with a small order to test the marketability of your products. Although any sale at all should be encouraged, you may choose to implement a minimum order requirement to make deals worth your time. If the product sells, the buyer will increase orders later. The important thing is to get the buyer to order *something* right away.

A good salesperson walks a fine line between being persistent and being pushy. Don't put buyers off with constant calls asking for orders, but do make sure they keep you in mind. If you leave materials for a buyer to look over, call back in a few days just to say, "Hello, I just wanted you to know that if you have any other questions, or comments, about our products, I would be glad to help you." Ask the buyers some questions, too. Let them know that you value their opinion on your products, whether they decide to buy any or not. You may get some valuable, honest feedback from the types of people you will need to please, and the buyers will feel important because you show trust in their expertise.

The best way to sell is simply to provide what the buyers want. This is your ultimate goal. If the buyers don't want what you have to offer, find out what they *do* want. Before long, you will be able to gauge what products the market wants the most, and you'll be able to respond with products that will take advantage of those opportunities.

WORKING WITH EXPORT DISTRIBUTION SYSTEMS

Your business is set up, you have chosen the perfect product to sell, and you know exactly what countries have the most responsive markets. Now comes the most important question of all: How are you going to generate sales? Even if your business organization is rock-solid, you can't make a living if you don't make a sale.

Import sales is essentially hands-on selling, which includes cold calling and meeting with retailers and wholesalers. It is much more difficult to organize export sales: you are selling in foreign countries around the globe. For exporters, the job of selling usually falls to a foreign sales agent or distributor. How you decide to set up your distribution network will depend on what you are selling and how closely you want to be involved in the sales.

As an export management company, you will be working with several intermediaries and buying sources. They make up the distribution channel you will use to place your clients' products in foreign countries. They will be representing your client to other connecting channels through which the product will reach the end user. Because you are the agent of the manufacturer and bear responsibility for distribution in foreign countries, their performance will be a direct reflection on you.

Competent trading partners will make your job much easier and boost sales for your clients. But what distribution channel is going to be most effective for you as an exporter? This depends a great deal on your evaluation of the market, and your prospective trading partners, but the three most common options for distribution are:

1. Sell directly to foreign markets. (Hire your own people to work in the country as sales agents.)

2. Hire a commission representative or agent company.
3. Work with a distributor.

Selling directly to foreign markets is very difficult, even for a large export management company. Most companies choose to work with a foreign representative who acts as an agent or distributor. In both roles, representatives work to find sales in their respective countries. The main difference is that the distributor buys goods from you and resells them at whatever price it can; the agent merely finds sales for you in the foreign country and is then paid a percentage as a commission.

Selling Directly

Selling directly can work for products that have a substantial price and are offered to a very limited market. For example, if you are selling jet engine nozzles, you can hire your own sales reps, who can travel to the very limited number of jet engine manufacturers. If you make a sale, you will most likely have repeat business and can continue selling directly to this customer. For most products, however, the markets are so large and complex that this method is not feasible.

Agent

Your agent abroad will make sales calls to wholesale or retail buyers. When he or she is successful, sales are passed on to you. In most cases, you will then send the goods directly to the buyer. Once the deal has been completed, you pay the agent a commission on the sale. A typical agent's commission is 5% of the cost of the goods sold, but this varies slightly from one part of the world to another, and from product to product. Compare several agents before you choose one. You will want an agent who is experienced in selling your type of product. Try to find someone who has valuable contacts in the industry—the kind of contacts that could take an outsider years to make.

Distributor

A distributor is a company that buys your goods and resells them, determining the resale price independently. A distributor may purchase the goods first and warehouse them, acting as a wholesaler (in which case the company is known as an "import house"). With a distributor, you will not have as much control as you would with an agent, but the distributor will take care of all advertising, promotions, returns, and customer service.

Finding Representatives

Finding a good sales rep is just as important as finding a reputable manufacturer. Some reps are better than others at distributing different types of products. The trick is to find one who best complements the goods you have for sale. If you plan to export to several different parts of the world, you may need to find several representatives. If you are planning to sell to several countries that are in close proximity to one another, it will be easier for you to find a distribution company that works in all of the countries in which you plan to do business.

The best place to begin your search for representatives is with the International Trade Administration (ITA), a division of the U.S. Department of Commerce. The ITA's U.S. and Foreign Commercial Service (US&FCS) has several resources through which you can locate foreign buyers:

- Agent/Distributor Service.
- Export Contact List Service.
- Matchmaker Trade Delegations.
- Commercial News USA.
- Trade Opportunities Program (TOP).

After you have the names and addresses of reputable distributors and agents, the real work in finding representation begins: narrowing the field down to the best choice for your company and products. You will want as much information as you can get about the reps: their current product lines, rep history, compensation terms, and marketing plans. Conversely, they will want as much information as possible about your company and products. Once you've collected some good possibilities, trim your list to those you think have the most potential. These individuals should be contacted by letter and a version of Package 39, described in Chapter 2, should follow.

Written Agreements

After you have decided what reps you want to work with, you must draw up written agreements with them. These contracts will clarify the responsibilities and duties of each party. All language should be specific and clear. It is strongly advised that anyone entering into such an agreement should consult with an attorney familiar with international law. Without the help of an attorney, it is easy to overlook details that may turn into major headaches.

The exact details of any agreement will vary from situation to situation, but most basic agreements cover a similar core of information that includes:

- *Responsibilities of the exporter and the buyer/sales rep.* Make sure these items are clearly delineated; parts of this agreement will serve as a legally binding contract.

- *Term of the contract.* Include compensation and any bonus or incentive programs.

- *Territory.* Does the buyer/rep have exclusive or nonexclusive rights to a particular region? This is an important matter that you must decide first. Most reps prefer to have exclusive rights to market a product in a given territory. At first glance, this arrangement might seem to limit you and your products, but exclusive rights are often a good way to create mutually beneficial relationships, raising the marketing power of both you and your sales rep.

- *Pricing.* Often, price is the most significant variable determining sales success. Price your product carefully, not too low or too high. Keep in mind that your agent will earn a specific percentage, and a distributor will pay only the prevailing wholesale market price.

- *Warranty and returns.* Who is responsible for returns or repairs and what is the policy? This can be a crucial section of your agreement, depending on what type of item you're selling. Sometimes, the seller also will have to provide product liability insurance.

- *Intellectual property.* Does the rep have the right to use trademarks, patents, and copyrights in advertising? Does the product require protective registration? Make sure that the product doesn't infringe on any trademarks, patents, or copyrights.

- *Who is responsible for marketing and advertising?* You may have to help defray some of the marketing costs involved with your products.

- *Recordkeeping.* Both parties should keep simultaneous records and reserve the right to see each other's documents.

- *Language.* Which language in the agreement is legally binding?

- *Contract termination.* If certain stipulations are not met, or if no sales or less-than-average sales occur within a specified period of time, termination of the contract may be justified.

Stipulate what to do if there is a disagreement about the contract sometime in the future. In most cases, a third-party arbitrator is called in. The major arbitrator in international trade disputes is the International Chamber of Commerce (refer to Appendix A). The Chamber has a great deal of information and books available on writing contracts with foreign representatives. These publications can be helpful in writing up your own contract.

INVENTORY ACCOUNTING SYSTEMS

As mentioned earlier, you will sometimes act as a distributor for your clients: you will actually buy products from the manufacturer and sell them to your buyers, or offer commission to reps for moving the product. As a distributor, you are taking title to the product. Although you may still represent the manufacturer, you will often be free to price your goods and sell them to any buyer you can find. Once you take title in this situation, the goods are yours, for profit or for loss.

Remember this important point: If you don't have buyers lined up before you take title to products, you will be stuck with an inventory. You will have to arrange for warehousing of the product and handle all the costs associated with maintaining inventory. The danger here is that your capital is tied up with your inventory. If you have to maintain large inventories for a prolonged period of time, you may run into cash flow trouble. Be careful not to miss any loan payments or extend your letters of credit beyond your given terms. Nothing will doom a new business more quickly than bad credit.

Inventory costs can be substantial if you don't practice effective inventory control techniques. To avoid those costs, install a good manual method or a computerized system. Keep in mind that some merchandise may be perishable or may be subject to a certain limited shelf life. Be sure to monitor these items carefully, or you may be left with a warehouse full of useless merchandise. If you maintain accurate inventory records, you'll be able to apply to your purchasing process the knowledge gained from your inventory control.

Basic Stock

The first step in learning to master inventory control procedures is to establish a foundation, or frame of reference, regarding your business's inventory needs. This frame of reference is known as *basic stock*—the number of items required to cover normal sales demands of a particular company.

To make an accurate calculation of basic stock, you must review actual sales during an appropriate time period, such as a full year of business. You won't have previous sales and stocking figures to guide you during your start-up phase, so you must make your best projections of what your first year's sales will be, based on your marketing plan for that particular product.

Lead Time

Lead time—the length of time between reordering and delivery of a product—must be included when you calculate basic stock. For instance, if your lead time is four weeks and a particular product line requires 10 units a week in inventory, then reordering must take place before the basic inventory level falls below 40 units. It takes only common sense to realize that if reorders are not made until the stock is actually needed, the basic inventory will experience a shortfall and you'll lose sales, not to mention customers.

Many small business owners protect themselves from shortfalls by factoring a safety margin into their basic inventory figures. The percentage of safety margin that's right for a particular business depends on the number of external factors that can contribute to delays, and must be determined by the individual owner based on past experience and any future delays that can be projected accurately.

Hidden Costs

Excess inventory creates extra overhead, and that costs you money. Inventory that sits in a warehouse does not generate sales or profits; it generates losses that will shrink your bottom line by burdening you with:

- Debt service on loans to purchase the excess inventory.
- Additional personal property tax on unsold inventory.
- Increased insurance costs on the greater value of the inventory in stock.

One merchandise consultant has indicated that it costs the average retailer from 20% to 30% of original investment in inventory just to maintain it. If you turn your inventory four times during your fiscal year, it will cost you from 5% to 7.5% of your sales just to maintain your inventory.

The natural reaction of any merchant to excess inventory is: MOVE IT OUT. Although moving it out at any price acts to solve the overstocking problem within your inventory, it also contributes to a vicious cycle by reducing your return on investment. In all your projections, you based your figures on receiving full price at the time of purchase. If you overstock and must reduce your prices by 15% to 25% to clear out the excess inventory, you're ultimately taking money out of your own pocket.

The typical reaction of an inexperienced distributor to an excess in inventory is overly cautious reordering. When you reduce your reordering, however, you run a significant risk of creating a shortage in stock. That is another hidden cost of attempting to maintain more inventory than your business needs.

When you combine the costs of all these factors, it's easy to see how quickly overstocking can spell disaster. To avoid all these pitfalls of purchasing excess inventory, plan well, establish a realistic safety margin, and only order what you know you'll sell.

MANAGING INVENTORY

The ideal inventory scenario is: always having sufficient products on hand to meet customer demand while avoiding either shortage or excess. In the course of operating a real business, both shortage and excess will occur. Rather than viewing these as mistakes, a smart entrepreneur will use shortage and excess as indicators of sales trends and will alter the inventory control system to correct the immediate problem and avoid it in the future.

If a shortage occurs, the small business owner can place a rush order, but even a rush can take a great deal of time to fulfill with international trade. Another alternative is to employ a different supplier, although the uniqueness of the product and the manufacturer's brand name are generally attractive to buyers.

Excesses or overstocking can be addressed by:

- Reducing prices.
- Increasing sales incentives.
- Creating a promotion to stimulate demand.

In either case, the first order of business you must address is to *analyze* your reordering system. If purchasing and reordering are conducted correctly, shortage and excess will not occur. Your goal should be to keep these troublesome (and costly) mistakes to a minimum. The mechanism you must employ to keep supplies up and excesses down is your inventory control system.

Inventory Turnover

Sales liquidate inventory. When 100% of your original inventory has been replaced, you have turned over your inventory. You must now determine the period of time it will take to replenish your inventory, known as your *needs period.* The needs period is calculated by adding together your cost cycle, order cycle, and delivery cycle:

Count Cycle + Order Cycle + Delivery Cycle = Needs Period

To illustrate, suppose you decided to count inventory once every four weeks (the count cycle). From the time it took you to process paperwork and place orders with your vendors, the time was two weeks (the order cycle). The order takes six weeks to get to your business (delivery cycle). Therefore, you need 12 weeks of inventory from the first day of the count cycle to stay in operation for the next 12 weeks.

You could improve your inventory turnover, however, if you counted inventory more often—every two weeks instead of every four weeks—and worked with your suppliers to improve delivery efficiency.

Inventory Accounting

As discussed, if you purchase import goods from your own account and then sell them as a wholesaler or distributor, you will have to keep track of your inventory and its value. An accountant can be invaluable in this operation. As noted earlier, inventory valuation uses LIFO and FIFO methods.

LIFO (last in, first out) assumes that the goods most recently received are the first to be sold to your customers. An easy way to grasp LIFO is by considering two lots of 10 widgets each. You purchased the first lot of 10 widgets a year ago at a cost of $1 each. A week ago, you purchased a second lot of 10 widgets at an inflated price of $2 each. Employing the LIFO method, you sell your customers the $2 widgets first, which allows you to keep the less expensive (in terms of your inventory cost) units in inventory. When you have to calculate inventory value for tax purposes, LIFO allows you to value your remaining inventory (the $1 widgets) substantially below the current price of $2 per widget.

FIFO (first in, first out) was the traditional method used by most businesses prior to recent years of rapid inflation. Under FIFO, inventory is priced at its most recent cost, which more closely matches the actual physical movement of inventory. FIFO is usually employed during periods of relatively low inflation. High inflation and increasing replacement costs for inventory tend to skew inventory accounting figures toward an inaccurate profit picture.

To differentiate between the two methods, keep this in mind: LIFO establishes the value of your inventory based on the last quantity received, and FIFO establishes the value of your inventory based on the oldest item in it. Either dollar control or unit control can be employed with the LIFO or FIFO methods. Match your system to your needs, based on your accountant's recommendations.

Ordering and Receiving Goods

It's important for you to learn each of your suppliers' order-filling priorities. Some suppliers fill orders on a FIFO basis; others give first attention to the larger orders while customers with smaller orders wait. Consequently, many importers specify a cancellation date on their orders. By including such a cutoff date, you increase the probability that orders will receive prompt attention and that goods will arrive in time for the selling season.

Give careful attention to arriving shipments. Check that the correct amount of merchandise is delivered and that the quality of the goods matches the samples shown.

Even if you are acting as a representative and selling on commission, there are times as an importer when, if you don't have buyers lined up when a product clears customs, you will have to arrange for temporary warehousing, for yourself or your client. At almost all U.S. ports of entry, there are temporary warehousing spaces for rent. You can ask the Customs Service how long a particular product will take to clear customs at the particular port of entry you will be involved with, and how long the product can be warehoused at the port after its arrival. Often, that time frame will be long enough to find buyers who will pick up the product at the port of entry, eliminating any additional warehousing needs.

Figure 8–1 is a sample packing list order form. Figure 8–2 is a sample receiving report form. You can customize and reproduce these forms for your import/export business.

Figure 8–1   Sample Packing List Form

PACKING LIST
ORDER

DATE: _____

TO _____   FROM _____

_____   _____   SHIP DATE: _____

_____   _____   SHIP VIA: _____

_____   _____   F.O.B. SHIPPING POINT: _____

_____   _____   ACCOUNT NO.: _____

_____   _____   ORDER NO.: _____

_____   _____   DEPARTMENT: _____

TERMS - NO ANTICIPATION

QUANTITY ORDERED	QUANTITY SHIPPED	PRODUCT NUMBER	DESCRIPTION	UNIT WEIGHT	TOTAL WEIGHT	TOTAL CUBIC FT.
		TOTALS			TOTALS	

COMMENTS

Figure 8–2   Sample Receiving Report Form

RECEIVING REPORT

PURCHASE ORDER NO.: _____

INVOICE NO.: _____

INVOICE AMOUNT: _____

SHIPPED BY: _____

_____

WORK ORDER NO.: _____

RECEIVED FROM: _____

RECEIVED AT: _____

PREPAID ☐   CHARGES $_____

COLLECT ☐   CHARGES $_____

Report all damages (including damage to cardboard boxes and crates) and shortages on all copies of the delivering carrier's freight bill and have the delivery person sign his/her name and date on all greight bill copies. Send the freight bill to the Purchasing Department with the Receiving Report. (Include Expense Report for collect payments.

P.O. ITEM	QUANTITY RECEIVED	STOCK NUMBER	UNIT OF MEASURE	DESCRIPTION	CONDITION

Comments (Explain damages, shortages, substitutions, etc.)

Action to be taken

☐ COMPLETE ORDER

☐ PARTIAL SHIPMENT

RECEIVED BY _____   DATE _____

REPORTED BY _____   DATE _____

CREATIVE SHIPPING TECHNIQUES

Getting your goods from Point A to Point B can be an intricate process. If you're an exporter, your goods first will have to be packaged for international shipping, with the correct export permits, documentation, and marine insurance verified. Next, you'll have to transport the goods over land from the manufacturer to a port. Finally, the goods must be moved by ship (or plane) to a foreign port, where they will go through customs and move along to the buyer's warehouse. Figuring out these shipping costs is a big part of your sales strategy. Your price quotation will vary, depending on how much you wish to involve yourself in the shipping process. There is a marked price difference between a quotation that is offered F.O.B. your port of origin and one that is C.I.F. the port of destination. If you're a Texas-based importer, for example, and you quote a price that is F.O.B. Houston, you are telling your buyer that the price includes the cost of goods plus freight only to the port at Houston. If your price is C.I.F. Barcelona, however, you are quoting a price that includes cost of goods, marine (or air) insurance, and freight. (These shipping terms are discussed in greater detail below.) You can ask your international freight forwarder for help in arranging these designations. Whether you use a freight forwarder and customs broker (to clear imports through Customs) or not, we will discuss the ins and outs of shipping, customs, and trade barriers.

Ocean Carriers

An importer or exporter will use any of three types of ocean carriers. These are:

1. *Conference lines.* Some ocean carriers join together in Ocean Freight Conferences to establish common shipping rates and conditions. Often, if the exporter signs a contract to ship all of its goods on member lines, it is offered reduced rates.

2. *Independent lines.* These lines operate on their own and usually offer rates that are lower than conference line rates to exporters who have not signed a conference contract.

3. *Tramp vessels.* These can be conference or independent, but are called tramp vessels because they do not operate on a fixed schedule. Instead, they simply find what they can to ship, and take the goods to the exporters' desired destinations. For this reason, they usually carry only bulk cargoes.

Air Carriers

Air freight is beneficial if your products need to get to their market in a hurry—certain perishable goods, for example. Air transport responds to market demands quickly and efficiently, but, understandably, is much more costly than ocean freight and might effectively price your product out of the market.

Rail and Motor

How you move your goods over land will depend on where they need to be delivered. Rail transportation is generally less expensive than truck transport, but trains rarely pick up and drop off freight at the exact locations of delivery. Some combination of the two types of transport may be the best alternative, and many shipping companies are turning toward *intermodal* service—a combination of truck and rail in a full-service shipping company—as their method of choice.

International Freight Forwarder

Early in the export business, you should learn that one of the most valuable and helpful sources of information and assistance is the international freight forwarder/customs broker. The freight forwarder/customs broker acts as an agent for exporters in moving cargo to overseas destinations. With few exceptions, it is recommended that a freight forwarder licensed by the Federal Maritime Commission be engaged to move your cargo from the U.S. port of export.

These licensed agents are familiar with the import rules and regulations of foreign countries, all methods of shipping, U.S. government export regulations, and documents connected with foreign trade. They can also assist exporters in computing freight costs, port charges, consular fees, special documentation and insurance costs, and their own handling fees, all of which will help in preparing the price quotation to the buyer.

In addition, a freight forwarder can provide routing and scheduling information, book ocean cargo or air freight space, prepare all necessary shipping documentation, handle shipping insurance, and arrange for warehouse storage. As a customs broker, he or she can route merchandise through ports with the lowest duties and can assist in using the most advantageous designation for the goods.

Freight forwarders and/or customs brokers can be found by looking in your local metropolitan telephone directory or by contacting the local ocean shipping lines, a rail shipping agent, or an airline freight agent. The cost for freight forwarders' services is a legitimate export cost that may be figured into the contract price charged to the customer.

Most forwarders' rates and services will be competitive. Some are even regulated by federal law. However, it is recommended that several different bids be obtained: there may be some variation in price. For a fair rate comparison, make certain that all of the services being compared are equal.

Packing Goods

Goods must be packed and marked properly to make sure they arrive at their destination in good condition. What packing materials you use will depend on what you are sending. Protection can vary from fiberboard boxes to wooden crates or metal drums. The manufacturer should be able to advise on packaging, especially if all packaging takes place at the point of manufacture, and domestic shipping is established. Freight forwarders can also offer information regarding international packing and marking symbols.

Collection Documents

In Chapter 5, we discussed collection documents, the documents submitted to the importer or the importer's bank by the exporter in order to receive payment. The importer then takes these documents to the dock and uses them to claim cargo. If you use a freight forwarder, he or she will fill out and process all of these forms. Although these documents will vary from country to country and from importer to importer, you can request a list of specific documents that must be presented as terms of your letter of credit. In general, the list will include all or some combination of the following forms (see Chapter 5 for explanation of each document):

- Bill of lading.
- Commercial invoice.
- Consular invoice.
- Certificate of origin.
- Inspection certificates.
- Certificate of manufacture.
- Packing list.
- Insurance certificate.

Shipping Terms

Designations adopted by the National Foreign Trade Council specify the different states (toward the final destination) to which the U.S. exporter will transport goods at his or her expense. These terms were adopted to clarify what was meant by various abbreviations commonly used by U.S. exporters. The obligations of the seller and buyer under each of these quotations are set forth specifically. The most common designations are listed below:

- *C. & F.: Cost and Freight.* All shipping costs (except for cargo insurance) are paid by the U.S. exporter from his or her warehouse to a port of the importer's country.
- *C.I.F.: Cost, Insurance, and Freight.* All shipping costs are paid by the U.S. exporter, including cargo insurance.
- *Ex-Factory:* Seller's responsibility ends when merchandise is accepted at the point of origin (i.e., the factory). Alternate terms are: Ex-warehouse, Ex-works, and so on.
- *F.A.S.: Free Along Side.* An example is: F.A.S. New York. This means that if goods are shipped from Nevada to Spain, no charges for shipment are payable by the Spanish importer until the goods are free along side the vessel in New York. After this point, some charges may be applied to the importer.
- *F.O.B.: Free On Board.* An example is: F.O.B. New York. This indicates that the price quoted includes the cost of loading the merchandise into an international carrier at the specified place.
- *F.O.R.:* Goods will be delivered by the exporter to a foreign railway station. The U.S. importer is responsible from this point on.

These terms are critical to establishing your buying or selling price. They determine not only price but also the parameters of responsibility between seller and buyer. If you're the importer and you want to receive shipment with the least amount of hassle and greatest amount of safety, you might want to ask for pricing that is C.I.F. whatever port you wish to receive the goods. For example, if you're a Seattle-based importer buying from a Japanese manufacturer, you might request pricing that is C.I.F. Seattle. This means that the seller will pay for and arrange all costs associated with the manufacture and insured shipping of the goods to the port in Seattle. Understandably, this buying price will be higher than if the goods were priced F.O.B. Kobe, Japan, meaning paid delivery only to the port in Kobe, Japan. For the beginning importer, it will be easier to deal with pricing that is C.I.F. your port until you gain enough experience to handle the other elements of overseas shipping.

WHY GOOD IMPORTERS/EXPORTERS FAIL

Most small business surveys show that the primary reasons for business failure lie in the following areas:

1. Inefficient control over costs and cash flow.
2. Poor inventory management.
3. Underpricing of goods sold.
4. Poor customer relations or lack of customer service.
5. Failure to promote and maintain a favorable company image.
6. Poor relations with suppliers.
7. Inability of management to reach decisions and act on them.
8. Failure to keep pace with management systems.
9. Illness of key personnel.
10. Reluctance to seek professional assistance.

These failure factors are not listed to put a damper on your entrepreneurial spirit, but should be viewed as reminders of the importance of preplanning. Use them as preplanning guidelines so that your business will *not* fail.

HOW TO SUCCEED IN THE IMPORT/EXPORT BUSINESS

Although we have tried to cover the critical points for starting and operating a successful import/export management company, this is a complex business. An important point to keep in mind is that the United States and every other government wants to increase exports; banks look on importers/exporters as businesspeople who can be potentially big accounts (if things develop well), and freight forwarders/customs brokers help to secure clients who will generate continuing and growing shipping needs (which is where their profits lie) in the future.

The U.S. government is promoting exports and can be a valuable trade partner in your import/export business. It offers a wide variety of consulting, financial, insurance, and supporting services at minimal cost to those engaged in improving trade with other countries. It is especially tempting to promote exports to the burgeoning markets in Asia, Latin America, and the former Eastern bloc countries, as all are large and emerging economies. The U.S. government also can help you understand what can and cannot be exported to and imported from areas such as the Middle East, North Korea, and other unfavored countries.

Your tools are information, determination, creativity, salesmanship, and perseverance. You must develop your capabilities as an intermediary, and your knowledge of markets, banking, and shipping. These, coupled with ever-increasing networks of contacts and your ability to match producers with purchasers, will determine your ultimate success.

Appendix A

IMPORT/EXPORT BUSINESS RESOURCES: GOVERNMENT AGENCIES*

Export-Import Bank of the United States (Eximbank)
811 Vermont Avenue, N.W.
Washington, DC 20571
(202) 565-3900

International Chamber of Commerce
156 Fifth Avenue, Suite 308
New York, NY 10010
(212) 206-1150

U.S. Department of Commerce
Herbert C. Hoover Building
14th Street and Constitution Avenue, N.W.
Washington, DC 20230
(202) 482-2000

U.S. Bureau of the Census
Public Information Office
Washington, DC 20233-8200
(301) 763-4040

U.S. Department of Commerce
International Trade Administration
Washington, DC 20230
(202) 482-2000

U.S. Patent and Trademark Office
Office of Public Affairs
2021 Jefferson Davis Highway
Arlington, VA 20209
(703) 557-4636

---

*Although the author and editors have made every effort to verify the following information to assure its accuracy at the time of publication, businesses and other organizations do move or cease to conduct business.

U.S. Small Business
    Administration
409 3rd Street, S.W.
Washington, DC 20416
(202) 205-7701

U.S. Department of Agriculture
Foreign Agriculture Service
14 and Independence Ave.
Washington, DC 20250
(202) 720-9445

U.S. Government Printing Office
Department 33
Washington, DC 20402
(202) 275-3054

Appendix B

U.S. CUSTOMS REGIONS AND DISTRICTS

Headquarters

U.S. Customs Service
1301 Constitution Ave., N.W.
Washington, DC 20229
(202) 927-6724

Northeast Region

Boston:
10 Causeway, Room 801
Boston, MA 02222-1056
(617) 565-6147

Districts:

Portland:
312 Fore St.
Portland, ME 04112
(207) 780-3328

St. Albans:
50 S. Main St., P.O. Box 1490
St. Albans, VT 05478
(802) 524-6527

Boston:
10 Causeway, Room 601
Boston, MA 02222-1059
(617) 565-6147

Providence:
49 Pavilion Ave.
Providence, RI 02905
(401) 528-5080

Buffalo:
111 W. Huron St., Room 416
Buffalo, NY 14202
(716) 846-4375

Ogdensburg:
Bridge Plaza
Ogdensburg, NY 13669
(315) 393-1390

Philadelphia:
200 Chestnut St., Room 103
Philadelphia, PA 19106
(215) 597-7480

Baltimore:
200 St. Paul Place, 28th Floor
Baltimore, MD 21202
(410) 962-2666

New York Region

New York:
6 World Trade Center
New York, NY 10048
(800) 697-3662

Jamaica:
Bldg. 77, JFK Airport
Jamaica, NY 11430
(718) 553-1585

Newark:
Hemisphere Center, Routes 1 and
    9 South
Newark, NJ 07114
(201) 645-3760

Southeast Region

Miami:
6601 N.W. 25th St.
Box 02580
Miami, FL 33102
(305) 869-2657

Districts:

Charlotte:
501 Nation's Crossing Road,
    Suite 203
Charlotte, NC 28219
(704) 527-0151

Old San Juan:
La Pontilla #1
Old San Juan, PR 00902
(809) 729-6977

Charleston:
200 East Bay St.
Charleston, SC 29401
(803) 727-4157

Savannah:
1 East Bay Street
Savannah, GA 31401
(912) 966-0557

Tampa:
311 Park Place Blvd., Suite 600
Tampa, FL 34619
(813) 799-4060

St. Thomas:
Main Post Office, Sugar Estate
St. Thomas, VI 00801
(809) 774-2510

Norfolk:
200 Granby St.
Norfolk, VA 23510
(804) 543-2033

South Central Region

New Orleans:
423 Canal St.
New Orleans, LA 70130
(504) 589-2021

Districts:

Port Arthur:
4550 7th St.
Port Arthur, TX 77642
(409) 724-0087

Houston:
1717 East Loop, Suite 201
Houston, TX 77029
(713) 671-1000

Laredo:
Lincolnwood Waters Bridge,
   Bldg. #2
Laredo, TX 78040
(210) 726-2267

El Paso:
9400 Viscount Blvd.
El Paso, TX 77925
(915) 540-5700

Irving:
1205 Royal Lane
Irving, TX 75063
(214) 574-2170

Pacific Region

Terminal Island:
300 South Ferry, Room 1001
Terminal Island, CA 90731
(310) 514-6231

Districts:

San Diego:
610 W. Ash St., Suite 1200
San Diego, CA 92101
(619) 557-5360

Los Angeles/Long Beach:
1 World Trade Center
Los Angeles/Long Beach, CA
   90731
(310) 514-7007

San Francisco:
555 Battery St.
San Francisco, CA 94126
(415) 744-7741

Honolulu:
Prince Kuhio Federal Bldg.,
   Room 7309
Honolulu, HI 96806
(808) 541-2623

Portland:
511 N.W. Broadway
Portland, OR 97209
(503) 326-2871

Seattle:
1000 2nd Ave., Suite 2200
Seattle, WA 98104
(206) 553-4676

Anchorage:
605 W. 4th Ave.
Anchorage, AK 99501
(907) 261-2675

North Central Region

Chicago:
610 South Canal St., 9th Floor
Chicago, IL 60603-5790
(312) 353-6100

Districts:

Chicago:
610 South Canal St., 3rd Floor
Chicago, IL 60607
(312) 353-6100

Pembina:
112 W. Stutsman
Pembina, ND 58271
(701) 825-6201

Minneapolis:
110 South 4th St.
Minneapolis, MN 55401
(612) 348-1670

Duluth:
515 W. 1st St.
Duluth, MN 55802-1390
(218) 720-5204

Milwaukee:
P.O. Box 37260
Milwaukee, WI 53237
(414) 571-2860

Middleburg Heights:
6747 Angle Road
Middleburg Heights, OH 44130
(216) 891-3800

St. Louis:
4477 Woodson Road
St. Louis, MO 63134
(314) 428-2662

Detroit:
477 Michigan Ave.
Detroit, MI 48126
(313) 226-3138

Great Falls:
300 2nd Ave. South
Great Falls, MT 59405
(406) 453-7631

Southeast Region

Miami, FL 33131

Districts:

Charlotte, NC 28219
Old San Juan, PR 00901
Charleston, SC 29401
Savannah, GA 31401
Tampa, FL 33605
Miami, FL 33102
St. Thomas, VI 00801
Norfolk, VA 23510
Washington, DC 20166

South Central Region

New Orleans, LA 70130

Districts:

Port Arthur, TX 77642
Houston, TX 77029
Laredo, TX 78041-3130
El Paso, TX 77925
Dallas/Ft. Worth, TX 75261
Nogales, AZ 85621

Pacific Region

Los Angeles, CA 90831-0700

Districts:

San Diego, CA 92188
Los Angeles/Long Beach, CA
    90731
San Francisco, CA 94126
Honolulu, HI 96806
Portland, OR 97209
Seattle, WA 98104
Anchorage, AK 99501

North Central Region

Chicago, IL 60603-5790

Districts:

Chicago, IL 60607
Pembina, ND 58271
Minneapolis, MN 55401
Duluth, MN 55802-1390
Milwauke, WI 53237-0260
Cleveland, OH 44114
St. Louis, MO 63105
Detroit, MI 48226-2568
Great Falls, MT 59405

Appendix C

U.S. PORTS OF ENTRY

Alabama

Birmingham
Huntsville
Mobile

Alaska

Alcan
Anchorage
Dalton Cache
Fairbanks
Juneau
Ketchikan
Sitka
Skagway
Valdez
Wrangell

Arizona

Douglas
Lukeville
Naco
Nogales
Phoenix
San Luis
Sasabe
Tucson

Arkansas

Little Rock–N. Little Rock

California

Andrade
Calexico
Eureka
Fresno
Los Angeles–Long Beach
Port San Luis
San Diego
San Francisco–Oakland
Tecate
San Ysidro

Colorado

Denver

Connecticut

Bridgeport
Hartford
New Haven
New London

Delaware

Wilmington (see Pennsylvania:
    Philadelphia)

District of Columbia

Washington

Florida

Boca Grande
Fernandina Beach
Jacksonville
Key West
Miami
Orlando
Panama City
Pensacola
Port Canaveral
Port Everglades
Port Manatee
St. Petersburg
Tampa
West Palm Beach

Georgia

Atlanta
Brunswick
Savannah

Hawaii

Honolulu
Hilo
Kahului
Nawiliwili–Port Allen

Idaho

Boise
Eastport
Porthill

Illinois

Chicago
Peoria
Rock Island–Moline (see Iowa:
    Davenport)

Indiana

Evansville/Owensboro (KY)
Indianapolis
Lawrenceburg/Cincinnati (OH)

Iowa

Davenport–Rock Island–Moline
Des Moines

Kansas

Wichita

Kentucky

Louisville
Owensboro/Evansville (IN)

Louisiana

Baton Rouge
Gramercy
Lake Charles
Morgan City
New Orleans
Shreveport/Bossier City

Maine

Bangor
Bar Harbor
Bath
Belfast
Bridgewater
Calais
Eastport
Fort Fairfield
Fort Kent
Houlton
Jackman
Jonesport
Limestone
Madawaska
Portland

Rockland
Van Buren
Vanceboro

Maryland

Annapolis
Baltimore
Cambridge

Massachusetts

Boston
Fall River
Gloucester
Lawrence
New Bedford
Plymouth
Salem
Springfield
Worcester

Michigan

Battle Creek
Detroit
Grand Rapids
Muskegon
Port Huron
Saginaw–Bay City/Flint
Sault Ste. Marie

Minnesota

Baudette
Duluth and Superior (WI)
Grand Portage
International Falls–Ranier
Minneapolis–St. Paul
Noyes
Pinecreek
Roseau
Warroad

Mississippi

Greenville
Gulfport
Pascagoula
Vicksburg

Missouri

Kansas City
St. Joseph
St. Louis
Springfield (temporary)

Montana

Butte
Del Bonita
Great Falls
Morgan
Opheim
Piegan
Raymond
Roosville
Scobey
Sweetgrass
Turner
Whitetail
Whitlash

Nebraska

Omaha

Nevada

Las Vegas
Reno

New Hampshire

Portsmouth

New Jersey

Newark
Perth Amboy

New Mexico

Albuquerque
Columbus

New York

Albany
Alexandria Bay
Buffalo-Niagara Falls
Cape Vincent
Champlain–Rouses Point
Chateaugay
Clayton
Fort Covington
Kennedy Airport Area
Massena
New York Seaport Area
Ogdensburg
Oswego
Rochester
Sodus Point
Syracuse
Trout River
Utica

North Carolina

Beaufort-Morehead City
Charlotte
Durham
Reidsville
Wilmington
Winston-Salem

North Dakota

Ambrose
Antler
Carbury
Dunseith
Fortuna
Hannah
Hansboro
Maida
Neche

Noonan
Northgate
Pembina
Portal
St. John
Sarles
Sherwood
Walhalla
Westhope

Ohio

Akron
Ashtabula/Conneaut
Cincinnati/Lawrenceburg (IN)
Cleveland
Columbus
Dayton
Toledo/Sandusky

Oklahoma

Oklahoma City
Tulsa

Oregon

Astoria
Coos Bay
Newport
Portland

Pennsylvania

Chester (see Philadelphia)
Erie
Harrisburg
Philadelphia/Chester/Wilmington
Pittsburgh
Wilkes-Barre/Scranton

Puerto Rico

Aguadilla
Fajardo
Guanica

Humacao
Jobos
Mayaguez
Ponce
San Juan

Rhode Island

Newport
Providence

South Carolina

Charleston
Columbia
Georgetown
Greenville–Spartanburg

Tennessee

Chattanooga
Knoxville
Memphis
Nashville

Texas

Amarillo
Austin
Beaumont*
Brownsville
Corpus Christi
Dallas/Ft. Worth
Del Rio
Eagle Pass
El Paso
Fabens
Freeport
Hidalgo
Houston/Galveston
Laredo
Lubbock
Orange*
Port Arthur*
Port Lavaca–Point Comfort
Presidio

Progreso
Rio Grande City
Roma
Sabine*
San Antonio

Utah

Salt Lake City

Vermont

Beecher Falls
Burlington
Derby Line
Highgate Springs/Alburg
Norton
Richford
St. Albans

Virgin Islands

Charlotte Amalie, St. Thomas
Christiansted
Coral Bay
Cruz Bay
Frederiksted

Virginia

Alexandria
Norfolk-Newport News
Richmond–Petersburg

Washington

Aberdeen
Anacortes*
Bellingham*
Blaine
Boundary
Danville
Everett*
Ferry
Friday Harbor*
Frontier

Washington (Continued)

Laurier
Longview*
Lynden
Metaline Falls
Neah Bay*
Nighthawk
Olympia*
Oroville
Point Roberts
Port Angeles*
Port Townsend*
Seattle*
Spokane

Sumas
Tacoma*

West Virginia

Charleston

Wisconsin

Ashland
Green Bay
Manitowoc
Marinette
Milwaukee
Racine
Sheboygan

---

*Consolidated port.

Notes:

1. Columbia River port of entry includes Longview, WA, and Portland, OR.
2. Beaumont, Orange, Port Arthur, Sabine port of entry includes ports of the same name.
3. Port of Puget Sound includes Tacoma, Seattle, Port Angeles, Port Townsend, Neah Bay, Friday Harbor, Everette, Bellingham, Anacortes, and Olympia, all in the State of Washington.
4. Port of Philadelphia, PA, includes Wilmington, DE, and Chester, PA.
5. Port of Rock Island, IL, Moline, IL, and Davenport, IA.
6. Port of Shreveport, LA, includes Bossier City, LA.
7. Designated User-fee Airports: Allentown-Bethlehem-Easton, PA; Casper, WY; Columbus, OH; Dona Ana County, NM; Fargo, ND; Ft. Myers, FL; Ft. Wayne, IN; Jackson, MS; Klamath County, OR; Lebanon, NJ; Lexington, KY; Midland, TX; Morristown, NJ; Oakland-Pontiac, MI; Rockford, IL; Sanford, FL; St. Paul, AK.

Appendix D

IMPORT/EXPORT TRADE ASSOCIATIONS

National Customs Brokers and
  Forwarders Association
  (NCBFAA)
1 World Trade Center, Suite 1153
New York, NY 10048
(212) 432-0050

National Association of Export
  Management Companies
17 Battery Plaza, Suite 1425
New York, NY 10004
(212) 809-8023

American Association of
  Exporters and Importers
  (AAEI)
11 W. 42nd Street, 30th Floor
New York, NY 10036
(212) 944-2230

Federation of International Trade
  Associations
1851 Alexander Bell Drive
Reston, VA 22091
(703) 620-1588

International Trade Council
  (ITC)
3114 Circle Hill Road
Alexandria, VA 22305-1606
(703) 548-1234

International Traders Association
  (IT)
c/o The Mellinger Co.
6100 Variel Avenue
Woodland Hills, CA 91367
(818) 884-4400

National Foreign Trade Council
  (NFTC)
1270 Avenue of the Americas
New York, NY 10020-1702
(212) 399-7128

International Union of
  Commercial Agents &
  Brokers
Herengracht 376, 1016 CH
Amsterdam, The Netherlands

Manufacturer's Agents National
    Association (MANA)
23016 Mill Creek Road
P.O. Box 3467
Laguna Hills, CA 92653
(714) 859-4040

Appendix E

IMPORT/EXPORT TRADE PUBLICATIONS

Global Trade and Transportation
North American Publishing
    Company
401 N. Broad Street
Philadelphia, PA 19108
(215) 238-5300

Business America: The Magazine of
    International Trade
Superintendent of Documents
P.O. Box 371954
Pittsburgh, PA 15250
(202) 512-1800

Commerce Business Daily
Superintendent of Documents
P.O. Box 371954
Pittsburgh, PA 15250
(202) 512-1800

Export
Johnston International
    Publishing Company
25 N.W. Point Blvd., Suite 800
Elk Grove Village, IL 60007
(708) 427-9512

Export Briefs
Foreign Agricultural Service
U.S. Department of Agriculture
14th Street and Independence
    Avenue
Washington, DC 20250
(202) 720-9445

Export Bulletin
Journal of Commerce
2 World Trade Center, 27th Floor
New York, NY 10084
(212) 837-7000

Export Shipping Manual
Bureau of National Affairs, Inc.
1231 25th Street, N.W.
Washington, DC 21137
(202) 452-4200

The Exporter
Trade Data Reports
6 West 37th Street
New York, NY 10084
(212) 837-7800

Import Bulletin
Journal of Commerce
2 World Trade Center, 27th Floor
New York, NY 10005
(212) 425-1616

International Trade Alert
American Association of
    Exporters and Importers
11 West 42nd Street
New York, NY 10036
(212) 944-2230

*International Trade Reporter—
    Current Reports*
Bureau of National Affairs, Inc.
1231 25th Street, N.W.
Washington, DC 20037
(202) 452-4200

Journal of Commerce
2 World Trade Center, 27th Floor
New York, NY 10048
(212) 837-7000

Overseas Business Reports
Superintendent of Documents
P.O. Box 371954
Pittsburgh, PA 15250-7954
(202) 512-1800

Trade Opportunities Magazine
International Traders Association
c/o The Mellinger Company
6100 Variel Avenue
Woodland Hills, CA 91367
(818) 884-4400

Import/Export Trade Directories

Australian Exports
Croner Publications, Inc.
211-03 Jamaica Avenue
Queens Village, NY 11428
(718) 464-0866

*International Intertrade Index of
    New Imported Products*
International Intertrade Index
Box 636, Federal Square
Newark, NJ 07101
(201) 686-2382

Taiwan Importers Directory
Croner Publications, Inc.
211-03 Jamaica Avenue
Queens Village, NY 11428
(718) 464-0866

Canadian Trade Index
Croner Publications, Inc.
211-03 Jamaica Avenue
Queens Village, NY 11428
(718) 464-0866

World Trade Index
Eagle Publishing Company
63-B Lansdowne Place
Hove, East Sussex BN3 1FL,
    England

Trade Directories of the World
Croner Publications, Inc.
211-03 Jamaica Avenue
Queens Village, NY 11428
(718) 464-0866

*Scott Directory of Argentine
    Exporters and Importers*
Croner Publications, Inc.
211-03 Jamaica Avenue
Queens Village, NY 11428
(718) 464-0866

GLOSSARY OF KEY INTERNATIONAL TRADE AND BUSINESS TERMS*

accounts receivable: A record used to account for the total number of sales made through the extension of credit.

accrual basis: An accounting method used for recordkeeping purposes where all income and expenses are charged to the period to which they apply, regardless of whether money has been received.

acid-test ratio: An analysis method used to measure the liquidity of a business by dividing total liquid assets by current liabilities.

ad valorem: According to value. See *duty.*

advance against documents: A loan made on the security of the documents covering the shipment.

airway bill: A bill of lading that covers both domestic and international flights transporting goods to a specific destination.

asset earning power: A common profitability measure used to determine the profitability of a business by taking its total earnings before taxes and dividing that amount by its total assets.

Audit Bureau of Circulation (ABC): A third-party organization that verifies the circulation of print media through periodical audits.

balance sheet: A financial statement used to report a business's total assets, liabilities, and equity.

---

* For additional terms, see *Dictionary of International Trade,* by Jerry M. Rosenberg, published by John Wiley & Sons, Inc.

balance of trade: The difference between a country's total imports and exports. If exports exceed imports, a favorable balance of trade exists; if not, a trade deficit exists.

bill of lading: A document that establishes the terms of a contract between a shipper and a transportation company under which freight is to be moved between specific points for a specified charge.

bonded warehouse: A warehouse authorized by the U.S. Customs Service for storage of goods on which payment of duties is deferred until the goods are removed.

bonding: Generally used by service companies as a guarantee to their clients that they have the necessary ability and financial backing to meet their obligations. Bonds are also used to guarantee payment of duty for U.S. Customs entry.

break-even analysis: An analysis method used to determine the number of jobs or products that need to be sold to cover all expenses and begin to earn a profit for a business.

business plan: A plan used to chart a new or ongoing business's strategies, sales projections, and key personnel in order to obtain financing and provide a strategic foundation for the business's growth.

Business Publications Audit (BPA): Similar to the Audit Bureau of Circulation, the BPA is a third-party organization that verifies the circulation of print media through periodical audits.

C & F: Cost and Freight: All shipping costs (but not insurance) are paid by the exporter from his warehouse to a port in the importer's country.

capitalization: Capital may be in the form of money, common stock, long-term debt, or some combination of all three. With too much capital, a firm is overcapitalized; with too little capital, it is undercapitalized.

carnet: A customs document permitting the holder to carry or send merchandise temporarily into certain foreign countries without paying duties or posting bonds.

cash basis: An accounting method used for recordkeeping where income is logged when received and expenses are charged when they occur.

certificate of origin: A document, required by certain foreign countries for tariff purposes, certifying the country of origin of specified goods.

chattel mortgage contract: A credit contract used for the purchase of equipment where the purchaser receives title to the equipment upon delivery but the creditor holds a mortgage claim against it.

CIF: Cost, Insurance, and Freight: All shipping costs are paid by the exporter, including insurance.

clean bill of lading: A receipt for goods issued by a carrier that indicates that the goods were received in apparent good order and condition, without damages or other irregularities.

collateral: Assets used as security for the extension of a loan.

commercial loan: A short-term loan, usually issued for a term of six months.

conditional sales contract: A credit contract used for the purchase of equipment where the purchaser doesn't receive title of the equipment until the amount specified in the contract has been paid in full.

confirmed letter of credit: A letter of credit issued by a foreign bank whose validity has been confirmed by a U.S. bank.

cooperative advertising: A joint advertising strategy used by a manufacturer and another firm that distributes its products.

copyright: A form of protection used to safeguard original literary works, performing arts, sound recordings, visual arts, and renewals.

corporation: A legal form of operation that declares the business a separate legal entity guided by a group of officers known as the board of directors.

cost-of-living lease: A lease where yearly increases are tied to the government's cost of living index.

Cost Per Thousand (CPM): Terminology used in buying media. CPM refers to the costs it takes to reach 1,000 people within a target market.

current ratio: A ratio used to determine the difference between total current assets and total current liabilities.

demographic characteristics: The attributes such as income, age, and occupation that best describe a target market.

depreciation: The lessening in value of fixed assets that provides the foundation for a tax deduction based on either the declining-balance or straight-line method.

disability insurance: A payroll tax required in some states that is deducted from employee paychecks to ensure income during periods when an employee is unable to work due to an injury or illness.

disclosure document program: A form of protection that safeguards an idea while it is in its developmental stage.

dollar control system: A system used in inventory management that reveals the cost and gross profit margin on individual inventory items.

drayage: The hauling of a load by dray—a low, sturdily built cart with detachable sides for carrying heavy loads.

Dun & Bradstreet: An agency that furnishes subscribers with market statistics and the financial standings and credit ratings of businesses.

Duty: A tax imposed on imports by the customs authority of a country. Duties are generally based on value of the goods (ad valorem duties), some other factor such as weight or quantity (specific duties), or a combination of value and other factors (compound duties).

equipment loan: A loan used for the purchase of capital equipment.

equity capital: A form of financing where equity in a business is sold to private investors.

exchange rate: The price of one currency in terms of another.

Ex-Factory: Seller's responsibility ends when merchandise is accepted at point of origin, i.e., factory. This can also be written as Ex-Warehouse or Ex-works.

exploratory research: A method used when gathering primary information for a market survey, where targeted consumers are asked very general questions geared toward eliciting a lengthy answer.

export license: A government document that permits the licensee to engage in the export of designated goods to certain destinations.

Fair Labor Standards Act: A federal law that enforces a group of minimum standards that employers must abide by when hiring employees.

F.A.S.: Free Along Side: Such as F.A.S. New York. This means that, for instance, if goods are shipped from Nevada to Spain, no charges for shipment are payable by the importer until the goods are free along side the vessel in New York. After this point, some charges may be applied to the importer.

Federal Insurance Contributions Act (FICA): A law that requires employers to match the amount of Social Security tax deducted from an employee's paycheck.

fictitious name: Often referred to as a DBA (Doing Business As). A fictitious name is frequently used by sole proprietors or partnerships to provide a name, other than those of the owners or partners, under which the business will operate.

first in, first out (FIFO): An accounting system used to value inventory for tax purposes. Under FIFO, inventory is valued at its most recent cost.

fixed expenses: Expenses that must be paid each month and do not fluctuate with the sales volume.

flat lease: A lease where the cost is fixed for a specific period of time.

F.O.B.: Free On Board: Such as F.O.B. New York. The U.S. would pay all costs for shipping from this point (New York) on to the final destination.

F.O.R.: Goods will be delivered by the exporter to a railway station. The U.S. importer is responsible for them from this point on.

free trade zone (FTZ): A port designated by the government of a country for duty-free entry of any nonprohibited goods. Merchandise may be stored, displayed, or used for manufacturing within the zone, and reexported without duties being paid.

freight forwarder: An independent business that handles export shipments for compensation.

frequency: The number of times you hope to reach your target audience through your advertising campaign.

401K plan: A retirement plan for employees that allows them to deduct money from their paychecks and place it in a tax-sheltered account.

income statement: A financial statement that charts the sales and operating costs of a business over a specific period of time, usually a month. Also called an operating statement.

inventory loan: A loan that is extended based on the value of a business's inventory.

inventory turnover: An analysis method used to determine the amount of capital invested in inventory and the total number of times per year that investment will revolve.

investment tax credit: A tax credit that allows businesses to write off the first $10,000 of equipment purchased for business use.

investment turnover: A profitability measure used to evaluate the number of times per year that total investment or assets revolve.

irrevocable letter of credit: A letter of credit in which the specified payment is guaranteed by the bank if all terms and conditions are met by the drawee.

Keogh: A pension plan that lets business owners contribute a defined portion of their profits toward a tax-sheltered account. There are several Keoghs to choose from, such as profit-sharing and defined-contribution plans.

last in, first out (LIFO): An accounting system used to value inventory. Under LIFO, inventory is valued according to the remaining stock in inventory.

leasehold improvements: The repairs and improvements made to a facility before occupation by the lessee.

letter of credit: A document, issued by a bank per instructions by a buyer of goods, authorizing the seller to draw a specified sum of money under stated terms (usually, the receipt by the bank of certain documents within a given time).

liability: A term used when analyzing insurance risks; describes possible areas of exposure. While a business may be liable for numerous comprehensive and special coverages that blanket almost every known exposure, there are three forms of liability coverage that insurers usually will underwrite: (1) *general liability,* which covers any kind of bodily injury to nonemployees except that caused by automobiles and professional malpractice; (2) *product liability,* which covers injury to customers arising as a direct result of goods purchased from a business; and (3) *public liability,* which covers injury to the public or visitors when they are on your premises.

manual tag system: A system used in inventory management that tracks inventory using tags removed at the point of purchase.

market survey: A research method used to define the market parameters of a business.

markup: The amount added to the cost of goods in order to produce the desired profit.

measure of liquidity: An analysis method used to measure the amount of available liquid assets to meet accounts payable.

media plan: A plan that details the usage of media in an advertising campaign, including costs, running dates, markets, reach, frequency, rationales, and strategies.

Modified Accelerated Cost Recovery System (MACRS): Used in accounting to define the rate and method by which a fixed asset will be depreciated for tax purposes.

net leases: Typically, there are three net leases: (1) a net lease, (2) a double-net lease, and (3) a triple-net lease. A net lease is a base rent plus an additional charge for taxes. A double-net lease is a base rent plus an additional charge for taxes and insurance. A triple-net lease is base rent plus an additional charge for taxes, insurance, and common area expenses.

net profit on sales: A profitability measure that determines the difference between net profit and operating costs.

Occupational Safety and Health Act (OSHA): A federal law that requires employers to provide employees with a workplace that is free of hazardous conditions.

ocean bill of lading: A bill of lading indicating that the exporter consigns a shipment to an international carrier for transportation to a specified foreign market.

open to buy: The dollar amount budgeted by a business for inventory purchases for a specific time period.

overhead: All nonlabor expenses needed to operate a business.

partnership: A legal form of business operation between two or more individuals. The federal government recognizes several types of partnerships. The two most common are general and limited partnerships.

patent: A form of protection that provides a person or legal entity with exclusive rights to exclude others from making, using, or selling a concept or invention for the duration of the patent. Design, plant, and utility patents are available.

percentage lease: A type of lease where the landlord charges a base rent plus an additional percentage of any profits produced by the business tenant.

personal loans: Short-term loans that are extended based on the personal integrity of the borrower.

point-of-sale (POS) systems: A computerized network that is operated by a miniframe computer and linked to several checkout terminals.

profit: There are generally two kinds of profits: (1) gross profit, the difference between gross sales and cost of sales, and (2) net profit, the difference between gross profit and all costs associated with operating a business.

pro-forma invoice: A form of price quote that is written up as an invoice, and in effect says, "This is what the price will be."

quota: The quantity of goods of a specific kind that a country permits to be imported without restriction or imposition of additional duties.

reach: The total number of people within a target market to be contacted through an advertising campaign.

return on investment (ROI): A profitability measure that evaluates the performance of a business by dividing net profit by total assets.

return on owner's equity: A profitability measure used to gauge the earning power of the owner's total equity in a business by dividing the average equity investment of the owner by the net profit.

signature loans: See *personal loans.*

sole proprietor: A legal form of operation where only one owner can exist.

specific research: A method used when gathering primary information for a market survey. Targeted consumers are asked very specific, in-depth questions geared toward resolving problems found through exploratory research.

Standard International Trade Classification (SITC): A standard numerical code system developed by the United Nations to classify commodities used in international trade.

Standing Rate and Data Service (SRDS): A company that produces a group of directories that list rates, circulation, contacts, markets serviced, and so on, for different types of media.

step lease: A type of lease that outlines annual increases in the tenant's base rent, based on an approximation of what the landlord thinks maintenance and repair expenses may be.

Subchapter S: Under federal law, small corporations in this category can pay out all income proportionately to their shareholders, who then claim the income on their personal income tax returns.

sublet: The leasing, by the original lessee, of space within a rented facility.

unit-control system: An inventory management system that tracks inventory using bin tickets and physical inventory checks.

variable expenses: Business costs that fluctuate in successive payment periods according to the sales volume.

venture capital: A source of financing for either start-up or expansion capital that is based on providing private investors with equity positions within the business.

workers' compensation: A privately managed or state insurance fund that reimburses employees for injuries suffered on the job.

working capital: Net current assets required for a company to carry on with its work; the surplus of a firm's current assets over its current liabilities.

INDEX

1995 Expo Schedule

CHICAGO
April 8-9, 1995
Rosemont Convention Center

ATLANTA
May 20-21, 1995
Cobb County Galleria

DALLAS
Sept. 30-Oct. 1
Dallas Market Hall

SAN FRANCISCO
October 28-29, 1995
Moscone Center

PHILADELPHIA
November 18-19, 1995
South Jersey Expo Center

MJWE

Entrepreneur Magazine's
SMALL BUSINESS
EXPO

**Save $5.00
when you bring this
ad to any Expo.**

**For more
information, call
(800) 864-6864.**

Get your FREE Small Business Development Catalog today!

Name: _____

Address: _____

City: _____

State/Zip: _____

MJWC

To receive your free catalog, return this coupon to:
ENTREPRENEUR MAGAZINE,
P.O. Box 50370, Boulder, CO 80321-0370.
OR CALL (800) 421-2300, Dept. MJWC
Step-by-step guidance to help you succeed.

Get the book.
FREE!